Poets Beyond the Barricade

Poets Beyond the Barricade

Rhetoric, Citizenship, and Dissent
after 1960

DALE M. SMITH

THE UNIVERSITY OF ALABAMA PRESS
Tuscaloosa

Typeface: Bembo

∞

The paper on which this book is printed meets the minimum requirements of
American National Standard for Information Sciences—Permanence of Paper for
Printed Library Materials, ANSI Z39.48-1984.

Library of Congress Cataloging-in-Publication Data

Smith, Dale, 1967–
    Poets beyond the barricade : rhetoric, citizenship, and dissent after 1960 / Dale M.
Smith.
        p. cm. — (Rhetoric, culture, and social critique)
    Includes bibliographical references and index.
    ISBN 978-0-8173-1749-2 (cloth : alk. paper) — ISBN 978-0-8173-8592-7 (elec-
tronic) 1. Protest poetry, American—History and criticism. 2. American poetry—
20th century—History and criticism. 3. American poetry—21st century—History
and criticism. 4. Literature and society—United States. 5. Politics and literature—
United States. 6. War and literature—United States. 7. Dissenters—United States. 8.
Persuasion (Rhetoric) in literature. 9. Persuasion (Psychology) in literature. 10. Poets,
American—20th century—Political and social views. I. Title.
    PS309.P7.S65 2012
    811′.54093587392—dc23

                                                                            2011027438

Cover image: "Protest," Jaume Ventura, 2006
Cover design: Suloni Robertson

It is that we are told we are free, and that we are shaping
our common destiny; yet, with varying force, many of us break
through to the conviction that the pattern of public activity has,
in the end, very little to do with our private desires. Indeed the main
modern force of the distinction between "the individual"
and "society" springs from this feeling.
—Raymond Williams, from *The Long Revolution* (1961)

The nation is like our selves, together
seen in our various scenes, sets where ever we are
what ever we are doing, is what the nation
is
doing
or
not doing
is what the nation
is
being
or not being
—Amiri Baraka, from "The Nation Is Like Ourselves" (1970)

Contents

Acknowledgments

Poets Beyond the Barricade addresses the rhetorical and cultural strategies of poetry during an era in which revolutionary events are noticeably absent. As I stress throughout this book, poetry after 1960, when used to respond to public situations, intervenes to engage our awareness, to challenge our assumptions about civic space and civil action, and to provoke us to act on behalf of our convictions. While writing this book, I often recalled those moments in my own experience when I had been moved by words I encountered in a poem and had thus been urged toward some better attitude or apprehension of the ethical possibilities that existed for me in public contexts. If, as Kenneth Burke argues, literature is "equipment for living," then I am gratified to have encountered it through the attentive efforts of my teachers and friends—men and women who took seriously the inquiries of art that alerted me to self-capacities I had yet to realize. It is, perhaps, this constant tension between the personal and public, between communal enjoyment and popular comprehension that drew me into this study. So in a sense, it is to the deliberate, though often random, encounters with the authors and instructors of my adolescence and undergraduate years that I owe the most gratitude for this project.

Continuing in this vein of camaraderie and social exchange, many friends, colleagues, and teachers have read portions of this manuscript as it developed along the way. But I want to give special thanks to Jeffrey Walker, whose care and attention to this project helped me realize the full scope of my arguments throughout the writing process. His own work in rhetoric and poetics provided me with a model for scholarly investigation, and his encouragement along the way has been invaluable. I would also like to thank Marjorie Perloff for her critical insights and challenges through many stages of this project, and Robert J. Bertholf for his conversations and comments that helped me more carefully attend the disciplinary divisions between rhetoric and literature. On that account, too, I want to acknowledge

Joshua Gunn, Mark Longaker, Samuel Baker, Brian Bremen, Roberto Tejada, Lisa Moore, Laura Smith, Kyle Schlessinger, Jeffrey Pethybridge, Nate Kreuter, Joe Ahearn, Roger Snell, Richard Owens, David Hadbawnik, Michael Kelleher, Boyd Nielson, Kent Johnson, Farid Matuk, Susan Briante, Patricia Roberts-Miller, Linda Ferreira-Buckley, and Gerrit Lansing, who offered valuable comments, bibliographical help, and generous encouragement and advice.

Chapter 1 owes a debt of gratitude to Peter Anastas, whose editorial presentation and comments on the poems and letters of Charles Olson in *Maximus to Gloucester* enabled my research significantly, and I am grateful for his permission to include portions of that work here along with significant details of our correspondence. David Rich's *Charles Olson: Letters Home (1949–1969)* also enriches the context of Olson's relationship to the city of Gloucester in the 1960s, and I am thankful for his leads and conversation. A portion of chapter 2 began as a presentation to the Summer Writing Program at Naropa University in 2009, and I am grateful to Anne Waldman for inviting me to participate. I also thank the organizers of the Rhetoric Society of America for recognizing part of chapter 3 with a Gerard A. Hauser Graduate Scholarship at RSA's 2008 Conference in Seattle. Additionally, I want to thank Aldon Lynn Nielsen and the executors of the estate of Lorenzo Thomas for permission to quote from *The Bathers* and to reproduce images from that book. I likewise appreciate Maria Damon's permission to quote from a paper she delivered for the Lorenzo Thomas Panel at the American Studies Association Conference in Houston on November 15, 2002. Jim Brown's reading benefited my discussion of the Internet and public space in chapter 4, and I'm thankful for his attentive contribution to my understanding of the horizontal and vertical forces of the web. Finally, I want to extend a note of acknowledgment to John Tranter who published a small portion of chapter 4 in *Jacket Magazine*.

I benefited from two excellent readers' reports from The University of Alabama Press by Maria Damon and James Arnt Aune. Both reviews challenged me to articulate more fully my commitments and provided detailed suggestions for revision. I thank my editor, Daniel Waterman, who has been supportive of this project and who helped me see it into print. I also thank Dawn Hall, Rebecca Todd Minder, Joanna Jacobs, and others in the marketing and production departments at The University of Alabama Press for their help in putting *Poets Beyond the Barricade* into the world.

This book is dedicated with much love to Hoa Nguyen and our children, Keaton and Waylon.

Poets Beyond the Barricade

Introduction

"The Press of Possibility": Poetry, Public Culture, and Modality

> Rhetoric performs in a strange domain of motivated possibilities, all needed in some civil scheme, all imbued with value colorations: attributions of purpose, cause, destiny, praise, blame, all embedded in scenarios of realization.
>
> —Nancy S. Struever

American public culture requires the social possibilities expressed through civil activism and dissent. Examples of such potential are especially abundant in the last century, ranging from the heroic Seattle General Strike of February 1919 to the Vietnam-era resistance efforts so broadly publicized by the print and broadcast media of the period. Poets, artists, novelists, filmmakers, and musicians have accompanied many violent and peaceful struggles. Art, broadly speaking, contributes to how public protest and dissent renew political possibilities when confronting forms of postindustrial repression. While artists and writers may have provided a compelling counterpart to situations requiring revolutionary struggle in the past, scholars and critics of contemporary culture are hard pressed to see relationships between poetry and social movements now. Who, outside of the numerous though relatively isolated poetry communities today, can even name a living public poet who associates with vibrant or contentious political messages?[1] Allen Ginsberg perhaps was the last poet of protest held in regard by a mass audience. But since the 1960s and '70s such literary figures have faded from popular scenes of engagement. Many wonder what happened to poetry, and to the poet's responsibility for shaping the possibilities of the nation's political and social life. Has poetry failed to put forward the actions and capacities required for successful public engagement?

The answer that motivates the commitments of this book is no: Poetry remains active in the imagination and enactments of public space. Open-mic readings in coffee shops, bars, and cafés, the publicity generated by poetry slams and the spoken word movement televised by shows like HBO's *Def Poetry* series, and the robust cultural significance of the St. Mark's Poetry Project, the Nuyorican Poets Café, or Bob Holman's recent projects with the Bowery Poetry Club have all kept poetry thriving within popular imagination.[2] National Poetry Month each April is celebrated with community-sponsored readings, lectures, workshops, prizes, and events. Every week around the country there are readings and lectures devoted to poetry. The growth of creative writing programs and community outreach through poetry instruction in public schools and many prisons also has made it possible for poetry to reach a wider number of readers than ever. Even communities of poets once considered to be on the political or formally experimental fringe now find popular and professional acceptance as teachers and editors at many universities and public institutions across the country.[3]

But how does poetry engage public culture? How does it contribute to the ways we understand our social and political commitments? Is such understanding even possible or necessary through poetry today? Since the hope for revolutionary change that once associated with poetry now seems remote, it is often common to deny poetry's public effects on contemporary culture.[4] Certainly poetry possesses a place in the public imagination, but in a world profoundly shaped by an ongoing War on Terror and an often predatory and seemingly indefatigable capitalist system, poetry can disappoint those looking for ways to enact art's modernist heritage of revolutionary change.[5] Poets are not so much considered "legislators of the world," as Shelley saw them; they appear more like cultural shopkeepers, managing inventories of literary value. By this I mean poets often only engage those communities in which the status of literature as an aesthetic object or popular artifact remains beyond question. But too often poetry is overlooked in terms of what it can accomplish beyond the literary community so that it may contribute to more radical social or political confrontations.

Poetry, however, is not alone in its perceived failure to inspire the revolutionary event. Radical confrontations of power are only marginally evident on the cultural horizon.[6] Whether we look to visual artists or to filmmakers, to musicians or to social activists, no one in the West agitates for a coherent and widespread social, political, or economic revolution. Why, then, should poetry be held accountable for this seeming failure? Perhaps, instead, our questions should ask how poetry accomplishes certain significant public work, composing actions and capacities in some readers and auditors. The result might be a rhetorical poetry—an art that is motivated to address public concerns and to increase possibilities of social action through persistent performative inquiry. This kind of rhetorically motivated poetics, in many ways, resembles the "tactical media" of Internet-based activism, where hackers, performers, and digital artists often leverage critical social and political confrontations. While "tactical media," much like rhetorical poetry, contributes temporal and ephemeral encounters with a localized and specific audience, it can nonetheless expand critical awareness for certain technology users and witnesses of these discrete social performances. Tactical media does not, however, pursue the many fantasies of the romance of the revolutionary event. "The right question to ask is not whether tactical media *works* or not, whether it succeeds or fails in spectacular fashion to effect structural transformation," Rita Raley argues, "rather, we should be asking to what extent it strengthens social relations and to what extent its activities are virtuosic."[7]

Poets Beyond the Barricade contributes to conversations in rhetorical studies and literary history by showing how social relations in public culture are strengthened by specific actions produced within the often-rigid parameters of postindustrial society and public culture. The rhetorical poetry in the pages of this book is similar to the tactical media Raley describes in that both of these public strategies rely on specific forms of engagement that contribute to public culture, education, and an expansion of capacities prior to deliberative moments of rhetorical debate.[8] Specifically, as I will elaborate, modalities of rhetorical intervention in poetry can enact gestures that allow new civic possibilities to persist within the contingent situations and specific pressures of contemporary North American and global culture. The goal for the poets discussed in this book is not to change the world, broadly speaking, but usually to accomplish specific objectives that can encourage possibilities in public situations. There are, however, problems to address before describing in greater detail how rhetorical poetic engagement in public events can work: We must, for instance, consider our demands of poetry as a public art in a postindustrial social and political milieu that is realized by such terms as *administered world, biopolitics, control society,* and *public sphere;* we must also consider how the cultural legacy of poetry and rhetoric in contemporary culture creates a significant division in attitude toward formalist gesture and aesthetic *production* on one hand and symbolic acts or interventions in language on the other. Beyond these, specific instances of public engagement suggest what, indeed, poetry in today's public culture realistically can accomplish.

Postindustrial Society and Art

Contemporary poetry adheres through a mixture of lore, institutional literary study, popular culture, personal affinity, and in-group identifications. These diverse associations invite many misconceived practices as well as misunderstood perceptions of poetry's cultural significance. Theodor Adorno observes how the separation of poetic practice from its cultural reception increased significantly after the tumultuous and horrific conflicts of the Second World War. He describes how "everything about art ha[d] become problematic: its inner life, its relation to society, even its right to exist."[9] The "administered world" in which art and poetry struggled to establish positions in society often compromised revolutionary commitments that became increasingly reified in the context of popular culture entertainment. Intellectual and artistic commitments soon gave way to performances of political spectacle. If the poems of Anna Louise Strong reinforced the commitments and political solidarity of workers early in twentieth-century Seattle, by midcentury the political poetry available for public consumption spoke not to workers, but addressed the capacities of a cultural market that reproduced political sensibilities and social values—values that were changing in a Cold War society. Allen Ginsberg did not inspire revolution; he reinforced certain social possibilities, helping to establish permission for readers to consider new relationships between the individual and society. Part impresario, part cultural prophet, he spoke not to the revolutionary moment but to its latent possibilities within a postwar situation of economic prosperity filtered through the conservative political paranoia of communist invasion. The success of the Beats was in part generated by a popular aversion to prescriptive Cold War–era social and moral attitudes. The performance of political beliefs through poetry helped shape the emergent social attitudes of the 1950s and '60s. But rather than confronting power in the form of worker solidarity, poets like Ginsberg validated broader cultural impulses for personal experiences through sex, drugs, religion, and other cultural expressions of the individual. While revolution may have animated the art house conversations of the Bohemian dives in San Francisco's North Beach or New York's Lower East Side, the political purpose was often lost in the exchange for new forms of self-expression.[10]

This narrative of the corruption of the poet or artist as a fallen demigod, whose political voice is absorbed into the commodification of its forms in the cultural marketplace, associates with Michel Foucault's notion of *biopolitics*, a term that describes the disciplinary functions of the individual in industrial societies.[11] While notions also like Gilles Deleuze's "control society" portray the kind of technological and biological union of discipline and desire that describes postindustrial society and the failure of the revolutionary event's emergence, the poets I turn to retain a faith in public possibilities; they employ, moreover, rhetorical gestures that align these hopes within actualities of existing conditions.[12] Some are difficult to characterize in modernist literary traditions, and many disassociate from publicity-driven forms of technocapitalism by focusing their efforts on specific targets well beyond the concerns of popular culture.[13] If the Beats adapted public forms of poetry to engage the preoccupations of a changing mass culture in postwar America, many poets after 1960 similarly adapted to the shifting social features of the nation: Charles Olson, Denise Levertov, Diane di Prima, and LeRoi Jones (now Imamu Amiri Baraka) advanced new perspectives of civic engagement, war protest, and racial conflict at the outskirts of public culture. Just as the workers strikes and commitments to solidarity of the early twentieth century no longer provided an audience for the poets of the 1950s, so too the popular sentiment of the 1960s, '70s, and '80s soon revived in the Reagan era a conservative ideology opposed to "tales of Beatnik glory."[14] No longer motivated by free love in a period where HIV/AIDS made headlines, or compelled by experimental drug use and self-exploration in an era that witnessed the rise of the Religious Right, the radical and experimental cultural optimism that greeted the Beats slowly dissipated. Instead, a conservative Cold War sense of values was reestablished in dominant cultural narratives. Poets after 1960, therefore, whose work evolves out of the social struggles for justice in the Cold War, slowly find their audiences changing, and as a result they discover strategies that let them adapt new public gestures even as the features of public culture necessarily shift.

I linger over these descriptions of poetry and postindustrial society to point out the great difficulties activists and artists face in contexts that certainly are compromised by thorough extensions of power. The vast systemic and internalized processes that shape contemporary society make social and political activism fraught with conflicts, internal strife, prejudices, and self-corrections. The situations such conflicts and contradictions reveal are best understood by examining the motives and strategies that often produce public forms of engagement. Thus, the poetic activism that surfaces in this book is largely dependent on communicative situations where possibilities for intervention are present in the attitudes and beliefs of particular poets: their attempts to intervene in specific situations are motivated by a need to voice their dissent and to perform their citizenship with the tools of their art. Indeed, new actions and capacities grow from the kinds of confrontations with belief and desire many poets today encourage. My own concern, however, about how such change takes place, leads me to sympathize with those looking for the revolutionary event in contemporary culture, even as this book departs from that theoretical optimism. I retain, however, insofar as rhetorical theory reveals the possible successes or failures of particular poetic engagements in US society after 1960, a firm commitment to showing how these practices inform public life and give shape to emergent social possibilities. For their part, the authors and activists who appear in this book theorize their rhetorical-poetic practices based on public models of engagement, and so while it is important to recall the ways in which an "administered world" may inform a good deal of what goes on in contemporary life, as well as provide a context in which to consider poetic work, it leaves little space for public engagement in ways the poets here imagine their own contributions. Public culture, then, acts as the rhetorical-theoretical site of engagement for the poets whose efforts animate the concerns of this book.[15]

Rhetorical Modalities

One way to understand poetry invented for specific forms of public engagement is to investigate the kinds of rhetorical modalities that enable this specific form of verbal art to produce actions and capacities in readers and auditors.[16] Nancy S. Struever strongly informs how I approach modality in rhetoric as a method for describing the ways in which poetry can initiate site-specific actions in public culture.[17] By adapting her arguments—arguments that for her derive from the quarrel of philosophy and rhetoric, and are, in many ways, associated with the philosophical writings of C. S. Peirce—*Poets Beyond the Barricade* shows how possibilities can be announced in situations of social conflict between committed public actors. Sharing similarities with modal logics, Struever's adaptation of modality for rhetoric focuses on "the press of possibility, the discrimination of the actual, the response to necessity and contingency. And rhetoric as hermeneutic, as a specific, traditional contribution to understanding civil interests, tasks, performances, carried in texts, signs, deeply engages modality as primary quality of civil experience."[18] Modality as Struever presents it establishes a useful strategy for understanding poetry because of its own complicated historical relationships to philosophy and rhetoric, relationships I will outline briefly in a moment. For now it is important to show the ways in which a hermeneutical rhetoric of modality—or a rhetorical poetics—presses upon public culture through temporal and spatial shifts as well as through investigations that disclose unrealized possibilities by "a code of gestures" adapted for "intervention, interference, [and] 'acting up.'"[19]

Although he is not a poet, the German social and aesthetic critic Walter Benjamin is presented by Struever (along with Kafka), as an "example of rhetorical brilliance in investigation," and her description of his critical work affirms the kinds of rhetorical-poetic engagements I will pursue later on.[20] Benjamin's "post-Kantian engagement with defining conditions of possibility" also maps onto a "post-Nietzschean 'philology of the future.'"[21] Such an association within a philosophical tradition lets Struever cast Benjamin's significance as a cultural critic within a rhetorical tradition of performance and "beliefs generating rhetorical habits of action in his criticism." She is then able to connect this modernist tradition with the Roman rhetorician Quintilian, for whom "gesture, *gestus* or *actio,* was the preeminent rhetorical skill."[22] As Struever continues, "gesture," for Benjamin, "describes the most basic unit of rhetorical effect, of material force in communication, and, still, only loosely attached to semantic structures; and, he regards gesture, surely, as timeful practice, not pure, stop-time visuality."[23] Through "gesture" Struever relates "discursive force" as "a complicity with the modality of contingency: the inquirer works in 'accidental, external, and even strange aspects in bond with the historical process.' The task is to confront 'the capacity to be at home in marginal domains.'"[24] Benjamin, as collector, translator, and cultural critic, provides a model of rhetorical modality, too, because he stresses "the materiality, [the] physicality of thinking-gesture as rubric." Struever continues, writing: "As opposed to systemic classificatory habits that relegate, deposit, these are *topoi* that rhetorically work in reverse: requesting links, threads of argument; they supply substance, ends, but not means; and, lacking means, they provoke our connection-making by the absence of explicit connections, soliciting, in short, possible arguments in response."[25] Benjamin's habits of investigation "energiz[e] belief." And Struever reminds us "that belief in possibility as primary domain of operation generates particular habits of action in rhetorical inquiry."[26] For Struever, Benjamin is engaged in "literature and criticism as intervention, yet the modal status of the intervention is precisely what is at issue. Not only are the demarcations impossible/possible insecure, but the actuality, the direction of the gesture is troublesome, descriptions are reactive, expositions too reflexive to place." Benjamin, then, is the preeminent rhetorician for Struever because of "the appreciation of the primacy of gesture" and for "his wild originality in generating possibility in response to contingency as context."[27]

I have spent time with Struever's arguments about Benjamin's rhetorical modalities of possibility and gesture because the German iconoclast provides an example that literary critics, poets, and theorists of cultural studies and communication will all recognize. I hope also by taking the rhetoricized version of Benjamin as a critical model for many of the poets I describe below, certain disciplinary divisions that often accompany boundary-crossing works such as this may be suspended, at least temporarily. Modality helps show how literature can be focused in particular moments to pursue new outcomes in situations that reveal new possibilities, or that realize actualities nascent to ideological conflict. The basic strategy of the gesture produces public conflict and initiates ethical procedures between poet/performer and reader/audience in certain situations of print, digital media, and other performative spaces. Modality is the expressive force issued in certain contexts that require interventions to address the actions and capacities of public participants. Modality also enables investigations of the possibilities available to participants in social and political situations, and it encourages gestures that can shape or enhance the potentials available to public actors. For these reasons, the rhetorical poetry in this book reveals responses in literature today that are significant for their commitments to community formation and public culture.

Rhetoric, Poetry, and Modern Social Movements

But why poetry? Of all the ways an activist might influence contemporary debate, why turn to this ancient and often remote aesthetic, an art that is largely alien from more common kinds of communication in postindustrial societies? One reason, perhaps, is the specific kinds of pressure it can provide in particular situations; thus, the poets considered in this book share more in common with the rhetorical-poetic traditions that predate romanticism and modernism.[28] Indeed, distinctions between rhetoric and literature, public engagement and aesthetic form, were less evident in the Renaissance, for instance. Poets and other writers were all formally trained in rhetoric, and without a concept of "literature" as we understand it today they did not distinguish readily between poetry and other manifestations of the rhetorical arts.[29] While the more recent poets considered here may not understand rhetoric in the ways of their early modern forebears, they do often explore new cultural and social possibilities by creating a kind of liminal space wherein public action can be modeled, explored, and invented for particular public audiences.[30] And yet the three-hundred-year gap between the end of the Renaissance and the present often complicates poetry's relationship to rhetoric in the present. Today, poets tend to identify more closely with philosophical traditions, or adhere to strict literary values of aesthetic practice. In part the invention of literature in the eighteenth century intervenes on poetry as a public art, bringing with it traumatic consequences.

The eighteenth century, for instance, was the beginning of a shift away from the modeling of rhetorical situations in drama and poetry toward fundamentally new conceptions of rhetoric as a mode of expression that established a clear path of understanding between author and auditor. For Adam Smith, George Campbell, and Hugh Blair, argues Barbara Warnick, three "critical senses" came to dominate rhetorical instruction: "propriety, sublimity, and taste."[31] These senses profoundly affected poetry in that the domain of literature became strongly associated with aesthetic experience and an audience's capacities for developing correct forms of taste. For belletrists like Smith and Blair, the sublime contributed "a touchstone of creativity, grandeur, and uniqueness."[32] While propriety and the sublime formed qualities of discourse for the belletrists, "taste was viewed as a capacity of the recipient."[33] Such emphasis leaves behind the Aristotelian theory of persuasive possibilities that had animated the Renaissance notion of poetics and develops instead what Warnick describes as "an empiricist tendency to equate taste with sensory capacity and a common-sense impulse to stress the importance of cognition and judgment in taste. All of the belletrists agreed, too, that there was an elite somewhere to which one could look to establish a taste standard."[34]

With literary study devoted to the development of a reader's sense of taste, something one learns according to various methods of textual engagement, situational models of rhetoric as a practice of civic life waned in pedagogical significance during the nineteenth and twentieth centuries. The division transacted between author and audience created an awareness of the author as separate from the culture that supported notions of genius. By the romantic period this leads to the harmonious play of the imagination on one hand and emancipatory pursuits on the other, all of which are found in the works of Coleridge, Wordsworth, Blake, and Shelley. But the belletrist emphasis on the sublime creativity of the writer and the evolution of taste in readers stressed the genius or special vision of the poet over others. In the nineteenth century this leads to an understanding of literature as "the best that has been thought or said," putting special stress on the hierarchy of relations between author and readership.[35] This in part contributes to the cultural and creative development of what Jeffrey Walker calls a "sacerdotal literatus" who, "as the representative of a higher self maintained or proposed against the actual downward drift of national culture, turns aside to cultivate the sensibilities of the worthy part of the public world from which he necessarily stands aloof."[36] This literatus, in an American modernist tradition, contributes, moreover, to "an evangelical and charismatic theory of literature and of national culture."[37]

While this sacerdotal literatus informs the making of many of the American modernist epics like Ezra Pound's *Cantos* or William Carlos Williams's *Paterson,* a critical subversion of social and cultural attitudes began to appear in Zurich after the First World War. Tristan Tzara, Hugo Ball, Emmy Hennings, Gottfried Benn, George Heym, and others performed at the opening of Cabaret Voltaire on February 15, 1915. This theatrical and public performance reintroduced the liminal experience of Renaissance drama with the radical experimentation of formal expression appropriate to polyglot Zurich—a city of refugees during the horrors of war.[38] These performances invited audiences into the spectacle of art, thus limiting the division between it and public life. The social and political upheaval of Europe at this time found relief in the deliberate reconfiguration of established values and social structures, offering instead a connection to the revolutionary social and political possibilities latent during this cultural era.[39] While Dada conflicts in significant ways with the American modernist tradition, the appearance of its creative strategies in the United States after 1960 helps to explain the historical background that made the countercultural movements of the period possible. Dada can be seen as a popular, public form that at least initially attempted to downplay social hierarchies and canon formations.[40]

Attempts have been made to revise how poetry contributes to social culture in the early decades of the twentieth century. For instance, literary recoveries of social histories in US poetry from 1910 to 1945 illustrate the great social and political possibilities that existed for many writers. The social reconstruction of poetic texts Cary Nelson assembles shows how "literary 'taste' is not a superficial phenomenon but one embedded within the productive relations of our history."[41] His arguments about canon formation in American literary history enable the evaluation of other voices—voices marginalized by social and political circumstances that prevented legitimization by cultural or literary critics. Nelson's pivotal work makes it possible, as he writes, "to propose a general reconsideration of the relations between poetry and the rest of social life," and initiates my investigation of certain poets after 1960.[42] If his work considers the significant social address and broad popular readership of underrepresented texts, such as the *Little Red Song Book,* published by the Industrial Workers of the World (IWW) during the early years of the twentieth century, the writing I address in public situations similarly pursues specific social commitments. My claims are made, however, to increase our knowledge of contemporary public space and the modalities available in activist engagements. I do not attempt to correct the canons of literary history; instead, I present situations of engagement and consider the possibilities such literary gestures initiate in public contexts.

Joseph Harrington also addresses the distinction between US academic and popular poetry in relation to social movements in the first decades of the last century. While he is concerned with a generic and social consideration of poetry of the period as it was being fashioned into "a popular art form—either in terms of the number of readers or by way of some inherent connection to 'the people,'" I make a distinction between public and popular writing.[43] The poets I examine in the postindustrial, postwar society in America do not all have a popular following, nor are they particularly concerned with widespread publicity. Instead, confrontation with public culture requires different rhetorical strategies. Harrington, however, enables our understanding of the social history and tensions that produced a division in the American modern canon between populist poets and modernist authors. In many ways, the Beats of the 1950s finally embody both possibilities, taking direction from Ezra Pound and William Carlos Williams as much as from the particular experiences and concerns of contemporary social and political life. As Harrington observes, "genteel and newspaper poets, communists and New Poets, [B]eats and the Poetry Societies of America all share one thing in common: they all, in one way or another and to a greater or lesser extent, agreed that poetry possesses an intrinsic or potential duty toward or power among reading (or listening) publics. Accordingly, they all became suspect in the eyes of the institutionally ascendant modernist critics."[44] Unfortunately, this suspicion persists, particularly in the case of the Beats, who, while maintaining a significant presence in popular culture, have yet to be fully addressed by academic literary critics and historians.

While others have contributed greatly to our understanding of the social relationships of poetry, popular culture, and canonization in postwar culture,[45] I pursue slightly different relationships to social action in public spaces in order to elaborate on specific strategies by poets who confront public situations with gestures that expand possibilities, actions, and capacities in social contexts. By focusing on unique public situations, rather than on larger social movements or categorical descriptions of kinds of social action, we can derive an understanding of how publics are engaged rhetorically, and how rhetorical poetry, applied through the modalities of possibility, confronts the temporal and contingent public spaces we inhabit.

Rational-Critical Debate and the Epideictic Mode

While public sphere studies, following the lead of Jürgen Habermas and others, have been concerned largely with rational-critical debate, such approaches link also to the disparate disciplines of rhetoric, literary theory, communication, cultural studies, philosophy, and others.[46] The terms of this debate frequently overlook the role of epideictic modes of communication in the rhetorical making of public attitudes and beliefs. Although Aristotle defined the epideictic as a mode of "praise and blame," it has been expanded in contemporary rhetorical study to be read as a mode of discourse that addresses belief and desire.[47] The public and private environments we inhabit, then, are striated with claims and imaginings that outpace critical debate in an orgy of textual and visual stimulation, acting on the ongoing transformation of civic space, democratic institutions, and global markets. Public decisions that arise through legitimate institutions are sustained in part by a collective fiction, a belief in the process of debate frequently mediated by actors who perform our democratic duties for us in print and digital spaces. The increasingly vibrant and dizzying array of textual and visual material, much of it in the form of advertising that has recontextualized and coordinated the work of twentieth-century modernist literary practice, pleads for public attention and addresses some of the desires that form the basis of key ideologies.[48] While the model of rational-critical discourse gives us a useful set of tools to investigate how we arrive at decisions and how policies are implemented, we must account also for how public space is prepared, in advance, for deliberative processes. In an era of digital technologies and stunningly vivid visual depictions of the publics we inhabit, temporality trumps tempo: our global capacity for rapid communication suggests a preference for velocity over pace, which relates to economic models that value growth over fruitful production and meaningful labor.[49] As long as a sense of connection at ever-increasing speeds of transmission advances communication into all spheres of private and public life, an illusion of participation accompanies voyeuristic contributions to democracy. With traditional media outlets such as radio and television we now include online sources for news and debate. Blogs, Facebook, Twitter, and other digital media provide public spaces for individuals to participate in divergent communities interested in politics, travel, art, food, sex, and almost any other division of the vast array of public or private experience imaginable.

But the story told about rational-critical debate in the public sphere is only partially accurate, for public spaces are invested with ideological values that are formed prior to deliberative modes of discourse. The preparation of public space by epideictic discourse to ready an audience for other forms of debate should be scrutinized, for much is at stake when we stop to consider how belief and desire can spill over into acts that are often irrevocable. This book considers the limitation of the rational-critical model by looking at how the epideictic shaping of our belief and desire by poetic texts and performances can prepare cultural actors for participation in public life.

The modalities of rhetorical engagement described by Struever let us expand the rhetorical potential in public spaces to include more than rational-critical discourse in the terms of public debate. The epideictic mode, in particular, shows how belief and desire filter arguments prior to the deliberative moment. Indeed, the realm of epideictic discourse figures prominently as a mode of public communication. As textures or "coloration" of the symbols, images, commonplaces, discourses, and performative acts correlate to represent and persuade individuals about belief, poetry can expand actions and capacities in particular situations of public encounter where new arguments and gestures form. While film, drama, music, and many other disciplines contribute to the reinforcements and expansions of belief in public life, poetry, when used as a public art, engages situations in ways that can transpose private feeling into public affect. After 1960, for instance, poetry entered Cold War popular consciousness through figures like Allen Ginsberg, Jack Kerouac, Galway Kinnell, Robert Bly, W. S. Merwin, and Adrienne Rich. Their personal engagements with social, political, and feminist encounters informed public expression and belief during a culturally repressive moment in US history. No longer within the provenance of the academy, or associated only with the coteries of postwar American poetry, writers like the Beats became popular icons of a much larger social movement that prefigured the social upheaval of the latter half of the 1960s.[50] While my concern now is not with this popular expression of cultural and public literature, or with the academic and community-oriented poetics of the period, I pursue the work of poets who envision a public and its possibilities at concrete moments of social engagement. Neither popular culture nor private expression answers the question of how epideictic modes engage public space. As the work of the Frankfurt school shows, mass culture is fraught with ideological compromises that reify public action into cultural products for popular consumption. By contrast, communities, or subaltern counterpublics, while potentially able to provide leverage in public situations, more frequently exist to support and reinforce shared values and beliefs without engaging more specifically the larger cultural and political domain in which they reside.[51] While poetry, since the time of Plato, often has held a complicated position in relation to public discourse, the rhetorical poetry I turn to addresses public life in ways that can prepare actors for deliberation in specific situations. As the history of poetry in Western culture has endured a long and complicated relationship to social and political institutions, certain poets after 1960 began to revise poetry's role in relation to democratic public discourse, and their work is the focus of this book.

The following chapters look to poetry in the United States for arguments about the influence of epideictic communication, about the structure of the public sphere, and about private interventions in public spaces that orient attention to social and political issues. This book offers a rhetorical study of poetry in several public contexts, showing how a rhetorical poetics can lead actors to engage public situations with new and meaningful strategies of communication. And based on this exchange, I argue that the rational-critical model of the public sphere should be modified to include other modes of communication relevant to cultural and ideological formations. Despite the tendency of much public-rhetorical theory to focus on rational-critical debate, poetry can make unforeseen connections, and these effects surface in peripheral exchanges that compose and describe cultural values. While there is no doubt that the model of rational-critical debate accounts in many ways for how public spaces develop in cultural influence, I argue that a poem is meaningful to public knowledge insofar as it is capable of preparing an audience for the possibilities that are latent in how circulations of discourse and other symbolic forms are valued.

Rhetorical-Poetic Engagement

While *Poets Beyond the Barricade* is motivated in large part by public address, it investigates, more importantly, public actions through the models of rhetorical theory and literary analysis, disclosing modalities that are shaped by poetic engagement. Such actions in writing focus on the making and reception of poetic texts that reveal the discordant values of democratic feeling in conflict with global policy, and in the kinds of responses these invite. While many competing theories describe public space and the political potentials enabled by it, the accounts here consider also the global and historical dimensions of public culture, for poets participate in many social situations, and their work invites reflection and evaluation of historical and cultural experiences.

A significant effort of this book is to explore a recent historical period, providing a view of the development of poetry and the rhetorical-theoretical concerns it has encouraged in the last half century. I look at moments of public confrontation in the United States as socially and rhetorically engaged realities that are projected in the writing of poets against a social and economic background of global markets and ideological conflicts. I move between several fields that intersect with rhetorical theory, too. These include cultural studies, activism, and literary studies. In this respect, my hope is to reflect the current challenges of rhetorical-critical thinking within an interdisciplinary methodology.

When we defer the culturally conservative obligation to recite the values that will turn readers into good citizens, we can see how literature, read rhetorically, prepares room for deliberation in the various occasions of public life. For poetry and other forms of literature can associate personal experiences with the lives of others, and this in turn can lead to reconsiderations of habits of thought and feeling that interfere with contested public space. Literature remains an important part of rhetorical education not because it only avows the timely truths of the humanities, but because it also instructs us on strategies of seeing ourselves in a world composed of many communities and public situations. The poets after 1960 whose work I address in this context begin from rhetorical assumptions about what poetry can achieve in a given context, not what it represents in terms of broad cultural value.

The portrait of contemporary writing I offer is not glamorous. Few of the poets I discuss receive national or global attention for their particular social goals or the rhetorical approaches they take in their work to achieve them. Some strategies, too, are counterintuitive to our understanding of how we judge particular public interventions. I argue, however, that poetry can create possibilities and expand actions and capacities from its humble origins on the page of a small press book or in the mouth of a public speaker.[52] Size and scale for public messages frequently shift. Many of the writers addressed in this book deliberately find ways to maximize the spatial impact of their engagements through print and web documentation. Strategies, moreover, exist in cultural geography that accounts for how audience formation grows over a period of time. Jules Boykoff and others argue that efforts by key people such as editors or other cultural actors can help a speech, poem, performance, or commercial product reach a larger audience over a short period of time.[53] They show how the context in which something as seemingly ephemeral as a poem can influence an audience or a larger public with its argument. This, in large part, helps explain the efforts of Charles Olson's editors in the pages of a small daily paper to bring his arguments into a civic context. It shows, too, how Denise Levertov's peace movement activism during the Vietnam War carried her political poetry beyond specifically literary situations into larger social confrontations.

If poetry can be viewed as a powerful tool for interacting with the social history and everyday life of a place and its peoples, the poets under consideration here bring attention to communal and social selvages that connect with other narratives striating public spaces in the United States to-day. This book explores the relations between poetic documents and public engagement, and how public spaces are reflected and transformed in the context of globalization that characterizes US culture since 1960. From the Vietnam War to the occupation of Iraq, a rhetorical poetics that is moti-vated by social and political issues of local and global significance shapes how we understand civic protest, public formation, ideological narratives, and cultural history, asking us to look more closely at specific public envi-ronments and social relations. Since it often works against legitimate pub-lic records, exposing personal claims about shared environments, poetry in-fluences how we understand modal rhetorical interventions that make new options, reflections, actions, or capacities possible. The following chapters pursue certain situations in which poetry has been used to enhance per-spectives on public space. Poetry is not a method for creating deliberative exchange, but rather it is an epideictic discourse that prepares readers and auditors to confront the notion of public addressees. *Poets Beyond the Barri-cade* investigates rhetoric's position in the structure of poetry as well as the place of poetry in the rhetorically formed spaces of public culture.

Rhetorical Poetry after 1960: Investigating Public Possibilities

The first of these studies, "Dear Gloucester," attends the civic poetry of Charles Olson. Better known for his modernist epic, *The Maximus Poems,* Olson contributed a series of letters and poems to the *Gloucester Daily Times* that drew attention to styles of city management, land-use issues, and ar-chitectural restoration and preservation. I look primarily at how Olson went from engaging a small, literary audience to addressing the civic decisions that faced a New England coastal community. Significantly, the specific ef-forts and support of publisher Philip Weld and editor Paul Kenyon made Olson's editorials and poems effective for a Gloucester public situation, help-ing to transform his writing into effective civic advocacy for a larger pub-lic audience. Weld and Kenyon supplemented Olson's writing with edi-torial design features that enabled readers to better understand the poet's positions on current issues vital to urban change in Gloucester, Massachu-setts. These included images that reinforced Olson's claims and commen-tary from outside sources to help legitimize his public move from modern-ist visionary to civic orator. I investigate also the rhetorical strategies Olson used to situate his civic concerns within the historical and geographic con-texts of New England cultural values, as he crossed the line that separated poet from orator. Although he failed to achieve many of his goals at civic preservation in Gloucester, we can see strategies for public address through poetry, and how rhetoric contributes modalities that enable self-reflection and awareness in citizens confronting necessary urban changes. His writing in the editorial pages of the paper helped citizens develop capacities to acknowledge urban transformations imposed by an ideology of global economic expansion. This conflict between an expanding global marketplace and local, communal values shows how individual authors can bring attention to civic decisions in a postwar cultural and ideological context.

The next chapter, "Rhetorics of 'Advantage' and 'Pure Persuasion,'" takes place during the divisive years of cultural debate and change generated in large measure by the Vietnam War, and addresses public intervention during a time of social crisis. Here I look to the wartime correspondence (1968–71) and poetry of Robert Duncan and Denise Levertov to focus on rhetorical strategies associated with Kenneth Burke's description of a "rhetoric of advantage" and a "rhetoric of pure persuasion." While the first of these rhetorical models considers social change and public engagement, the other investigates persuasive strategies developed for their own sake. These allowed both writers to create divergent poetic paths in their protest of the war and in their address to social movements and literary public spaces. Their close friendship and intimate correspondence arrived at a crucial impasse in the late 1960s as both writers struggled to theorize an appropriate response to the war and the culture around them. While Levertov, with activist Mitchell Goodman, increasingly announced her role in the peace movement, addressing the concerns and sentiments that created bonds and reinforced the ideological commitments of a broad cultural protest, Duncan grew distrustful of the ideological climate that validated activist participation in the publicity that mobilized opinion against US imperialism abroad. Although both writers were critical of the war in Southeast Asia, they arrived at diametrically opposed responses in their work: Levertov embedded her efforts in the peace movement, writing poems that spoke to the beliefs and desires of activists, while Duncan sought to bring awareness to the condition of war as an attribute of human "order and strife." His presentation of the poet's role conflicted with Levertov's, and he located their difference in theoretical and practical uses of the poem. "The poet's role is not to oppose evil," he cautioned her, "but to imagine it,"[54] thus increasing the situational context for poetic labor to include social, historical, and psychological possibilities. Their competing views were grounded in rhetorical and literary assumptions that helped to illuminate the methodological differences both encountered: Levertov exploited the motives many shared in a popular resistance to war, while Duncan found this ideological condition to be yet another component in the spread of Western-led globalization. Levertov brought forward lyrical-expressivist modes in popular contexts that showed the limitations and successes of such rhetoric in this volatile period. By contrast, Duncan continued in many ways a modernist project of collage, hermetic investigation, and hyposyntactic methodology that identified with a modernist literary program. While such literary high modernism would seem to resist rhetorical approaches to the modalities contingent on actual conditions of war-era stress, Duncan placed emphasis on the situational contexts of war as motive in modern democracy. By showing how public intervention, formed in response to war, adheres within particular historical conditions, Duncan and Levertov provide a compelling orientation for readers of cultural history as well as rhetorical and literary studies.

While the previous investigation acknowledges a divide between rhetoric and literature, personal vision and public action, the following chapter, "Public Witness/Public Mind," considers how poetry is used to query race, politics, and mass media in the work of Lorenzo Thomas and Edward Dorn. By looking at interventions in the public events their sardonic writing addresses, we can see how popular discourse and imagery can be claimed for other public purposes of social engagement. If rhetoric provides strategies of interpretation and public engagement in a field of discourse, then the work I describe here seeks to contextualize cultural possibilities in the proliferating occurrence of mediated images and texts that filter through the poetic imagination. Thomas, for instance, notes the discord between the private perspective of poetic labor and the intrusion on it by televised broadcasts of social images that disturb domestic experience. His work looks at how public images, distributed by mass media, can distort the identity and history behind the social contexts that generate such imagery. By reclaiming potent public images for particular social and historical situations, Thomas recreates meaningful public narratives for his audience. In one telling instance, he appropriates volatile public images generated by the May 1963 segregation protests in Birmingham, Alabama, to address an African American audience about the extensive history of race and enslavement in the United States. The poem for Thomas becomes a kind of intermediary discourse wherein communal vision is reconciled with public claims of legitimacy on social differences of race and class.

Facing a similar problem of reconciliation between public enactments of national ideologies, Edward Dorn's satirical epigrams project an image of a public mind in the discourse of Reagan-era social and economic policy. His rejection of expressivist poetry led him to develop a satirical voice that could negotiate public and private spaces for particular audiences. By taking a rhetorical-hermeneutic approach to the images, texts, and speech generated in specific public instances, Dorn contextualized public issues for readers skeptical of the dominant ideologies of the period. Combining humor, sarcasm, and inappropriate and transgressive content, Dorn fully exploited the satiric epigram to reveal a dissonance between private feeling and public acts. By isolating particular media-generated items for his satiric performance, he contextualized public content within a rhetorical-hermeneutic methodology to increase awareness of the ideological limitations of global capitalism.

Chapter 4, "Poets Against War," attends formations of temporary public alliances as public possibilities for action and capacities that contribute strategies of protest to recent wars in Iraq and Afghanistan. The chapter establishes a meaningful juxtaposition between poetry as social documentation in light of contemporary poetic practice and modernist rhetorical discourse. I begin by looking at the response by poets, gathered under the aegis of Sam Hamill's Poets Against War website, to protest military action in Iraq prior to the March 2003 invasion, and I query the public uses of poetry on the web to establish a rhetorically meaningful site of engagement. To further elucidate the difficulty of forming messages of protest in an ideological climate that, unlike the one during the Vietnam War protests of the '60s, supported US interventions in the Middle East, I investigate public actions taken in New York City by activist groups like Poetry Is Public Art (PIPA) and "Debunker Mentality." Describing strategies of public engagement to define meaningful modalities of social inquiry and protest, I look at how these groups' rhetorical efforts are reconciled with the literary traditions that inspire much of their commentary. Further, I investigate PIPA's efforts at documentation, following the transformation of public interactions as they become catalogued for a larger print audience. From this process of documentation, I assess the Iraq War poems of Kent Johnson, who questions the privilege claimed by literary perspective. By questioning the political commitments of a contemporary avant-garde, he invites his audience to see how events in the Middle East, caused by recent US aggression, require social and political attention. Moving discussion in his poems away from interpretive strategies toward phronetic social solutions, Johnson's satire draws attention to war as a cultural event for which all are responsible: no one remains innocent in his argument; instead, it becomes the responsibility of those who possess the means to act in ways that bring attention to the suffering of others abroad.

The rhetorical nature of the poems I look at contradicts the common assumption that literature provides only an aesthetic experience, and that poetry lies beyond the grittiness of day-to-day life, with its concomitant arguments and reconciliations regarding the public spaces we inhabit. The contrast between the Vietnam War poetry and correspondence of Robert Duncan and Denise Levertov, next to the efforts of PIPA, Kent Johnson, and others, shows distinctions between rhetorical and literary methodologies, even as it reveals the active and agonistic debates that shape these public situations.

Poets Beyond the Barricade examines the relationship of literary documents and rhetorical strategies to show how activist poets have addressed US public spaces. From Vietnam to more recent wars in the Middle East, poetry invites us to renew public perspectives on institutional legitimacy, disciplinary practice, and citizenship. This book looks at late twentieth- and twenty-first-century poetic engagements between local activists and global entities, between the United States and its economic claims on other areas of the world, between the interpretive strategies of literary critique and the motives that underlie rhetorical investigations of cultural phenomena. I suggest ways to develop a theory of rhetorical poetics significant to the potentials in public culture that are produced between institutional identities. While poetry's uses and definitions vary, it remains a vital cultural art that, understood in the register of epideictic rhetoric, gives us opportunities to receive a "reflexive circulatory field" of texts, images, and performances that both comment on and contribute to our knowledge of the various modalities of public space we inhabit.[55] To further our understanding of civic practice, public intervention, and the agonistic discourse of democratic societies, strategies adopted by poets to pursue critical debates in contemporary culture advance our appreciation of local and global citizenship. At a divide between not only the disciplinary intersections of the academy but also notions of local, national, and global citizenship, poetry rhetorically used to further itself as a "field of action" shows how the personal interface of the individual affects the structural reality of institutions.[56] With this in mind, I hope to show how a rhetorically motivated poetics can offer a critical opportunity to reconfigure our approaches to public spaces, and that the intertextual exchanges these methods promote can modify our various social and aesthetic assumptions. The artifacts of rhetorical and literary studies lead us to encounter the world in symbolic forms, appraising our public and private responsibilities and perceptions by examining the motives we do and do not value. At stake in the seams of institutional discourses are evaluations of modes of possibility, contingency, necessity, and actuality. The rhetorical poetic histories here offer insight to the profound personal labor undertaken to sharpen and illumine the public spaces revealed by the textual and symbolic fields we encounter. Through these we discover how different rhetorical modes of critical engagement in many ways give form to the public environments around us.

I

"Dear Gloucester"

Poet Charles Olson has issued a last desperate appeal to the public . . .
—Editors, *Gloucester Daily Times,* August 8, 1967

While best known for his epic *The Maximus Poems,* a work that self-consciously engages a modernist tradition in the spirit of William Carlos Williams, Ezra Pound, and others, Charles Olson modified the practice of modernist pastiche and assembly to establish a voice that was plausibly competent as a vehicle of public consciousness. His complicated practice as a poet-orator—a man committed to poetic production, literary criticism, radical pedagogy, and civic engagement—provides insight to how poetic gestures in public contexts can motivate reflection on issues important for civic awareness and social environments. Through Olson's letters and poems in the 1960s written for the *Gloucester Daily Times* we see also how poetry can take on a new audience, moving from a literary context to one of municipal debate. If Olson's modernist literary practices restricted his access to a larger public audience, his writing for the town daily narrowed distances between personal vision and communal realization, and with the help of key public figures he was able to bring a historically grounded perspective to the Massachusetts community where he lived in the 1960s. By looking closely at his gestural shifts away from literary coterie to civic space, we can discover how civic possibilities are maintained through poetry in the controversial situations Olson addressed. While contingent public concerns provoked responses in him that narrowed the distance between private experience and more integrated social textures, his actions contributed to a lasting regional legacy.[1] Through his relationship with concerned citizens, editors, and local publishers, Olson's community advocacy invited reflection and demanded action over the inevitable urban changes Gloucester faced in the 1960s.

While he negotiated the distance between literary vision and public argument in powerful and iconoclastic ways, the intervention of editors at the town daily in Gloucester ensured a public reception for his civic address. In particular, Paul Kenyon, the paper's editor, and Philip Weld, publisher, contributed greatly to the preparation of Olson's idiosyncratic literary style for a large public audience, and a portion of this chapter looks at that task while considering the results and municipal possibilities Olson enabled. In terms of extending knowledge of public culture and the rhetorical methods available to someone like Olson who, in many ways, addressed a community's sense of values, the situations described here suggest modal possibilities inspired by contingent local issues of ecological preservation, urban planning, and architectural development. While not all of Olson's advocacy projects were successfully realized, he left a record of public inquiry that complicates deliberative discourse based on actualities of existing civic discussion; he established, moreover, a record of committed gestures, performative acts, and strategic interruptions that move between literary claims of authority and public capacities for engagement.[2] Like Walter Benjamin, Olson pursued a "contextualist program" and was "antiformalist" in his approach to a poetics grounded in a materiality of communication.[3] The archive of these actions provides a public record for understanding how such strategies influenced a region of the American Northeast, and it preserves events of keen interest that enable the public queries pursued here.

But as a writer who is often associated with many aspects of Ezra Pound's version of modernism, it is possible to overly identify Olson's "code of gestures" with the strong, performative presentations in the *Cantos,* or to those vituperative radio broadcasts transmitted from World War II Italy. Both authors privilege conservative instincts of preservation, and both are critical of business interests (or of what Olson calls "merchandise men, / who get to be President,"[4]) that intervene on prior cultural traditions. Olson's critical perspective, however, is directed at formations of capital that had been imposed on geographies that, to him, once bestowed identity and purpose for communities, and he integrated these into historic public and personal legacies. But the tendency in both men to idealize the past creates what can be seen as a romanticized reaction to the industrial and postindustrial forms of modernity each responded to. This cultural stance is echoed, moreover, in the writing of Olson's student Edward Dorn, whose penetrating analysis of US society critiqued instead postwar commodity culture, focusing especially on what he called (echoing Pound), its "ruinous increase."[5] This criticism of the proliferation of postwar consumption—a contrived system of growth leading to environmental devastation and disciplined socioeconomic relationships—correlates closely with Olson's own responses in the pages of the *Gloucester Daily Times.* While certainly a strong play is made by these writers to exert literary authority for their claims on behalf of idealistic, prewar visions of a socially integrated American polis, Olson's postwar criticism, unlike Pound's, focuses on the practical benefits of conservation, resource management, regional identity, and urban planning, not on idealistic notions of order, tradition, and anti-Semitism.

But the macho voice Olson creates associates strongly with Pound, whose own masculinist performances may have been derived, like other modernists, from fears of "the distance between aesthetic sterility and artistic authority" in a new era that broke radically with the past.[6] As Michael Davidson explains, machismo in the writing of postwar male poets paid homage "to the old guys of modernism . . . by reinstating an ideal of heroic masculinity and by returning to romanticism's cult of energy, orality, primitivism, and expressivism."[7] For Davidson, the "compulsory character of homosocial literary communities" created "innovative poetic practices," too. He claims, moreover, that these "communities saw themselves in direct contrast to more public agendas of consolidation and consensus," and this certainly will be evident in the voices Olson constructs for his public writing.[8] The thing to note for the purposes of this chapter is that Olson's construction of masculinity is complicated by cultural attitudes, literary homage, class identification, and other values that shaped the potentials in his poetic vocabulary. The very male voices that Olson and other New American poets create in the Cold War era are in many ways reactive to systemic social and economic changes in America at that time. But Olson also registers a different kind of voice—one that is vulnerable and less certain than the many performances that animate Pound's shifting social and creative masks.

Another difference was Olson's obvious political and ethnic commitments. As a New Deal Democrat working under the FDR administration during World War II, Olson supported Roosevelt's social policies and actively addressed first-generation ethnic groups regarding the Democratic Party's position on the war. Olson identified with many of the issues immigrants faced, while Pound's rigid screed against "a botched civilization" betrayed a serious rift between the poets: one engaged in the social and political particularities of US citizenship, the other from a great distance lamenting the decline of tradition and values. Consequently, Olson self-consciously stepped away from Pound's influence; thus, after World War II, when the elder poet had been incarcerated at St. Elizabeths Hospital in Washington, DC, Olson wrote of him as a "traitor" who "stood with the lovers of ORDER."[9] It is worth noting also that Olson, the New Deal Democrat, and Robert Duncan (whose work will be considered in chapter

2), share much in common with Dorn's critical observations of a heedlessly expanding American culture and economy. This is a very different socio-critical affinity for postwar interventions in poetry than the openly fascist, cultural-traditional establishment of literary objectives sustained by Pound and others of his generation.

I have lingered over Olson's relationship to modernism because he did little to modify his writing for a public medium, using instead modernist strategies of montage along with disruptive syntax and tonal registers that colored the process of his writing in deliberate ways. Because of these literary commitments, his public presentation allows a rare opportunity to observe the rhetorical effects of a marginal voice making arguments in a more culturally accessible venue. While Olson's letters and poems to the *Gloucester Daily Times* focus on local issues, particularly on topics of architectural and ecological preservation, civic history, and the maintenance of common spaces, the occasions of his letters and poems provide insights to how rhetorical poetics influences public space. Primarily, I will explore how scale shifts[10] contribute to the transforming contexts of modernist public discourse, as well as show how poetic gestures in Olson's writing for a public audience could alter contingent plans with new possibilities of municipal action.

Guilt and Urban Change in Gloucester

Olson's letters to the *Gloucester Daily Times* provide a unique opportunity to witness a poet's attempt to shift scales in readership from a small literary community to a larger civic audience. Olson's letters should be looked at as an effort to bring arguments in poetry to a genre that typically allows some degree of epideictic discourse within the more deliberative and forensic modes of a daily paper. In its pages, editor Paul Kenyon and publisher Philip Weld encouraged Olson to express his views to a public audience invested in issues that were also significant to the poet, even offering, in 1963, to give the poet a regular column.[11] They provided print space for Olson's claims, frequently inserted photographs to illustrate some of the primary concerns in his letters, and on occasion, Kenyon provided editorial commentary to help interpret Olson for his local audience. In many ways we may think of this process as a collaboration between the poet and his editor, and as such the role of mediation plays a significant part in the scale shifts that occur for Olson's work. Moreover, Kenyon did not alter Olson's letters directly, most of which are written with the same poetic form and diction as *The Maximus Poems.* Taking the poet's concerns into account, Kenyon went so far as to even reproduce Olson's peculiar typography through facsimile reproductions. Some of Olson's letters, however, were framed with editorial comments to help readers understand the arguments better, and photographs of buildings important to Olson's arguments often accompanied his editorials, thus providing a link between the common experience of the city with the uncommon rhetorical gestures of the modernist poet. More about this editorial relationship will be described a little later, but for now let us begin with an exemplary editorial by Olson.

In his third letter to the paper from December 3, 1965, we get a sense of the clash of modernist montage within the editorial packaging for the *Gloucester Daily Times.* The occasion for Olson's letter is the destruction of the Davis-McMillan house, a town house at 69 Middle Street next to the YMCA in downtown Gloucester. Solomon H. Davis had built it in 1840.[12] Because of its ornamental Greek columns, the house was known locally as "Solomon's Temple." The Y wanted to replace the house with a new swimming pool.[13] Olson's response mixes outrage at the citizens of Gloucester for allowing the demolition of the house while providing a historical context for reading the value of local architecture. Written in the oratorical style of the early books of *The Maximus Poems,* Olson assumes a Maximus-like persona whose ethos is built on archival knowledge of town history. The first portion of the poem begins:

A *Scream* to the Editor:

Moan the loss, another
house
is gone

       Bemoan the present
which assumes
its taste, bemoan the easiness
of smashing anything

Moan Solomon Davis'
house, gone
for the YMCA, to build another
of its cheap benevolent places
bankers raise money for,

and who loan money for new houses: each destruction doubles
our loss and doubles bankers' gain when four columns[. . . .][14]

Here, with performed indignation, Olson "moans the loss" of a physical piece of the city's heritage. While he is sensitive to the details of Gloucester's architectural history, he is skeptical of the institutions of finance that support the replacement of historic structures with urban conveniences. He refers to the YMCA as a "cheap benevolent place," throwing into question any positive social effects the organization may offer the city. Olson is skeptical of the system of finance that seeks to replace historic property with structures the polis does not need, at least from Olson's informed historical perspective. In other words, a YMCA exists in Gloucester because bankers have persuaded the city to make room for it at the expense of historic structures. This interrogation of capital as a force of destruction motivates much of Olson's work and supports many of his angry addresses to the polis. He argues for the value of historic memory and the relations of that memory through civic space. For Olson, the city's expansion in the 1960s made room for new sites without a thorough reflective process on the value of historic structures and their revived possibilities in the present. To his perspective, the total environment provided a sense of individual value, and when the architecture changed, so too the people.

As the poetic epistle continues, Olson moves from the historic circumstance of the destruction of "Solomon's Temple" to address the people directly, writing:

> Bemoan a people who spend
>   beyond themselves, to flourish
> and to further themselves
> as well made the Solomon Davis house itself
> was such George Washington
> could well have been inaugurated
> from its second floor
>
>   and now it is destroyed because 70 years ago
> Gloucester already could build the Y, and Patillo's
> equally ugly brick front and building[. . . .][15]

Here Olson examines temporal scale in a civic context. The YMCA, built seventy years prior, and "Patillo's," a dry goods warehouse, constructed in 1895, "dwarfed the Davis-McMillan house."[16] Olson's argument "bemoans" the loss of Gloucester's original mercantile existence to the corporate interests of the late nineteenth and twentieth centuries. Here he returns to a theme prevalent throughout *The Maximus Poems,* wherein he argues to preserve an ideal of Gloucester as a village of fishermen and merchants, and he regrets the town's decisions to allow newer corporate expansions to transform his beloved polis.

The poem/editorial continues with considerable historic details that are relevant to his argument about the destruction of the Davis-McMillan house. Once he has provided the historical civic relation of the house to the history of Gloucester, Olson shifts tone from that of the concerned citizen interested in Gloucester's architectural history to a voice of outrage at the social catastrophe of the kind of historical erasure he perceives. He writes:

> oh city of mediocrity and cheap ambition destroying
> its own shoulders its own back greedy present persons
> stood upon, stop this renewing without reviewing
> loss loss loss no gains oh not moan stop stop stop this
>   total loss of surface and of mass,
>   putting bank parking places with flowers, spaces dead so dead
>   in even the sun one does not even know one passes by them
> Now the capitals of Solomon Davis' house
> now the second floor behind the black grill work
> now the windows which reach too,
>
> now the question who if anyone was living in it
> now the vigor of the narrow and fine clapboards on the back
> now that flatness right up against the street,
>
>   one is in despair, they talk and put flowers up
>   on poles high enough so no one can water them,
> and nobody
> objects
>   when houses which have held and given light
>   a century, in some cases two centuries,
>   and their flowers
>   aren't even there in one month[. . . .][17]

Here Olson amplifies his general theme of Gloucester's erosion under the encroaching demands of capital by shaming the town's citizens. He argues against the "total loss of surface and of mass, / putting bank parking places with flowers" in "spaces dead so dead." In many ways, the claim is incredible to our perspectives in the early twenty-first century, for Olson argues on behalf of the preservation of an eighteenth- and nineteenth-century conception of the city's coherence, even as new social needs were being created through an expanded notion of postwar capital. In this small municipality in 1965, such issues were relevant to citizens who were going along with changes that to them must have appeared necessary. Olson, as a voice of archival conscience, provided strong enough claims for this historic awareness in his poem to receive publication space in the daily paper. In fact, the press of his argument in the "scream" went beyond the usual civic protests found in the paper.[18]

Olson continues for a couple of stanzas to argue against the urban transformation "in one month" of centuries-old structures, claiming that "the Electric Company's / lights" even "destroy the color of color / in human faces."[19] As the poem progresses toward its bitter conclusion, one might begin to wonder what on earth such a tirade is doing in a newspaper.

> I'm sick
> of caring, sick of watching
> what, known or unknown, *was* the
> ways of life. I have no
> vested interest even in this which
> makes life.
> Moaning nothing. Hate hate hate
> I hate those who take away
> and do not have as good to
> offer. I hate them. I hate the carelessness[. . . .][20]

Then finally, after presenting the historic necessity of preserving the house and after a declaration of a hatred of "carelessness," he arrives at the final argument:

> For $25,000 I do not think anyone
> should ever have let the YMCA take down Solomon Davis'
> house, for any purpose of the YMCA.[21]

In order to understand the rhetorical strategies of the poem, we should consider more fully the situation in which it arrived to the citizens of Gloucester in 1965. Olson's letter was published under the headline: "Destruction of 'Solomon's Temple' Prompts 'Scream to the Editor' by Gloucester Poet Charles Olson."[22] Photographed from Olson's typescript, the letter occupied a full half page in the *Times's* editorial section. A photograph of the poet by William Greenbaum appeared with the caption: "The Poet in His Fort Square Home," a reference to Olson's Gloucester address. Another image of the "Davis–McMillan house at 69 Middle Street" reveals its partial demolition. Following Olson's "letter," an editor's note reads: "Charles Olson is the only living Cape Ann writer whose biography is included in the latest edition of the authoritative *Oxford Companion to American Literature.* His appeal for the appreciation of Gloucester beauty is presented in his distinctive projective verse technique."[23] A number of rhetorically interesting elements are at work here, for we have a situation in which community arguments are made through the words and actions of several actors, namely the poet, his editor, and, significantly, *Times* owner Philip Weld. Behind this immediate scene, the ethos-forming reference to Olson as a person listed in "the authoritative *Oxford Companion to American Literature*" lends the poem certain credentials for the editor, who shows familiarity with Olson's "projective verse technique," the word "technique" coloring Olson's theoretical proposal for writing with a tinge of local misapprehension for modernist formal innovation.

"Projective verse," following Williams's notion of the poem as a "field of action," was more than a "technique."[24] It proposed a radical compositional approach to writing that influenced the New American poetics and defined the Black Mountain project associated with Olson by encouraging poets to consider the rhetorical situation in which poetry operates. Its stress on the process-oriented and energy-driven "field" of the poem provided a way for authors inspired by the modernist tradition to address environments that constituted their social and physical experiences. To reduce unintentionally what was at the time a compelling statement of the New American poetics to a mere "technique" suggests that while Kenyon was sympathetic to Olson, he had to narrow the range of concerns dominating Olson's poetics for his Gloucester audience. While a small in-group of those already familiar with modern and contemporary poetry would recognize the richness of Olson's claims better than Kenyon, the editor, nonetheless, perceives the potential in Olson's "technique" and respects the poet as a leader of a literary community. He is willing to open up page space to this literary figure so that arguments on behalf of the city of Gloucester could be made from a unique perspective informed by a broad sociohistorical engagement with the potentialities of the landscapes of the Cape Ann region. While projective verse developed in literary contexts and conversations, its focus on the actualities of experience and potentials in writing to enable new social possibilities appealed to Kenyon, who certainly drew Olson's poetic voice into civic debates for these intervening capacities.

As the semifamous son of a small New England city experiencing rapid urban change, Olson's reputation as a poet of international recognition was enough to secure some special treatment in the editorial pages of the paper. The half-page facsimile copy of the poem with a brief editorial explaining it to readers indicates that Olson's work was received with considerable respect, even if it was written in a style that may have appeared obtuse, difficult to follow, and outraged at civic disregard for public structures. If this poem had appeared in a collection of poetry, it might be read with passing interest as a disgruntled and angry diatribe against civic change. In fact, it might be read as the conservationist social critique it is. In this way it would offer little by which an actual public could create social change, and only the initiated group of poets who understood Olson's project might find some value in its appeal to historic awareness and the kinetic scope of human activity within specific geographic coordinates.

Because Olson's "Scream" appears in the medium of a print daily, however, other perspectives emerge from the poem. For instance, in the context of a newspaper, the poem's language is certainly unusual. And yet, removed from the context of other modernist works, it is easy enough to read, with a little patience. Gloucester's public would have understood the immediate references to the city's architecture while poets or contemporary readers of poetry, persuaded by the New American poetics Olson helped inspire, might have missed the specific details without a bit of research on Gloucester history and urban planning. And while the effort of shaming citizens appears dogmatic and rhetorically undemocratic, Olson tapped into a sense of shared public guilt over the transformation of Gloucester's historic architecture. Although most of Olson's arguments regarding preservation failed to save Gloucester's most ancient structures, we should consider the civic possibilities produced by his letters. While they were placed in a deliberative context, and there is a sense in which Olson hopes to extend debate over issues, the reality of the situation exposes public guilt in the changes the city faced. Olson contributed to civic reflection in this instance by casting blame on the city for offending its heritage. The conservative message would have resonated with many reading the paper, and for this reason Weld and Kenyon perhaps felt justified in promoting Olson's arguments. While he did little to assuage the transformation of the polis into a more contemporary urban setting, he persuaded a town daily to publish his performative gestures in a public context. Even if he did little else other than promote a sense of regret in a people who could not help but contribute to the city's transformation, given the economic and political realities of midcentury New England, that blame from a poet of apparent repute may have been welcome as a way to openly state the guilt in such environmental transactions. And this sense of public guilt at civic transformation may have motivated the editors of the *Gloucester Daily Times* in this instance to publish Olson's poem. Psychologically, blame can provide purgative effects, awakening public feelings that may otherwise remain repressed. As a voice of public conscience, Olson challenged his city to better understand its urban and spiritual transformations.

This guilt Olson tapped into, however, also produced critical responses from Gloucester citizens who saw him as "the Jeremiah of the Fort [a reference to Olson's home at 28 Fort Square], Quixote of Gloucester, tilting at the windmills of our guilt, telling us what we hear but won't listen to, after saving us from ourselves / each other." These words, written in a January 29, 1968, letter to the *Gloucester Daily Times* by Cape Ann historian Joseph E. Garland, push against Olson's claims with invective arguments that match Olson's own critical gestures. Garland writes: "Solomon's Temple had to go because the Y is doing more for our beloved City. The Hardy-Parsons shack was an ugly afterthought, and now the house is virginal again, and gardened, and the Parsons-Morse place—broken-down, really, no proud relic at all—and one of the few creditable things the last Council did was to hold off destruction out of deference to you, oh Poet."[25] While he acknowledges the guilt Olson tries to produce in citizens of Gloucester, Garland's response invokes a modal rhetoric of necessity, arguing that the city simply had to make room for the YMCA building as its urban features changed. Garland also argues that the changes coming to Gloucester are paid for "from out of the [fishing] hold, where we have for 345 years" obtained it. It is not the venal interests of distant financial investors who produce these changes; civic need instead demands certain uses of the urban architecture.

Like Olson, Garland had studied at Harvard, and he was a historian of Gloucester, with several publications on the New England fishing industry.[26] Certainly it appears that a kind of rivalry with Olson over Gloucester's history and its future development is indicated in this letter and others. But the significant force of Garland's response comes in the acknowledgment of Olson's shaming of the citizens of Gloucester as well as the contradictory reaction to Olson by another committed stakeholder in the city's urban transformation. Both letters represent competing stances on Gloucester's development: one decried the removal and demolition of historic properties in order to accommodate a changing civic landscape that increasingly catered to tourism, the other valued progress and argued for the necessity and inevitability of change and urban transformation.

Ecology and Commons

In another editorial piece offered by Olson on December 28, 1965, the poet chooses a more conventional prose form in which to address his audience. The writing remains uniquely Olsonian, a kind of prose-poetry that mixes oratorical bluster and literary authority, thus moving beyond conventional news genres of deliberation. Under the heading "Poet Proposes Gloucester Restore Selectmen," Olson began his letter to the editor with sharp criticism in a language that appears deliberately rough:

> Editor, Gloucester Times:
> What bastard man today does not know, or his fellows who sell to him abuse in and for him, is the created conditions of his own nature. One of these certainly is topography, that is that the shape of things on earth, of his own tools and constructions, the paths he and animals made and the roads which followed on and after those earlier means of his own movement, have, like the air and odors of spring and fall, or the difference of light and color when Winter's air is cold, and like food, and love-making, and children, and a place he lives in, much to do with how alive he himself or her personally is.[27]

Although the eventual topic of this long letter will address the structure of city management (Olson favored a form of government instituted in 1873 that called for a board of selectmen to conduct business as directed by eligible citizens who equally participate in decisions that affect the commons[28]), he returns to a theme of historic awareness of city history established in his prior letter-poem of December 3. Olson's "bastard man" is a synecdoche for urban dwellers no longer connected to the natural rhythms of agricultural life. As an opening, the words attract attention, and the phrase indicates a lower position of rank for moderns who have been more completely absorbed into corporate (rather than mercantilist) systems of government and economic life. The address, while strong, possibly fits the tone of the rough-and-tumble working class that formed the base of Gloucester's fishing industry, the leading commercial enterprise there until recent years. Olson, as elsewhere in his writings, uses topography as a way to measure the "shape of things on earth." Through it he orients civic discussion to the physical stresses of season, labor, and family in what again begins as a conservative argument for appropriate cosmic orientations to the polis.

To understand his argument, we should briefly examine the political situation in Gloucester in 1965 that motivated Olson's letter. According to

Peter Anastas's editorial notes, Gloucester was operated by a city manager in 1957, the year Olson returned to live more or less permanently. The manager "served at the pleasure of an elected city council, one member representing each of the city's eight wards" established under what was called "Plan E."[29] According to Anastas, "Olson believed that under Plan E the city had gotten out of the people's control and into the control of managers, who had viewed her not as 'commonwealth' but as a purely fiscal entity, at worst as a 'business corporation' to be managed, with 'profits' to be gained in taxes as the result of an expanded industrial base. It was under Plan E that Olson's despised urban renewal—he called it 'renewal by destruction'—took place, chopping up the waterfront into commercial lots and destroying many of the city's most important architectural and historical landmarks, to say nothing of her traditional neighborhoods adjacent to the waterfront."[30] It was not until after Olson's death in 1970 that the city revoked Plan E following "an initiative to re-write Gloucester's municipal charter."[31]

After his initial orienting outburst against "bastard man," Olson draws upon personal experiences in the region, "driving Cape Ann's still often delicate roads." He goes on to name them, recalling the physical geography of urban Gloucester in order to impress upon his readers the physical coordinates of "East Main Street, which is almost or perfectly as far as East Gloucester Square the way the road to the Eastern Point followed the initial shore use."[32] He builds up from the place names of Highland, Mt. Pleasant Avenue, Rockport, and Mill Pond to argue for the stewardship of "ecology as man's own." He feared that "mostly stupid leadership" was mismanaging Gloucester's delicate, ecological balance. This form of leadership, more focused on economic development than on ecological "ways of his life,"[33] motivated Olson to write his letter. In it he reflects on "bastard man" for whom he cares for the same as "fish, and birds, and shellfish, and kelp," evening out the hierarchy of human relations within the natural world. He also cares for "flowers, which also live best, or even the way wheat, and oats and barley and corn, each cereal, as grass and as flowers, hybridized in the mixtures of nature and man's dumps. The hedgerow, they call it east of Buffalo, what is the unturned edge between adjoining plowed fields of two owners, are where, like I'm hoping Mill Pond will be left, because these places between places breed future."[34] After the opening outburst, Olson now begins to show more sympathy for his fellow Gloucesterites, and he stretches the epideictic mode from an initial position of blame to indicate a kind of praise for the locale. He argues for an appreciation of "places between places" that "breed future," a compelling, if strange, claim that relies on strategies of rhetoric similar to the Longinian sublime—an expansion of emotion and identification between author and audience through shared topoi.[35] Olson's amplification of topographical features invites readers to see Gloucester within a larger, cosmic context, rather than in a strictly social one. As we will see, the value of open spaces for Olson is located in human measurement within topography, and he relates this through a language of cosmic order that is transcendent only as a rhetorical performance, locating the specifics of place within a larger cycle of historic and cosmic significance. In a January 6, 1966, editorial he argues that "distance, in which a person can feel themselves and look, or move, has become so valuable . . . that the whole future of the human race depends upon them."[36] His concern over kinetic relationships to geographic space is complicated and appears throughout his writing. In his "Projective Verse" essay, he argues that "the projective involves a stance toward reality outside a poem as well as a new stance towards the reality of a poem itself."[37] This "stance" turns composition into an energetic and process-oriented task that interrogates space. By questioning his environment the poet derives content, and it organizes the operative norms of the poem. Similarly, his early study of Herman Melville, *Call Me Ishmael,* opens with the claim that space is "the central fact to man born in America." For Olson, "it is geography at bottom."[38] His argument calls for awareness of spatial topography as a way to measure human value. He wants such value to be considered as a way to bring pressure to "city managers" and "greedy present persons."[39]

To support his claim for the value of human relations to topography, Olson turns, again, to the history of the region to present an ideal use of land and its management for human purpose. This assumes that under twentieth-century corporate uses, human purpose is no longer operative. Agency is perceived broadly in institutional and social forces. And in the face of the progressive urban renewals to turn seaside-fishing villages into bedroom communities for Boston professionals, Olson argued for a more aggressive response to the transformation of the environs around Gloucester. What Olson hopes to persuade his audience of is the significance of the commons—the shared properties of life as an ecology of delicately balanced forces of trade, agriculture, and local culture. The corporate move to manage cities for profit rather than the welfare of its citizens pushed Olson to address his city as a civic orator who blamed and praised the efforts of all. He argued for a vision of Gloucester that included present social conditions within a larger frame of historic and geographic dimensions. The "cosmic" for Olson resided in natural conditions, but his appeal through a version of the Longinian sublime relied on a transcendent rhetoric that connected the past with the present, and the nonhuman with the social.[40] To provide some extrinsic evidence for his reading of Gloucester's topography, he narrates briefly (for Olson) the story of "a Gloucester captain of the China trade, who retired and lived on Washington there on the uplands going down to the marsh of Mill Pond."[41] This captain "so longed for the feeling of the view he knew he had a small junk made and floated her there in the pond for himself and anyone else who therefore had occasion to see. And watch and enjoy—or laugh at and scorn I should also suppose?"[42] In this image of the captain's junk Olson hopes to restore some sympathy for cosmic and human scales rather than for the permanent transformation of topography brought about by "city management." In his hopes for the commons, there is room for eccentric actions or displays, and yet these rhetorical gestures can be determined with pleasure or scorn by a public active in the uses of "Gloucester 'Commons.'"[43]

"I am proposing something," Olson writes, finally, after so many digressions, appearing to arrive at his claim. "Man today is so stolen and cheated of creation as part actually of his own being—gulls and fish and flowers and mussels and insects, and grasses and water ain't, nearly so much—that. . . ." Here Olson moves into a discussion of "universals," arguing against "the new crop of 20-year olds" who "think that the only universals which possibly can matter are those, like pot, say, which put one directly in touch, and only, with 'the universals.'"[44] While Olson risks the appearance of an old man shaking his fist at those "20-year olds," such sentiment against pot smoking youths might have appealed to an audience of conservative fisher families who traditionally composed Gloucester's residents. The curmudgeonly reference to youths might certainly motivate his older, more economically established working-class audience to hear his words, perhaps preparing them for his next appeal to cosmic identification, where he writes: "I am happy to offer Gloucester, in the guise of the very total I best think was and is man's interference with creation, his ecology (which is like the wife to the husband of his economics) can only come in again, or be drawn like Capt. Whose boat on Mill—or Jim Chum, which Gloucesterman's dory-mate caught in the hooks of a trawl. . . ."[45] Olson continues with an apocryphal local legend of a man caught in a trawl while fishing, another figure of appeal for members of Gloucester's fishing community. It is difficult to imagine these words in a newspaper today. Creation, ecology, and economics are argued by Olson to be the essence of topographical life, regardless of the many forms in which they occur. He appeals with folksy yarns to a people's sense of legend and local history, and they, perhaps instead of Olson's contemporary poet-audience, would identify more completely and easily with these shared situations of an imagined New England locale.

Following this cosmic, topographic proposal, Olson makes the more deliberative pitch, proposing that "Gloucester restore her original selectmen as her Governing Body solely to redeclare the ownership of all her public conditions—including the governance of anything in that Body's and the total Electorate's judgement / no longer any appeal to eminent domain, or larger unit of topography and environment than the precincts of the City's Limit—in other words to re-establish the principle of *commoners,* for ownership of *commons.*"[46] It is interesting to note that Gloucester did change its form of government in 1976. Olson's contribution to a public conversation can be seen in this instance as contributing to a broader understanding of ecological and historic relations of human uses of local space. Through recognizable modal gestures that increased perspectives of a contingent situation, he attempted to produce possibilities in an audience that in the mid-1960s was not used to the arguments of ecological preservation. The ecological perspective offered by Olson countered the more commercially minded efforts of the city's management, providing another basis from which to reflect on the transformation of a small city in the mid-twentieth century. By blending epideictic traits of praise and blame in the sublime, and modernized, rhetoric of Longinus with other more deliberative modes of rhetoric in an editorial for the town paper, Olson drew on a variety of oratorical tools to persuade an audience to reflect on their situation in a changing environment. He did this also by exploiting modal registers through performative appeals that drew on literary skills that he adapted for public display. His appeals through a sense of cosmic place, geographic beauty, cultural assumption, and local legend helped him reach an audience unfamiliar with his work as a poet in the modernist tradition, someone who sought social change through the modal registers available through poetry. By treating the public space of the editorial as a "field of action," Olson managed to address a public that was quite different from the modernist context in which he is customarily read.

The Agonistic Public Voice

With themes of preservation, ecology, and city stewardship established in his letters, Olson returned throughout the decade in the editorial pages to bring attention to these pet concerns and to a sense of life as it was changing in 1960s Gloucester. He received indication of the value of his editorials from the continued and increasing support of the paper, as well as from locals, such as "one of the police officers I haven't seen in several years," Olson noted in a January 3, 1966, letter to the editor. This officer "mention[ed] the two pieces [Olson] had in the *Times*" and indicated that "the Sargent house will be next" (the Sargent-Murray-Gilman-Hough house on Middle Street was constructed in 1768 by a leading Gloucester merchant).[47] Moreover, according to Peter Anastas, "few letters went uncommented upon." Olson's "letters and poems opened up a dialogue with the community which the poet would not otherwise have had in his lifetime."[48] Since this civic audience was composed largely of workers, Olson's more direct and accusatory language may have been aimed at them in a rhetorical style they would appreciate. Words spoken bluntly and with force might appeal to a Gloucester audience of fishers descending from working-class Italian, Greek, Portuguese, and British lines rather than for others who were more accustomed to the decorum of "polite" deliberative exchange (Joseph Garland's letter, as we saw above, also relies on this strong, masculine language of engagement). After concluding this letter with a typically Olsonian recount of Gloucester's history and then comparing it with a more tony coastal community to the south, Olson offers Bridgeport, Connecticut, as an example of the kind of change Gloucester would not want, and such a place "is happily something [Olson] can gladly kiss off."[49] Such rhetorical performance allows Olson to appear socially more in accord with the community. Indeed, a rereading of *The Maximus Poems* might lead to a reevaluation of some of the tone and performative gestures therein, since that epic, too, is informed by the largely working-class people of Gloucester.

Olson's agonistic language in his letters to the people of Gloucester, moreover, contributes to a community spirit of debate through performances of masculine authority. Rather than phrasing his letters in the measured and "objective" language of standard print media, Olson built an ethos of moral character, native intelligence, and social commitment that was backed by strong words that reoriented a sense of scale from corporate to cosmic space. The combination of macho performativity with civic oratory let Olson adapt modernist compositional methodology with the working-class vernacular of his audience.[50] In an October 25, 1967, open letter to Nick Taliadoros, a descendant of one of Gloucester's first Greek settlers and an owner of several gas stations, including one at 73 Essex Avenue,[51] Olson writes:

Please don't do it. Don't choke off
another Gloucester space. I don't care what
Julian has done to make the river side of
Essex Avenue look like a rubbish pile or dump,
don't you yourself take any more marsh away.
Just because you are a Tally, don't do it.
Your brothers and I were raised together. WE
go back at least to Pearl Harbor.[52]

In this passage Olson creates a trustworthy ethos through personal appeal to Taliadoros, reminding him of his family's connections with Olson. He also confronts him with a warning, demanding that he "leave not one inch more of marsh and creek invaded / by your automobiles. Leave the front lawn of / Apple Row no more hurt. Please, as a man of / a family of Gloucester men. Otherwise all will / be the same, all will be like Park Avenue in / Worcester."[53] The imperative force of his argument offers little space for negotiation, and adjectives like "invaded" and "hurt" publicly accuse Taliadoros of inflicting the city with damages. The public performance of this direct appeal to a local businessman with extensive familial ties to the region gives Olson an opportunity to establish an ethos of communal commitment. He offers up Gloucester as a shared resource to be respected as a common property, not one to be purchased for private gain. His case rests, however, not, as in previous letters, on ecological perspectives of topography but on shared terms of engagement as important Gloucester citizens. Olson seeks to raise his own status as a leading citizen of Gloucester by addressing Taliadoros as an equally important contributor to the community. The economically successful owner of auto repair shops and dealerships, however, in reality, thrives in a scale far removed from Olson's studious life as a modernist poet who occupied 28 Fort Street near the town harbor. Olson's communal influence through rhetorical strategies in the town paper, as well as through the poems he published among literary presses, is distant, too, from the daily, face-to-face conduct of business in a small New England city. Olson's need to establish a credible ethos, however, by paying respect to persons of community influence, offers a performance for his public that does more than address the particular issue of the conversion of wetlands at Essex Avenue. It also reveals Olson as a man of influence capable of addressing his equals, however imaginary that equality may be.

Supporting Olson, moreover, was the *Times*'s presentation of the letter in the editorial page. Along with Olson's letter an image of the disputed land was reproduced under the caption: "Picturesque Marshland on West Side of Essex Avenue." Another photo provided commentary under the heading: "Cluttered Area on Annisquam River Side of Causeway." Moreover, an editor's note was included next to Olson's letter, headlined, "Please Don't Do It." It reads: "Again poet Charles Olson speaks out for preserving Gloucester beauty and character. This time his appeal takes the form of an open letter to a neighbor, who proposes to fill marshland that he owns alongside the westerly side of Essex Avenue causeway. The Gloucester City Council held a public hearing Oct. 11 on a notice of intent to fill the marshland. The City Council voted to postpone action until the State Department of Natural Resources determines whether or not the area substantially contributes to the production of finfish and shellfish."[54] Kenyon's mediation of Olson's arguments marks a stark contrast to the poet's personal appeal to Taliadoros. The editor's position is not built on descriptions of "Gloucester beauty and character." By contrast, Olson remains concerned with specific ecological knowledge of the scale relations between civic and cosmic spatial perspectives, and he argues for the historical civic forms of life such topographies allowed in Gloucester. By reducing Olson's concerns to that of "beauty and character," Kenyon made the poet accessible, in a sense, to the paper's audience. Olson's rhetorical strategy, however, was to build the capacities of his audience for reconsidering the possible values of landscape and historic structures in their daily lives. By speaking in a public language of the working-class citizens of Gloucester, he hoped to appeal to their sense of identity. What the paper calls "beauty" and what Olson calls "a distance, in which a person can feel themselves and look, or move,"[55] are at odds. The former is abstract, meaningless except as a very general and universally regarded referent of pleasing visual effects. Olson wanted to produce awareness in an audience to help them understand his notion of topography as an essential ecological value of social and cosmic relation. While the *Times* generously supported Olson, mediating his arguments with photographs and editorial commentary, such legitimizing efforts also packaged Olson's arguments into fairly harmless statements of "Gloucester beauty." The contrast between Olson's rhetorical specificity within a notion of poetry as a "field of action" stands out remarkably from the homogenized forms of mediation offered by the paper. Kenyon's generosity and his trust in Olson's arguments must not be overlooked, for without the paper Olson's writing would not have been able to jump scale to receive a broader public audience. And yet, too, the citizens were attentive to Olson for his mixture of exotic modernist poetry layered with the language of a mass audience of uneducated fishermen. He attempted in his way to speak in their language and to appeal to their sense of masculine power in public speech while observing the goals of modernist convention that produced gestures and actions in order to disrupt the status quo. The paper appealed to a simplified universal of "beauty" when, in fact, the experience of life in Gloucester was probably far from beautiful. The combination, however, of Olson's unedited letters published within the legitimizing public space of the paper provided a rare rhetorical situation in which diverse public actors interacted with one another to address the very real effects of urban change in postwar New England.

Editorial Mediation

While Olson's rhetorical approach in the poems and letters to the *Gloucester Daily Times* was largely poetic and performative, through editorial mediation and support he was able to jump scales to reach a new audience. To this end, Paul Kenyon and Philip Weld proved to be essential and sympathetic agents in the process of presenting Olson's message to a new readership. For instance, Peter Anastas claimed that Kenyon had left a successful career at the *Boston Evening Transcript* during the 1930s to move to Gloucester. "He felt an affinity with Olson," Anastas continues, "because [he] was also a writer" of "a popular children's book, *Driftwood Captain* [Houghton Mifflin, 1954]." He also took an interest in the history of Gloucester, authoring a "memoir of economist and Gloucester native Roger Babson," as well as introductions to local books concerned with the town's history and fishing industry. Like Olson, Kenyon was "an old New Deal Democrat" who "would also have felt a political affinity with Olson."[56] Kenyon's literary interests and publisher Philip Weld's friendship with Olson guaranteed to an extent a reception for Olson's letters and poems. Beyond the personal interests in Olson's poetry, the editor and publisher worked to successfully contextualize the arguments offered by Olson for a larger audience.

The *Gloucester Daily Times* also provided precise information that Olson often neglected. In his efforts to save yet another historic structure from demolition, Olson offered a brief letter to the editor that was contextualized in the following manner:

> Poet Charles Olson has issued a last desperate appeal to the public to help him save the historic Parsons-Morse house at 106 Western Ave.
>
> The City Council has decided to have the house razed to straighten the curve on Western Ave. The neighbors said the house was full of rats.
>
> When Olson did not present architects' plans last week for mov-

ing the house, the council voted to have it razed despite an offer by Olson to put $2,500 in escrow as evidence of his good faith.

Today Olson urged citizens interested in saving the house to contact their city councilors and ask them to reconsider their action.

Olson's statement follows:

May I ask anyone in the city who believes as I do that to destroy the Morse house at 106 Western Avenue because 1) it is a wreck and 2) because it is on the curve, is to remove a hinge of the city which, once gone can never be restored, to write, call or visit personally and immediately, today, your councilor so that any last chance before the ugly destroyer's ball swings (the house) may be gained, acquired, and kept for persons unknown to us in the future who will never know what they have lost because easy contemporary ideas and persons dominate the land.

As the man who failed to promise, buy, beg, or convince, I appeal.

Signed Charles Olson.[57]

This situation stems from a month-long effort by Olson to prevent the demolition of the Parsons-Morse house. After his address to the City Council and an offer of the escrow amount indicated above all failed, the house was razed on August 9, 1967.[58] Rhetorically, the interesting aspect I wish to draw attention to is the continued legitimizing support of the *Gloucester Daily Times* for Olson's efforts to preserve the historic building. Olson's unmediated plea to preserve the house receives some much-needed contextual discussion by the editor and publisher of the paper. The paper's support of Olson reveals to the public that his position, while articulated in a forceful epideictic mode, remains relevant, and that it is backed by other town interests. Indeed, over the course of the decade in which he wrote to the editors of the *Times,* it seems as if Olson had been accepted as a kind of authority by the paper, which went out of its way to insure that Olson's arguments received full public presentation.

In a January 18, 1968, letter that appeared under the heading "Poet Begs for Action to Save Beauty," Olson appeals to the citizens of Gloucester to preserve significant architectural structures. He does so by recalling the town's history yet again, beginning with a "corner on which Abraham Robinson sat down as early as 1638." He concludes the letter by arguing that the city's beauty not be destroyed "forever simply to accommodate business men."[59] Accompanying this letter was a lengthy editorial in which the editor claims, "Olson sees more in past and future than less sensitive and knowledgeable people. Also, he sees Gloucester with the eye of a lover, eager to protect his loved one."[60] Kenyon goes on to list several of the projects Olson had opposed or brought attention to, including the YMCA's purchase of Solomon's Temple, Taliadoros's contract on disputed marshland and other historic sites that had been razed over the years to make room for new businesses. The final paragraph, however, reiterates the significance of Olson's arguments: "But now that Olson has sounded the alarm again, perhaps eyes will be opened at last, and one thing will lead to another to bring about a new appreciation of the good buildings along the West End and Main St. and up Washington St. and along Middle St."[61]

Although Kenyon confuses Olson's modernism with romantic ideals of the poet as being more "sensitive" than others, and that he strives, in the metaphoric vocabulary of courtship, "to protect his loved one"—the city of Gloucester—there remains a strong sense of fidelity to Olson's rhetorical strategies for producing awareness of historic preservation. He is able to perform as the archivist in his letter, detailing events about "the 1830 fire" at the Mansfield House in the West End of Gloucester, or commenting on "a half dozen of the rarest Federals or Colonials left anywhere," referring again to the city's historic architecture. In this way an interesting rhetorical relationship develops between Olson and Kenyon. Rhetorically, the paper provides the expected mediation and extends for Olson a sense of public legitimacy for his arguments. By contrast, Olson can expand the public's capacity for an interest in the historic development of its city by praising the city's past. By recounting the numerous architectural wonders of this small city, Olson could instill a sense of pride for Gloucester in his public audience. By recalling the physical beauty of the city that resulted from past decisions in favor of financially driven modernization, he hoped to generate reflection upon the current process of urban transformation.

The relationship between Kenyon and Olson allowed the scale shift necessary for Olson to address his civic concerns. Without the mediation of the *Gloucester Daily Times,* Olson would have been restricted to other writing communities, channeling his arguments for historic preservation and ecological awareness to audiences less intimately familiar with the civic changes citizens of Gloucester more immediately faced.[62] Although Kenyon projected Olson in a romantic vocabulary of sensitivity and genius— a vocabulary Olson's modernist theories of writing shunned—the editor was successful in preparing a print space through which Olson could perform a role as the archival voice of a city. Olson examined the often inert and half-formed responses to civic change that accompany the activities of daily life. He challenged his public audience to witness civic life in a broader cosmic context and provided a space for reflection on the complex urban changes transforming Gloucester. The collusion between Olson and Kenyon suggests ways to understand how scale shifts increase possibilities of modernist inquiry for new readership. Critics, poets, journalists, and others who produce cultural reflection in audiences push relatively unknown work into new spaces through their advocacy.

Social Rituals of Engagement

While Kenyon and Weld were committed to the city of Gloucester, providing news and earning profits for the paper, their 1960s New England community was a place undergoing ineradicable change. Because of these changes, the *Gloucester Daily Times* provided a space wherein personal values could argue against commercial interests. While there may have been some risk in providing Olson with print space in their paper, Kenyon and Weld were sympathetic to his literary stature and to his arguments regarding the historical value of Gloucester architecture. Without this sympathy it is unlikely that Olson's work would have received respectful treatment. And this perhaps is key to Olson's successful shift of scale from literary to civic communities. In Olson's case, his reputation as a leading poet engaged in other national and international literary scenes in part persuaded Kenyon and Weld to distribute his arguments in a wider field.

Since Gloucester in the 1960s faced changes in the form of a revised system of city management that valued profit and progress over community history and traditional industry, Olson's particular arguments may have appealed to the editors as an outlet for frustration over the changes coming to their city. As I discussed above, Olson tapped into a sense of collective guilt over changes that were only partially understood and inchoately felt by the citizens of Gloucester. As centuries-old houses were being razed to make room for parking lots, swimming pools, and other utilitarian civic structures, such progress appeared necessary and terrible at the same time. Since, as a poet, Olson could work within an epideictic mode to exert praise or blame in civic situations, he could bring up the issues confronting Gloucester, creating a situation wherein audiences could reflect upon the implications of the urban changes facing them.

As a poet committed to a project of social change, Olson's public letter-poems provided an opportunity to perform for a larger civic audience. While

The Maximus Poems was addressed to a smaller literary group of readers, Olson's concern with the polis of Gloucester remains central throughout the body of his work. Jeffrey Walker and others argue that the first two books of *Maximus* are more successful than the final third section because of this engagement with civic history, while the third book, assembled by editors after his death in 1970, seems to come unwound under personal constraints of growing isolation, declining health, and a sense of encroaching death.[63] Interestingly, during the years in which Olson wrote these late, more inwardly reflective poems, he still felt compelled to provide his civic arguments directly to the polis. Since Olson did not prepare a third book himself, it is compelling to consider how the inclusion of the poems and letters to the *Gloucester Daily Times* might influence readings of *The Maximus Poems*.[64] As it stands, the third book concentrates most intently on esoteric personal vision and its undoing through dreams, myth, and alchemical metaphors of cosmic movement; in the context of the paper he opts to speak directly to a living public. While Olson's modernist perspective consisted of varied bands of poets working within midcentury traditions of verse, Gloucester continued to occupy his attention. Through the *Gloucester Daily Times* his poems found a concrete audience to counterbalance the more inward and vulnerable impulses of the final movements of *The Maximus Poems*. Given the temporal correlation between the authorship of the third book and the arguments made to the people of Gloucester, a revision of the editorial construction of this portion of *Maximus* should include the letters and poems to the *Gloucester Daily Times*.

The final portion of *The Maximus Poems* can be read in sacramental terms, punctuating the public urge to speak with personal rituals of observance. The late work's engagement with myth and geographic space is located in a civic urge to extend protection to the polis through prayer. We might think of Olson's contribution to the *Times* as a civic complement to the late work's more personal, prayerlike function. An untitled poem in the third book reads:

> The hour of evening—supper hour, for my neighbors—quietness
> in the street, and kids gone and the night
> coming to end the day (which has piled itself up
> in shallows, and some
> accomplishment—sweet air of evening promises
> anew life's endlessness, life itself's
> Beauty which all forever so long as there is

a human race like flowers and, I suppose,
other animals—they too must know something
of what it is to love, to be alive, to have
life, to be on the sweetness of Earth herself.[65]

The observance of the "hour of evening—supper hour, for my neighbors," suggests a form of civic awareness that differs from the public engagements with historic preservation and the deliberative arguments that shape the architectural face of the city. Here and elsewhere in the third book of *Maximus,* Olson turns to the sacramental acts of community. These prayerlike observances serve to bring awareness to the daily rituals of social interaction—exchanges often taken for granted. And yet he employs the sublime rhetoric of the American bard, appealing to the modernist reader about what amounts to a fairly traditional plea for the observance of intimate social transactions. If one goal of the historical avant-garde socially is to infuse life with art—to produce new possibilities within the actualities of experience—here Olson turns to the basic transactions of the evening meal as an opportunity to address intimate social exchange.[66] Still, the conventional understanding of the self is disrupted. Olson identifies this "matins" poem with "the sweetness of Earth herself," intensifying the sublime range of identification through natural or cosmic elements in which the self is but a fluctuating part in the process of life.

With the last book of *The Maximus Poems* settling into reflective moods based in personal experience, the letters and poems to the *Gloucester Daily Times* provided an opportunity to remain in contact with the public performance of Maximus, the archival figure of the polis. A relationship forms through Olson's attention to two different scales of address: one inward, quiet, meditative; the other bold, abrasive, civic. He does this, he claims late in *The Maximus Poems,* so "that by your inner world you may / dwell in the outer as well without / any loss of your being."[67] The operative notion of self that Olson chooses to engage has private and public aspects. And yet, as we see above, the private is infused too with a public acknowledgment of the social rituals of exchange. The rhetorical approach for this observational and reflective mode of inquiry differs from the civic broadcasts of outrage, such as we see in his "scream" to the editor. Both rely on an oratorical strategy of appeal, but they are modulated differently, appealing, in one instance, to a broad social connectedness, and in another to the civic decisions that determine the spaces in which social life takes place. Olson's ability to shift scale to reach a civic audience is unique for a modernist poet. By comparing these different scales, we can perhaps address with better accuracy the diverse strategies of appeal generated by postwar American poets. In their attempts to infuse life with art many came to face a predicament of rhetorical procedure: How to adapt language for new audiences and situations? How to perform in modes that can produce new social possibilities and actions in public? How might a poet give shape and new senses of social access within the contingencies of civic deliberation, corporate determination, and public contradiction? No longer could the poem be thought of as a final product; instead, it became a record of rhetorical transactions at specific moments in the life of a community. These concerns will be apparent in the chapter ahead, where we will see how responses to the Vietnam War were devised in poetry to reinforce communal goals and commitments, or were used to expand the concept of public space to include a larger dialectic of cultural relationships.

Rhetorics of "Advantage" and "Pure Persuasion"

Robert Duncan, Denise Levertov, and Vietnam

My title for this chapter conveys certain flexibilities and potentials in poetry when it is used as a public art. Kenneth Burke's distinction of a "rhetoric of advantage" and the rhetorical possibilities based on "pure persuasion" suggests that public awareness can be produced on divisive topics by aggressively pursuing advantage over an audience, or also by seeking to follow the cohering relationships that emerge within certain contexts. Burke claims there often exists an "agonistic" purpose "to *gain advantage,* of one sort or another."[1] "Advantage," for Burke, is useful as a way to account for the "drives" and "urges" that motivate individual or group psychologies. Theorizing a modern rhetoric based on ancient models, he addresses rhetorical situations that are informed by the influences of Nietzsche, Marx, and Freud. A "rhetoric of advantage" also makes use of traditional rhetorical practices in which a writer or speaker attempts to move readers and auditors to act in some way based on a sense of shared motives. A person operating from the perspective of advantage does so with realizable purposes in mind.

Denise Levertov, for example, contributed arguments to social movements in the 1960s and '70s that protested war in Vietnam. The moral advantage she sought corresponds with Burke's reading of the Sophist rhetorician Isocrates, who "chose to spiritualize the notion of 'advantage' (*pleonexia*)."[2] Such spiritualization constitutes a "true advantage" in that it is based in a rhetorician's sense of "*moral* superiority."[3] Levertov's convictions about the immorality of war in Southeast Asia led her to address the antiwar movement through a poetics that derived its own rhetorical advantage from moral commonplaces. She restated these through textual and performative gestures that gave shape and resonance to debates over Vietnam.

Robert Duncan, by contrast, pursued different rhetorical possibilities in his war writing and in his personal response to the peace movement. His approach differs from Levertov's in that it displays keen similarities with what Burke called a rhetoric of "pure persuasion," and is most evident in Duncan's poems during this time, especially "Passages 25," which stressed the phatic role of the poet as seer. "Pure persuasion," Burke argued, "involves the saying of something, not for an extra-verbal advantage to be got by the saying, but because of a satisfaction intrinsic to the saying."[4] For Burke, "pure persuasion" underlies a commitment to artistic and religious impulses in which the motives of an artist proceed in a kind of dialectic between the individual and her rhetorical situation. His theoretical description of "pure persuasion" aligns with Bronislaw Malinowski's term, "phatic communion."[5] To Burke, Malinowski "refer[s] to talk at random, purely for the satisfaction of talking together, the use of speech as such for the establishing of a social bond between speaker and spoken-to."[6] Burke claims "pure persuasion" is "more intensely purposive," possessing "a kind of purpose which, as judged by the rhetoric of advantage, is no purpose at all, or which might often look like sheer frustration of purpose."[7] Next to "advantage," a rhetoric of "pure persuasion" seems feckless, even misguided, yet in its realm exist strategies that reinforce social bonds and relationships. It exhibits the rhetorical ground of the traditional relations of the artist to her work and to the larger social networks it engages. "Pure persuasion," moreover, enables relations of inquiry and relates to Nancy Struever's emphasis on modalities of investigation, expanded pursuits, gestures, and actions that lead to confrontation or challenge; it allows inquests that can provoke new perspectives and outcomes. By looking at Denise Levertov and Robert Duncan's public engagements through these possibilities of "advantage" and "pure persuasion," sharper distinctions of rhetorical poetry as a factor in citizenship and dissent may be shown.

Both approaches indicate ways in which modality in poetry contributes to certain kinds of public intervention: it gives coloration of value possibilities that can prepare audiences to understand controversial issues from different perspectives. Modalities of possibility also encourage social change, resistance, or future political engagement. If publics can be addressed through rhetorical modalities that shift attention from actual conditions toward other possible public actions, new social alternatives may be offered for public understanding, preparation, and future action; poetry in such instances produces capacities that enable an audience to receive ethical perspectives in complex systems of belief based on private and public feelings. The rhetorical modalities of intervention pursued here will illustrate processes of communication that empower speakers and writers to resist the unfair leverage of power that is often displayed in public situations. By turning to the Vietnam War era we may pursue an instance of public engagement that enhances our knowledge of communication during a period of social and cultural volatility. The public and private interventions made by Robert Duncan and Denise Levertov will help inform public participants with ways to direct arguments for constructive cultural purposes.

While much of their correspondence is preoccupied with the practical labor of publication, commentary on each other's work, and introductions to diverse communities of writers, it is their reaction to the Vietnam War that offers the greatest source of reflection on ways poetry can bring attention to divisive public topics. The extensive personal correspondence spanned several decades of the mid-twentieth century, and their commentary over the public and private uses of poetry at the height of the war reveals a dilemma in public engagement that many American poets have since continued to face.[8] Through their differences we can observe two competing approaches in contemporary literature that imagine how poetry works as a medium of public and social confrontation. It is instructive to see how in a private exchange of nearly five hundred letters these poets theorized the public influence of their art. If the notion of a public is a contested site inviting competing claims about its values and uses in particular situations, the letters between Duncan and Levertov provide unique insight into how poetry may advance claims that provoke public reflection.[9]

Positioning Poetry

> I have found myself a poet, long before this particular involvement, saying things in poems which I think have moral implications. I think that if one is an articulate person, who makes certain statements, one has an obligation as a human being to back them up with one's actions. So I feel that it is poetry that has led me into political action and not political action which has caused me to write poems more overtly engaged than those I used to write, which is something that has happened to me, but that is just a natural happening. I've always written rather directly about my life and concerns at any particular time.[10]

For Denise Levertov, one's word must be supported with action. During the Vietnam War she worked on behalf of the peace movement through the aid organization RESIST, devoting considerable energy to help young men who refused to register for the draft. She also attended rallies, participated in marches, and supported her husband, Mitchell Goodman, who

had been indicted in 1968 as part of the Boston Five for urging draft eva-
sion the previous year.[11] Arrested with Dr. Benjamin Spock, Yale University Chaplain William Sloane Coffin Jr., and others, Goodman's indictment
brought significant national attention to the peace movement and opposition to the war in Vietnam.[12] The national attention this brought to Levertov created a shift in scale for the reception of her poetry.[13] No longer
confined to smaller literary coteries, she now found a wider audience in a
popular social movement.

She claims also that poetry led her to activism, and books from the period, particularly *To Stay Alive* (1971), became what literary critic Marjorie Perloff has called "agitprop."[14] Because of the shift in social scale that
occurred with Goodman's indictment, Levertov's poetry became increasingly reflective of her activism. As her national reputation increased, attention came to her through other sectors of the public and she responded
by writing lyrical accounts of her activist engagements along with poems
that brought attention to the injustices of war in Vietnam.

In *To Stay Alive,* Levertov grounds her poetry in personal experience;
"individual history gives me [a sense] of being straddled between *places*"
and "straddled across *time.*"[15] She incorporates into her work "those public
occasions, demonstrations, that have become for many of us such familiar
parts of our lives." She is not only opposed to war, but also of "the whole
system of insane greed, of racism and imperialism, of which war is only the
inevitable expression." Her words extend to "all who struggle, violently
if need be, to pull down this obscene system before it destroys all life on
earth." She offers her work, "not as mere 'confessional' autobiography, but
as a document of some historical value, a record of one person's inner/outer
experience in America during the '60's [*sic*] and the beginning of the '70's
[*sic*], an experience which is shared by so many and transcends the peculiar
details of each life, though it can only be expressed in and through such
details."[16]

The tension she describes between the urgency of social action and the
"peculiar details of each life" stand out remarkably because those "peculiar" details offer insight to how social action forms through the beliefs,
feelings, and habits of individuals. Levertov wants poetry to contribute a
social document that addresses a shared body of private feeling in the hopes
of reinforcing communities that can influence larger political issues. By
making private beliefs known to others she anticipates poetry as a place
where private feelings find new life as public artifact. Her use of the poem
as the platform for such documentation leads her to seek "advantage" by
claiming a moral edge in the cultural debates around the Vietnam War. By

employing commonplace figures of pathos in her writing, Levertov seeks to gain an advantage over her audience as she persuades them to go along with her "war on war." And yet within the committed but often playful context of the social protest movement of the '60s, such figures of pathos did not always find advantageous positions in larger social movements or in the historical problems facing the nation.

The War on War

While poems in *To Stay Alive* are composed of a vivid language that powerfully appeals to a reader's ear, rhetorically Levertov's use of figures of pathos, along with a command of the "majestic plural" (or "royal we") burden her "documentation" with morally superior claims on behalf of an idealized citizenry—not an alert and willing public. In "Life at War," she speaks to "the disasters numb within us." Contributing to this emotional nullity, she argues:

> We have breathed the grits of it [war] in, all our lives,
> our lungs are pocked with it,
> the mucous membrane of our dreams
> coated with it, the imagination
> filmed over with the gray filth of it:

And toward the end of the poem she reminds her readers of the human capacity for both good and evil:

> We are the humans, men who can make;
> whose language imagines *mercy,*
> *lovingkindness;* we have believed one another
> mirrored forms of a God we felt as good—
>
> who do these acts, who convince ourselves
> it is necessary; these acts are done
> to our own flesh; burned human flesh
> is smelling in Vietnam as I write.[17]

In "Tenebrae" she likewise speaks for others in an attempt to criticize middle American indifference to the suffering she sees in Vietnam. But her dramatic repetitions and statements of pathos come off as heavy-handed. She writes:

Heavy, heavy, heavy, hand and heart.
We are at war,
bitterly, bitterly at war.

And the buying and selling
buzzes at our heads, a swarm
of busy flies, a kind of innocence.[18]

Her ironic use of "innocence" suggests that the middle class of her critique keeps busy with the national values of "buying and selling" and is thereby incapable of perceiving the full horror of Vietnam as a human travesty. "They are not listening," she says, because "they buy, they sell. / They fill freezers with food. Neon signs flash their intentions / into the years ahead."[19] In her quest for advantage she puts her perspective above those who remain indifferent to war, delivering a moral argument that shows how their "innocence" contributes to a kind of willful negligence of human responsibility. The distance she puts between herself and the subject of her criticism introduces other problems of ethos. Although her passionate response to the war is genuine, her inability to appeal to those "middle Americans" who may be indifferent suggests a limitation in the imagination of public potential. In pursuit of rhetorical advantage, Levertov resorts to using straw figures to represent an American middle class that adheres to its own unique value system. While she uses poetry to bring private perspectives into public associations, she maintains a certain moral high ground for readers who already share her political positions; this, however, causes her to risk the support of an important group of American citizens. While we may sympathize with Levertov's social vision, her poetry misses an opportunity to engage those with whom she disagrees. In her rhetoric of advantage she claims a moral position that must be met head on and accepted at face value. Those who may not publicly share her commitments are put down as passive supporters of the war.

The accumulation of pathos in her poetry attempts to startle readers, too. Aganactesis, a rhetorical figure of deep indignation ("breaking open of breasts" "entrails of still alive babies"[20]), is prominent here, along with congeries—accumulating images that are supposed to move a reader. The identification between author and audience in the first person plural is meant to establish sympathy while sharing indignation over the "breaking open of breasts" and "skinned penises." Such horrors are mitigated in her appeal to "humankind," an identity "we" all share. She appeals to an audience's sense of decency and outrage over acts committed in Vietnam by other fellow Americans. Pathetic accumulation and vivid descriptions are designed to bring an audience to identify with her moral position—to accept the version of "humankind" she identifies so righteously.

Levertov's appeal by pathos, however, runs counter to her claims that these poems are a kind of documentation of private feeling engaging public belief.[21] Before considering this more fully, the value of her pathetic accumulation should be observed in greater rhetorical detail. It certainly is appropriate for pathetic figures to populate a book of poetry, but for whom are these poems written? What public might Levertov imagine engaging with her descriptive imagery and passionate claims against war? Activists who read this will not need to be convinced of the horrors taking place in Vietnam, nor would a more conservative audience necessarily be persuaded by her attempts to humanize them through the establishment of her indignation as a transcendent rhetorical point of identification. Perhaps readers who are in sympathy with Levertov's cause but who have not yet been moved to act on its behalf will respond accordingly. But compared to other public forms—even other types of poetry—her figures of pathos violate the trust an audience might have in the valid expression of her experience. Her documentation does not reveal a personal struggle of apprehension of the complex social and political forces that shaped the period; instead, she determines for a reader how to feel rather than persuading them to act more comprehensively.

One potentially effective approach to the book of poetry as a public form of documentation comes toward the end of a poem written in response to the seizure of People's Park in Berkeley, California. After personal and public reflections on the transformation of the park by student activists in the spring of 1969, Levertov documents, with pathetic accumulation again, the taking of the park by police. "Bulldozers," she writes, "have moved in. / Barely awake, the people— / those who had made for each other / a green place— / begin to gather at the corners." The force of the stanza increases as her documentation shifts into indignant claims against the brutality that day:

> Their tears fall on sidewalk cement.
> The fence goes up, twice a man's height.
> Everyone knows (yet no one yet
> believes it) what all shall know
> this day, and the days that follow:
> now, the clubs, the gas,
> bayonets, bullets, The War
> comes home to us. . . .[22]

Although this stanza relies on uses of pathetic figures ("tears fall," "now the clubs, the gas," etc.), and it shifts perspective from Levertov's individual voice to include "everyone," hoping to build identification to illustrate war's domestic reach, the following page reproduces an actual document of the period:

WHAT PEOPLE CAN DO

1. Be in the streets—they're ours!
2. Report any action you have witnessed or been involved in that should be broadcast to keep the people informed. Especially call to report the location of any large groups of people, so those people who have been separated may regroup . . .
3. The Free Church and Oxford Hall medical aid stations need medical supplies, especially:
—gauze pads
—adhesive tape
—plastic squeeze bottles.
4. PLEASE do not go to the Free Church unless you have need to.
5. Photographers and filmmakers: Contact Park Media Committee.
6. Bail money will be collected at tables outside the COOP grocery stores:
—Telegraph Ave. store: Monday
—University Ave. store: Tuesday
—Shattuck Ave. store: Wed & Thurs.
7. BRING YOUR KITE AND FLY IT. Use nylon strings. Fly it when you are with a crowd. A helicopter cannot fly too near flying kites.
8. Be your brothers' and sisters' keeper.
9. Take care.[23]

As a social document, this contrasts starkly with the other lyric stanzas in the poem. It introduces a piece of agitprop to help situate the events and to provide useful information to participants in Berkeley at the time. It also presents an intimate exposure to student protest, and it suggests strategies other activists may use to achieve their goals. While this documentation is rhetorically and poetically provocative, it introduces specific actions that contrast with the accumulations of lyric imagery and commentary that comes in the preceding pages of *To Stay Alive*. In a quest for advantage, her passionate rhetoric contradicts the documentary genre she wants to create, and she confuses rhetorical and poetic possibilities for a public audience broadly conceived. While such documentary efforts can produce new potentials for some readers, Levertov identifies her public audience as one who will act in accord with her sense of "humankind." Her efforts to reach them are based on a faith in a sympathetic public readership, but by refusing to anticipate the responses of a more varied and complexly attuned readership, her lyric passion overtakes the book and renders even these moments of documentary effect into sympathetic pleas on behalf of the work of activists. But such simple awareness does not necessarily ensure the kinds of political opposition to war that forms the premise of her book.

Duncan's Response

Well before the decisive break in their friendship, Robert Duncan raised issues about Levertov's rhetorical intent in both her poetry and as a war activist, and she had largely ignored his concerns, working with tremendous energy, instead, at the serious tasks she faced as a public activist. Perhaps because of these odds at work in Levertov's poetry and her activism, Duncan noted a divide between the inner and outer lives his friend began living. Duncan, however, held a strong view of poetry that did not easily associate with revolution and activist engagement. Marjorie Perloff observes that unlike many poets inspired by the avant-garde who "claimed to be producing a new 'revolutionary' art," Duncan found the motives in poetry to precede political action. The revolutionary impulse for social or political reform betrayed the poet's language—a language composed of the history of cultural uses and values. Unlike Levertov, he was not concerned with one's willingness to act based on the testament of poetry: one's words *are* actions. But for Levertov, the revolutionary community became the subject of *To Stay Alive,* and she sought a more deliberate relation between her poetry and activism; Duncan, in contrast, argued for a poetics that contributed to communal vision.[24]

Throughout their correspondence of the mid- to late 1960s, as Levertov became increasingly active in the peace movement, Duncan grew ever more critical and reflective on the war and how poets could respond to it. "We are not reacting to the war," he wrote in one letter from 1966, "but mining images here the war arouses in us."[25] Levertov, however, responds the following week by locating her "participation in the Peace Movement . . . in a *real* relation to my feelings—this seems to me terribly important—& part of that, I feel, is a matter of trying to grasp with the imagination what does happen in war."[26] She uses the pronoun "we," moreover, as opposed to "they" because of "the common humanity of slayer & slain."[27] For Duncan, who questioned that commonplace, her poems bring "an agonizing sense of how the monstrosity of this nation's War is taking over your life."[28] He then, in what must seem a weak effort of protest to Levertov, announces that he and his partner, the collage artist Jess Collins, "will wear black armbands (as the Spanish do when some member of their immediate family has died) *always* and keep a period of mourning until certainly the last American soldier or 'consultant' is gone from Viet-Nam."[29] For Duncan, distinctions are drawn regarding the nature of a poet's task in a period of social upheaval—and this reveals his understanding of a public as communal presence activated in the poem rather than as a force outside the poem to be changed. Although he shares a similar ideological position with Levertov, he is concerned "with the imagination of what is going on in Man [*sic*]."[30] A poet's role is to provide reflective material through which a community can come to better understand its needs. A poet shapes communities with a more thorough sense of social obligations and by producing a larger context in which to prepare public action. Levertov, by contrast, hopes to move a community to act, and she seeks such action within the frame of a revolutionary event; Duncan merely asks that an audience look with comprehension at issues that may be decided in other moments without the aid of poetry.

So far we have observed two poets working through competing responses to public life during a period of social confrontation. Rhetorical poetry, whether used for advantage, as Levertov advanced it, or put to the more dialectical purposes of "pure persuasion," as Duncan understood it, provided a flexible public genre of communication. Both Duncan and Levertov take important steps to shape a community in opposition to a larger, more chaotic public threatened by war. But they intervene with different tactics that can help us see the possibilities available to speakers and writers in public space. To speak to a group of people in many ways shapes them, determines a collective nature in the moment of address. A poem like Levertov's "Tenebrae" is addressed to a community of people who identify with the antiwar message and the heaviness and dread of American occupation in Vietnam. It helped to reinforce the identity of the peace movement and gave form in poetic language to the sentiment felt by its members. This community, mobilized to oppose war, for Duncan, however, meets violence with rhetorical violence instead of actively reshaping actions and capacities through rhetorical modes of intervention. For Duncan, Levertov reinforced prevailing attitudes and positions on war; she did not expand the possibilities of her argument to include others outside of the peace movement. Duncan, instead of speaking *to* anyone, reflects on how to withhold judgment in order to satisfy a larger projective field of possibilities enabled by the poetic imagination. The imagined vitality and flexibility of the community in poetry provides the persuasive platform. Rhetorically, the community cannot be addressed because, in a sense, it does not exist except as an active potential. For Levertov, more practically, the issue was clear: war must be resisted with all available and willing voices.

"Kali Dancing"

> Dear Denny & Mitch,
>
> We saw the PBL report on the Rankin Brigade Washington protest and the sudden apparition of Denny in full ardor. The person that the *demos,* the *citoyen*-mass of an aroused party, awakes is so different from the individual person; recognizable—something of you, Denny that calls up the fondness of intimate continuities of feeling was very much there—and thrilling—it's the fieriness that all demotic personae have once they are aroused. As special an increase of commitment or earnestness over the fullness of commitment or earnestness [as always in the demotic urgency, the arousal of the group against an enemy— here the enemy clearly brings the whole state structure against our *humanity*—commitments must be withdrawn from the wholeness of the individual life to be focusst [*sic*], driven into the confinement of a single-minded purpose] as the erotic zeroing of a heightend [*sic*] and specialized power of the person. . . . In the PBL view of you, Denny, you are splendid but it is a force that, coming on *strong,* sweeps away all the vital weaknesses of the living identity; the *soul* is sacrificed to the demotic persona that fires itself from spirit.[31]

As this passage indicates, by March 1968, Duncan's critique of Levertov's war activism had sharpened significantly. In a portion of his poem, "Santa Cruz Propositions," Duncan also strikingly reveals his distaste for Levertov's "demotic persona," giving the public mask mythic and satiric form in the images of "Kali dancing," shouting "Revolution or Death!":

> She changes.
> Violently.   It is her time.   I never saw that dress before.
> I never saw that face before.

Duncan transforms Levertov into "Madame Outrage of the Central Committee" who "has put on her dress of murderous red" and "her make-up of the Mother of Hell, / the blue lips of Kore."[32] The poem offers quite a different perception than the one in the letter he wrote directly to her, and it presents a more disturbing sense, for us, of Duncan's own outrage—a sign of growing conflict in his imagination of poetic authority in a period of cultural stress. The feminine, monstrous "Mother of Hell" he associates with Levertov may be configured in part through cultural values that reinforced his own notions of public engagement.[33] As we will see a bit later, homosocial bonds among activists and poets restricted and shaped Levertov's public activism.

I want to focus on Duncan's argument, however, because it begins to articulate most fully his objections to a "rhetoric of advantage" in socially obligated poetry. The term Duncan uses—"demotic"—forms, in part, our word "democracy." The demotic signifies the populace—the people. And yet Duncan cautions against Levertov's assumption of their projective expectations by forming a persona they can appreciate. Duncan, in many ways, plays into an ancient argument against rhetoric, suggesting that beyond mere propaganda, Levertov engages in a kind of witchery, performing for the crowd to gain their support against the war.[34] The vulnerable aspects of her personality are forfeited to assume that public persona, taking on the role of the outraged protester, antiwar activist, and so on.

The problem for any speaker or writer, given particular social and cultural situations, is to speak through the chaotic accumulation of positions, offering a significant, if tentative, perspective the immediate value of which cannot always be determined. It is a compositional struggle to activate a presence of mind among others, reaching for the available means of persuasion, and perhaps, even then, still falling short of the necessary conditions of the public moment. Levertov's vulnerable demotic performance turns the power of language on an audience to claim authority in a moment of public activism. That growing sense of authority, validated by these public acts of protest, speeches, and readings of her work, in part caused her to turn from Duncan's arguments establishing, in anarchic and romantic spirit, the individual as the source of rhetorical agency—not the crowd or the institutional pressures forming the moment of conflict.[35] In contrast, Levertov derived her sense of purpose more explicitly from the peace movement and public instantiations of protest.[36]

As suggested earlier, the homosocial bonds of Black Mountain coterie poetics, as well as the compulsory sociality and hierarchy of male authority that emerged in Cold War–era culture, may have shaped, in part, Duncan's response to Levertov's performance on television.[37] His reduction of Levertov to "Kali," a witchlike and dangerous public presence whose face he no longer recognizes, can be understood as a reaction to his own threatened relationship to social agency and his claims to poetic authority in public culture. But he gives certain insights about how, in rhetoric, we adapt ourselves to particular situations in order to claim others. "It is hard, indeed, to write," he says in a June 1968 letter, "for you both stand now so definitely at the Front of—not the still small inner voice of conscience that cautions us in our convictions but the *other* conscience that draws us to give our lives over to our convictions, the righteous Conscience—what Freudians call The Super Ego, that does not caution but sweeps aside all reservations."[38] Duncan, "repell[ed]" by righteousness, instead, claims to "actively seek to keep alive all volitions."[39] For Duncan, there is a question of moral scale: "righteous Conscience" institutes a program to accomplish its goals while the "small inner voice of conscience" preserves its right to hesitate, reflect, and defer judgment for particular occasions in other contexts. This flexing of judgment in Levertov's speech is pivotal to Duncan's rejection of her poetic and activist performances. For him, poetry enacts possibilities; it does not bear judgment through stump performances.

While the "righteous Conscience" can focus intent and reinforce the appetite in others on behalf of an important cause, blunt assertions and single-minded drive more often interfere with greater possibilities. In demotic situations, where crowds gather for protest, authority (which is rhetorically and temporarily constructed in these instances) is only delicately maintained, and it is at times in jeopardy of abandoning the rhetorician. Despite one's personal conviction, the attitudes, desires, and responses of an audience can be difficult to anticipate, and spontaneous confrontations can disrupt the speaker's aim.

In response to one such disruption, a People's Park protester observed how the slogan "'the personal is political' extended its alliterative syllogism to include 'poetry.'"[40] And perhaps this "syllogism" can provide a cultural context for understanding Duncan and Levertov's conflict, for it suggests that, especially for the poet, the personal and the political are not maintained in easy isolation. They are related directly in the shared language of one's immediate community, if not, indeed, beyond to a larger public. This argument of the personal being political, with its larger connection to social activist groups and the women's liberation movement of the late 1960s and '70s, might help us also understand what poetry shared during this period with commitments to "consciousness-raising" by many on the left.[41] Efforts to expand consciousness correlate also with the possibilities expressed by modal rhetoric, with emphasis on performative opportunities, interventions, and dramatic gestures that confront an audience. Disruptions of daily practices with modal gestures, pranks, and performances provoke new responses, attitudes, and considerations of social order. But when everyday social relations are interrupted—such as during the carnivalesque atmospheres of large social protests—authority, as Mikhail Bakhtin observes, can be turned on its head. Such instances can test the orator's ability to maintain persuasive influence if the chain-reaction response of the crowd turns on her.[42]

The People's Prick

Consider one June 2, 1969, event—"Poetry Reading for the People's Park"—with performances by Levertov, Duncan, Lawrence Ferlinghetti, Gary Snyder, Michael McClure, and others. Here, Levertov's public authority came under question when the "personal is political" "syllogism" was challenged unexpectedly. As the poet and one-time student of Levertov's Aaron Shurin observes:

> As if on cue, up onto the stage from somewhere in the audience jumped an eight-foot pink felt penis, who grabbed the mike and announced to the crowd that he was "the People's Prick," bouncing around like a giant bunny on LSD. The audience roared their approval (the other operative syllogism extended "free all political prisoners" into "free love")—but not Denise [Levertov]. She was outraged. She was affronted. She knew better. She tried to take back control, hectoring the audience to behave with a puritan, if not Stalinist, regard that made it clear that Emma Goldman's revolution was not *her* revolution. But the *audience* was *not* hers. The Prick defied her, danced around her, as her sense of offence congealed and straightened her unbending spine into something far more disturbingly erect.[43]

The clash of personal authority, demotic personae, and the quick subversion of "righteous Conviction" meet here in the carnivalesque atmosphere of protest and amusement. A spontaneous moment like this tells us much about the role of poetry (and oratory) in public atmospheres, and about who controls it, claims authority for it, and appeals through it to the political values of others. While deliberative and forensic rhetorical contexts are far easier to locate and describe, the epideictic mode, in a chaotic observance of rhetorical power and vulnerability, reveals how images, symbolic acts, poetry, and protest meet, entangle, and disrupt conventional public expectations. The rhetor's sense of control within the playful context of the poetic can be wrested by the crowd, which is attuned in complex and unanticipated ways to the situation. While the "People's Prick" offers an image of humor, helping to deflate the social urgency, at least momentarily, of the People's Park situation, it also shows how volatile situations can spontaneously diminish the orator's authority and moral obligations, providing instead the scenes of *jouissance* and *carnival* commonly associated with demonstrations. Rhetoric in these instances becomes fluid and unstable, released by the images, words, and temporal eruptions of identity that mark an individual from the crowd. As Levertov's authority was questioned by the "People's Prick," her rhetorical quest of "advantage" was overcome with a more playful expression of poetic performance.

We also witness gender conflict of a most obnoxious sort. The phallus literally challenges the feminine claim to authority in an atmosphere where the body's symbolic form surely contributes to the tensions between the "prick" and the feminist activist. The "prick's" aggression can be read as a ploy to shut down Levertov's voice in a volatile moment. While Levertov's pursuit of rhetorical advantage was unable to gain the crowd's assent, the forceful intrusion of the "prick," aroused by the crowd's exhilaration and uproar, maximized the symbolic sexual division between feminine orator and masculine audience, reinforcing codes of male dominance through a performance of masculine tumescence.[44] While the scene illustrates the limitations of Levertov's moral incentives, it also reveals the power obstacles of gender and sexuality in the complex situation of her address. It echoes, moreover, Duncan's own virulent responses to Levertov as "Kali dancing," a pejorative appellation marked by his own claims to authority in existing poetic communities.

If poetry or performative acts can "raise consciousness" or build awareness in an audience, it can also reinforce positions of power maintained through Cold War cultural attitudes and practices. Rhetorical poetry offers two sharp edges: one that can address publics beyond the community, challenging them to consider new social or political possibilities, the other, however, reinforcing the in-group practices and commitments of poetry coteries. One such instance occurred when Denise Levertov visited San Francisco in 1957, and in a way it corresponds with the People's Prick confrontation in Berkeley a decade later. On this occasion Duncan had arranged a party to introduce her to the San Francisco community of poets whose most prominent figure, Jack Spicer, "directed a poem at the guest of honor, although its message was anything but honorific":[45]

People who don't like the smell of faggot vomit
Will never understand why men don't like women
Won't see why those never to be forgotten thighs

Of Helen (say) will move us into screams of laughter.
Parody (what we don't want) is the whole thing.
Don't deliver us any mail today, mailman.
Send us no letters. The female genital organ is hideous, We
Do not want to be moved.
Forgive us. Give us
A single example of the fact that nature is imperfect.
Men ought to love men
(And do)
As the man said
It's
Rosemary for remembrance.[46]

Spicer's misogyny inspired Levertov to reply later with her own riposte of feminine authority, writing that if "a white sweating bull of a poet told us // our cunts are ugly—why didn't we / admit we have thought so too? (And / what shame? They are not for the eye!) / No, they are dark and wrinkled and hairy, / caves of the Moon."[47] While the occasion for Spicer's outburst is situated in San Francisco coterie politics and perhaps presented an opportunity for participants to define their loyalties to Spicer, my point in bringing this up is that Levertov had encountered "pricks" prior to the People's Park event, and such confrontations could have left marks of resentment, anger, and frustration that emerged again at the People's Park event. On these occasions men asserted power over her claims to poetic authority, achieving an incongruent participation with her through gestures that proclaimed, loud and clear, who was boss. So while her attempts to regain control of the crowd at the People's Park event might make her appear "outraged," "offended," and "hectoring," she responded within coded social milieus that encouraged performances of masculine superiority and that frowned on women exerting their own claims of authority.[48]

To Sound Our Not Knowing

The aim of Duncan's letters to Levertov in the fall of 1971 reveals an unease with her use of poetry as a kind of rallying cri de coeur, particularly in *To Stay Alive*. By contrast, he articulated a role for poetry with roots in Pound's imagistic vocabulary and a compressed sense of history that is revealed through the poet's labor of imagination. Through these he claimed that poetry was an art capable of discovering motives behind political acts. He writes: "It's the deep-going and moving conjunctions in history—the seeing the poetic image—that the poet alone can precipitate (tho dreamers come close to it; and those monsters of history, the men in revolt against civilization—as the French Revolution, or Hitler in our own time—who write their nightmares in the actual instead of the fictional mode), the wanting everything flooded or swept by fire—that is the urgency that demands the poet to reveal what is back of the political slogans and persuasions."[49] For Duncan, the poet's work is located in these "moving conjunctions in history." The poet writes to realize them and reveal the pressure points "back of the political slogans and persuasions." Behind the "political slogans and persuasions" Duncan finds the emotions, dreams, and inchoate motives of broad political claims. While he does not elaborate more fully on what he means here, the rest of the letter offers a psychoanalytic reading of Levertov's work, and we can assume that his historical conjunctions are like psychic nodes, historically and socially active, by which the poet conducts her craft. At root, however, Duncan stresses revelation, admonishing Levertov for writing poems like "Tenebrae," where "it is moralizing that sets in." Such moralizing, for Duncan, is "vanity."[50] Poetry, he argues, is alert to the possible claims on the imagination made by a dialectic presentation of personal and cultural images and arguments. The immediate social hopes of the poet must be put aside in order to more accurately reveal the complex motives of a given situation, for the poem's architecture provides a self-fulfilling formal engagement with language, historical contexts, cultural possibilities, and social manifestations produced through the performative actions of recursive discourse.

For Duncan to go behind "the political slogans and persuasions" suggests indifference in his thought to rhetoric, if not outright hostility to it. If rhetoric, as Aristotle frames it, is a study of the means of persuasion (a definition that rhymes with Burke's rhetoric of "advantage"), how might Duncan's hermeneutical concerns contribute to our understanding of poetry's public role? Despite his claims to the contrary, he was interested in a kind of persuasive grappling with feelings and beliefs—the moral textures that accompany historical movements. And he certainly went out of his way in his correspondence to gain advantage in his arguments with Levertov.[51] He is concerned, however, with the motives behind situations, while Levertov is more interested in expanding an audience's capacities to identify with her feelings of moral certitude, thus basing her appeals in a personally defined *humanitas*. Duncan's strategy, by contrast, aims at informing readers of motives and perspectives that had been previously hidden. These disclosures enact a more reflective stance in the presence of volatile political positions. For Duncan, poetry's public value is its ability to ready a reader's attention so that it can be more fully engaged in the appropriate moments when decisions are made.

Another point of contention for Duncan is Levertov's involvement in People's Park and the poems she wrote about it. "The questions," he wrote to her, "are not ideological but have to do with where I feel you do not get to the truth of your ideology."[52] After reducing the People's Park activists to "deluded, self-deluded; [sic] hypocrites of the revolution," he goes on to argue that he is "outraged not only by the hypocrites and self-deluded, but by the innocent."[53] Instead, Duncan values "the truth of the unconscious," for, he tells Levertov, "the poetic truth of Viet Nam has to do with the deep well of your own life."[54] Such a committed perspective shifts the '60s-era slogan, "the personal is political," into a less obvious relationship to social formations, and instead suggests the power of personal psychology in the exertion of political will. Rather than giving the personal permission to relate its desires as political potentials, this view seizes on the horrors of war as an extension of the individual political alienation from real power. The violations abroad in Vietnam, then, confront the most intimate domestic spaces because of the shared possibilities that make connections across geographic spaces. Such potentials join most intimately the seemingly separated events of geopolitical design. They are linked through relations of rhetorical perspective. Poetry, for Duncan, provides access to such reservoirs of feeling in the self, though at a distance we may be trained, socially or politically, not to feel. The inquiring poet of pure persuasion cares not for mustering protest over injustices such as those bestowed on Vietnam by US force, but instead seeks to awaken an awareness of persistent human relations to such suffering.

In an earlier letter Duncan had written, "as workers in words, it *is* our business to keep alive in the language definitions as well as forces, to create crises in meaning, yes—but this is to create meanings in which we are the more aware of the crisis involved, of what is at issue."[55] To Duncan, Levertov does not "want to go into [her] own depth."[56] Her "verse form has become habituated to commenting and personalizing" rather than arguing for "a history beyond [her] idea of [her]self or [her] personal history."[57] The personal, for Duncan, was in service to an impersonal, or transpersonal, relationship to others. The "personalizing" for the sake of rhetorical advantage in Levertov's response to war neglected this awareness of the formative power of larger sympathetic relations. As a poet, Duncan did not want to represent the suffering of others for persuasive display; he, instead, sought ways of enacting the intense moral dilemmas and failures that underscored the futility of American efforts to eradicate communism from Vietnam.

As he argued, "the poet's role is not to oppose evil, but to imagine it." He asks: "Is it a disease of our generation that we offer symptoms and diagnoses of what we are in the place of imaginations and creations of what we are."[58] In other words, the imaginative possibilities of a purely persuasive rhetorical poetry far exceeded advantageous strategies based on commonplaces and similes.

He turns frequently, for instance, to the metaphor of the well. We "must go deep into . . . some imagination of what that depth would be if it weren't 'ours.'"[59] He urges Levertov to reflect on her uses of the poem that have become propaganda for a movement rather than a tool of interrogation and spontaneous eruptions of necessary images and arguments. Such "depth" correlates with the historic "conjunctions" noted earlier and contributes to a paradigm of documentation and confrontation, but the use of the poem differs from Levertov's "personalizing" values. Duncan argues that such psychic depth is crucial because it gives poetry the ability to invite reflective readings and for a number of readers to compare their perspectives with those delivered by the poet. Since an advantage is not sought over them, they can suspend judgment in order to follow the pure-persuasive means of the writer. "The idea of the multiphasic character of *language,*" writes Duncan, "and of the poem as a vehicle of the multiplicity of phases is more and more central to my thought." He continues: "The most important rimes are the resonances in which we sound these phases in their variety of depths . . . the resonances that depend upon our acknowledgement in our work of what we know of the range of meanings in the language so that we remain, beyond our intent, aware of our actions in the realm of words—for that we keep alive the historical levels of meaning, the sexual content so active everywhere in human discourse, the existential propositions of syntax, the changing concepts of the real."[60] These "rimes" argue for a deferral of judgment, or what Burke calls a "self-interference" in the process of "pure persuasion." Burke's claim that such interferences contribute to the process of "pure persuasion" by deferring judgment or action correlates closely with how Duncan sees the poet, who seeks to expand such "resonances" in an effort to overcome internal objections or personal prejudices. Such strides deepen a critical engagement with the terms of action realized as potential in the poem. The writer's "self-interference" obstructs determinative motives, leading her to pursue, instead, new perceptions that have been motivated by a suspension of personal values and beliefs in order to recall other shared affinities—"resonances" that invite reflection. An embodiment of social and historical "meanings in language" erupts in the syntactic "propositions" of the poem. Rhetorically, such "meanings" advance as claims about the nature of language, its use in social and historical contexts, shared cultural imagery, and arguments on behalf of how the poet understands "the changing concepts of the real." For Duncan, such engaged pursuits of the open potential in the "field" of the poem gave the poet a valuable cultural and social role. Levertov, preoccupied with addressing more immediate social conflicts, sustained a more purposive and localized strategy of public engagement; she sought a public audience, composed, for instance, of protesters at large events. Duncan, by contrast, addressed a public, or future public—readers whose assembly across geographic and temporal spaces form in less cohesive and apparent ways. He was, moreover, in service to the potential discovery of new positions. For him, Levertov's certainty of perspective cohered in figures of pathos and accumulations of metaphors that "no longer go deep into the well of knowledge to sound our not-knowing."[61]

Poet and "Private Citizen"

Although by December of 1972 Duncan would acknowledge his lack of tact and generosity in his initial outbursts against Levertov's war poetry, calling it "a projection of an inner disturbance with what the Jungians call the *Anima*," the ruin of their once close and deeply felt friendship was evident. Much as he would attempt to reestablish the familiar exchange in letters, Levertov distanced herself all the more, finally spelling it out in a February 1979 letter wherein she observes that their love had not been "shallow," and yet "it was not so deep that it had not a statute of limitation."[62]

In a long, October 25–November 2, 1971, letter wherein she responds to the strongest of Duncan's criticisms, Levertov discusses what can be seen as certain limitations on poetry's ability to act as a public vehicle of change: "*People's Park* What happened to the PP and Berkeley generally since the spring I was there has nothing to do with my poem. The experience of community I lived through there is inviolable, and in no way invalidated by whatever may have happened later. (In any case, if the city is now making more parks that's a victory not a defeat—and if they aren't the kind of parks people want then the people will have to make them so. But that's another story.) You were not a participant in the PP struggle, so what makes you think you know more about it than I do? It is damned arrogant of you."[63] The angry tone runs throughout the letter, but what's interesting to note is Levertov's ability to distinguish between her poem (the People's Park portion of "Staying Alive") and an "experience of the community."[64]

This tension between the private and the public in Levertov's work prevents her from truly addressing Duncan's critique, because he holds a view of the poem that while perhaps not public in the same sense as Levertov's more immediate public audience, is at least impersonal and readily available to a broad potential readership. More importantly, the poem is a direct relation—a commonplace argument regarding the nature of events that transpired at People's Park. Contra Duncan, she values the "experience of community" rather than the revelation of "conjunctions of history." Levertov views the poem as a reflective apparatus for personal experience. It is not public in the way her activist life is. But Duncan wants her to take the poem public with as much argumentative "depth" as her activist life.

Levertov also takes on his critique of her PBL performance as "Kali" in a red dress. After explaining some of the factional, behind-the-scenes politicking that went on between the rally's organizers, she says that "I was there not as a 'famous poet' but as a private citizen who had done what I was urging others to do and as the wife of a man at that time under indictment for doing likewise."[65] Rhetorically, whatever her intent had been, it is difficult to control such an image of self-presentation, poet or "private citizen." This also offers insight to the interesting problems of poetry as a public or political tool of documentation. At what point does the poet and "private citizen" lose control over identity? Again, in Levertov's case, the distinction between private poet and public activist-citizen is apparent, but for her audience, both roles are public. Indeed, an audience may operate under competing assumptions of public expectation, since notions of public space are so often in conflict with personal desire, social forces, and political interests. As she justifies her intent at People's Park, and in her poems, she reveals all the more how powerful Duncan's response is, because he takes the position of a reader, looking for evidence of public significance. For him, the notion of what constitutes a public is not so easily defined: he is not looking for the revolutionary event, but he is eager to see a public contribution. While in poems like "Tenebrae" Levertov claims not to be "moralizing," but to be "keening"[66] over the middle-class commonplace figures that illustrate the poem, it is difficult for Duncan to locate such a lament in the poem's angry tone.

For many poets in the 1960s, particularly those who identified with the New American poetics anthologized by Donald Allen,[67] poetry became useful as a way to address an expanded sense of community that could bring public matters to private audiences for further reflection.[68] This urge to document and make inquiries into the "conjunctures of history" requires assumptions about how poetry can affect the attitudes of an audience as well as elucidating the social and historical contexts that form cultural motives. Commonplace arguments about what exists or what did exist receive greater scrutiny in such contexts, as reflective readers labor to prepare themselves with knowledge of unique social situations. Duncan reads *To Stay Alive* in this way as a document of confrontation, as Levertov calls it in her introduction. In her private defense, though, she argues that her work is a personal response to daily life. This use of documentation provides for her a new possibility for poetry in public. "I have always had a strong preference for works of art in which the artist was driven by a need to speak (in whatever medium) of what deeply stirred him," she writes, "whether in blame or praise."[69] Moreover, she continues a bit later, "I do not at all have a sense of luring anyone into the poetic by catching hold of them through my subject matter. The idea appals [*sic*] me in fact."[70] The "poetic" then really is a kind of dramatic unfolding in language for Levertov, whereas for Duncan "subject matter," or the deep "well" where "conjunctions of history" form, is to be documented by poetry "to reveal what is back of the political slogans and persuasions."[71] As a writer Levertov possesses the organic groundwork of her particular body of feeling as the basis of political response but neglects other possible perspectives that might augment her feelings with other urgent sources of thought. Poems for Duncan still influence the attitudes and capacities of an audience. But as a work of inventive art, poetry's "pure persuasion" leads to greater engagements with public topics and discovers new questions or sources to consider in the ongoing confrontation between personal motives and the public knowledge disclosed through poetry. Since he did not seek advantage with an audience (although clearly he did seek advantage in correspondence with Levertov), he was compelled in his writing to prepare a public archive for consideration of social topics dear to him.

"Bending the Bow"

But what of Duncan's war poetry? Responding to the criticism of middle American life in "Tenebrae," he writes to Levertov: "While you tell us that 'they' are not listening, not hearing the war, I am listening and hearing more than you consider it legitimate to hear."[72] Instead of criticizing a group of people who do not belong to their community of writer-activists, Duncan argues that the common demands a kind of upkeep. He writes: "In the face of an overwhelming audience waiting for me to dare move them, I would speak to those alike in soul, I know not who or where they are. But I have only the language of our commonness, alive with them as well as me, the speech of the audience in its refusal in which I would come into that confidence. The poem in which my heart beats speaks like to unlike, kind to unkind."[73] This understanding of commonplace assumptions in an audience led Duncan to see poetry as "a field of ratios in which events appear in language."[74] An audience and author identify with each other through common assumptions about the reality of the world they inhabit. Against the mode of praise and blame, the poet, distant, looking down at the audience to tell them what they should know, Duncan presumes a common discourse and capacity in his audience to evaluate the evidence of his poetry. "Every present activity in the poem," he writes, "redistributes future as well as past events." His sense of commonality and community is based rhetorically on an approach to poetry that asks questions about the world, presents possible versions of it, and provides a commonplace vocabulary that lets readers compare perspectives.[75] Through these shared commonplaces, "like and unlike" can suspend their differences to enter a sphere of complicity and exchange.

Duncan's Vietnam-era book, *Bending the Bow*, practices what his poetic theory preaches, though with some noticeable exceptions. "The Multiversity: Passages 21" is a good example of the work in that volume, and in this poem he argues that the common must be defended as a space that fosters individual freedom. Unlike Levertov, he finds that a poetic vocabulary can only arise in opposition to the images and arguments of the state when individuals realize their commitments to one another. The identification of "like to unlike" and "kind to unkind" operates in opposition to Levertov's activist notion of public engagement as an opportunity to act out against powers of state. Although ideologically he agrees with Levertov, he finds her rhetoric limited by its insistence on meeting the power of the state with the power of the demos. Instead, he argues that communities must define their positions and work to support the individual as an agent in the changes they may initiate in social or political situations. "Where there is no commune," writes Duncan, "the individual volition has no ground. / Where there is no individual freedom, the commune / is falsified." For Duncan, the "hidden communit[ies]" that in part compose a public support individual agents who must persuade those with whom they have contact to promote change.[76] According to Duncan, the poem provides a common space through which communion can take place, giving strength to individuals to act according to their capacities to meet the demands of new situations. Such ideal communion, enacted through a purely persuasive rhetorical engagement within the terms of the poem, differs from the actual communities of antiwar protesters who composed much of Levertov's audience. What Duncan lacked in terms of immediate social engagement, he gains by preparing more widespread communities of readers for recurring issues of war and conflict that each generation faces on its own. The temporal and spatial scales of his engagement differed from Levertov's more immediate social confrontations, and through these differences of scale tactical interventions are seen to access immediate audiences as well as preparing a public readership for roles in future conflicts.

Duncan also can compose his own self-righteous outbursts. In "Up Rising: Passages 25," he compares President Lyndon B. Johnson to Hitler and Stalin, saying:

> Now Johnson would go up to join the great simulacra of men,
>   Hitler and Stalin, to work his fame
>   with planes roaring out from Guam over Asia,
> all America become a sea of toiling men
>   stirrd at his will, which would be a bloated thing,
>   drawing from the underbelly of the nation
>   such blood and dreams as swell the idiot psyche
>   out of its courses into an elemental thing
>   until his name stinks with burning meat and heapt honors[. . . .][77]

While he frames this critique of American political systems within totalitarian molds, he also invokes the literary figures of D. H. Lawrence and William Blake, hitching their radical social and political critiques to his nightmare vision. "As Blake saw America in figures of fire and blood raging," Duncan discovers, "the ominous roar in the air, / the omnipotent wings, the all-American boy in the cockpit / loosing his flow of napalm." The poem's violence rivals Levertov's, with "the burning of homes and the torture of mothers and fathers and / children, / their hair a-flame, screaming in agony, but / in the line of duty, for the might and enduring fame / of Johnson." More visually violent and startlingly vivid than other work, "Passages 25" attempts to situate the Johnson administration's commitment to war in Vietnam within literary, religious, and social history, despite the violent imagery he uses to make his claims. Indeed, if Levertov turned her anger upon the comfortable middle class, Duncan likewise speaks of "the fearful hearts of good people in the suburbs turning the / savory meat over the charcoal burners and heaping their barbecue / plates with what they can eat, / from the closed meeting-rooms of regents of university and sessions of profiteers." While his rhetorical aim is perhaps different from Levertov's, he tries to broaden the range of his critique and nonetheless retains the spiritually distant vision of the phatic seer who is removed from the transgressive America of his scrutiny. He continues, with powerful awareness, though very much in line with Levertov:

> —back of the scene: the atomic stockpile; the vials of synthesized diseases eager biologists have developt over half a century dreaming of the bodies of mothers and fathers and children and hated rivals swollen with new plagues, measles grown enormous, influenzas perfected; and the gasses of despair, confusion of the senses, mania, inducing terror of the universe, coma, existential wounds, that chemists we have met at cocktail parties, passt daily and with a happy "Good Day" on the way to classes or work, have workt to make war too terrible for men to wage—[78]

Echoing Pound, he invokes the names of Adams and Jefferson who "feard and knew / would corrupt the very body of the nation / and all our sense of our common humanity." The biologists and "people in the suburbs" preserve a world of universal terror, responsible for "America's unacknowledged, unrepented crimes."

This powerful poem attempts to widen the concerns of his commitments to include an audience separate from Levertov's. If she spoke to members of the peace movement as well as to a literary community, Duncan's devotions reside almost solely with a literary public. His theoretical complaint with Levertov seems only that: for they share so many similarities of judgment and execution that it is difficult to really determine expansive differences. This is but one poem, however, established within a larger, compelling suite of work that significantly complicates Duncan's poetic enactments. And yet poems in later books like "from Robert Southwell's 'The Burning Babe'" also situate "the broild flesh of these heretics, / by napalm monstrously baptized" within range of Robert Southwell's sixteenth-century poem, with "Truth's heat" and "a fuel of passion in which / the thought of wounds delites the soul. / He's Art's epiphany of Art new born, / a Christ of Poetry, the burning spirit's show; / He leaves no shadow, where he dances in the air/ of misery below."[79] While Duncan's poems in *Bending the Bow* persevere with attention to poetry as a spiritual art and a psychagogic engagement designed to lead attention from specific conflict in Vietnam and America into the larger spiritual upheavals of good and evil, his use of pathetic figures would seem at times to unite him in practice with Levertov.

The Risk of Authority

It is worth noting, too, that Duncan's reactions to her war poetry increased as Levertov gained ever-greater public acknowledgment, first as the poetry editor at *The Nation* and then as a public antiwar activist. Perhaps her successful ability to shift scales from a literary audience to ones motivated by other social causes inspired anxiety in Duncan. If strong bonds among male poets of Duncan's generation contributed to his sense of authority and gave him the ability to move within literary hierarchies, it is possible to understand Levertov's own claims of authority as a threat.[80] His strong reaction to Levertov also suggests that he sought ways to maintain personal and gendered authority over her. While much more is at stake, it is possible nonetheless that he felt Levertov threatened his power as a poet, for she expanded her readership, engaged new audiences, and adapted her writing to commit to new possibilities of action within the arenas of Vietnam protests and the peace movement. Despite his rhetorical motives to push poetry toward greater public conceptions, Duncan often relied on his authority as a literary figure to reach others. His authority required affirmation, at least here in a moment where poetry and activism began to enter new public contexts.

Duncan does, however, produce new ways of looking at Vietnam for his readers. He establishes ethical relationships between those in power like Johnson and the suburban makers of barbecue. Given his commitments to individual preparations for political realities, and for the open access of many perspectives within communities, ideal or otherwise, Duncan's arguments indicate ways to understand publics, communities, and individual attempts to subvert institutionalized forms of power. Levertov's use of poetry, by contrast, addresses significant processes of state-sanctioned power; for her the individual is possessed of the forms of her experience in such engagements with powerful institutions, and she dramatically embodies them. Duncan resists such dramatic embodiment, arguing instead that by looking for common ground in which to argue for our positions on social or political life, individuals may be able to influence other actors through an increasing movement of perspectives. Such individuals may not confront directly heads of state to oppose war, but through this communal vision of poetry's influence on readers, communities provide spaces for actors to more confidently reflect on the capacities poetry can produce.

Duncan's work in this period also takes seriously the problem of a public/private dialectic. While his poetic practice turned to a rhetoric of pure

persuasion, composed of textual layering, treating the poem as a dialectical strategy for understanding geopolitical strife, his work also argued for a
greater awareness of the social, historical, and psychological forces at stake
in private and public exchanges taking place in the daily life of the period.
His work takes seriously the circulation of imagery and other intervening
forms. By responding to these images, Duncan and others expanded capacities and knowledge of private and public life. Duncan, especially, asked that
we make sense of the daily barrage of circulating forms that we encounter, and poetry, with its flexibility as a written discourse, produces ways of
understanding present situations.

But Levertov, unlike Duncan, more radically put herself at risk as a public
figure. The legacy of her commitments can still be found in the works of
poets like Anne Waldman, Amiri Baraka, Clayton Eshleman, and younger
contemporary writers working with poetry in public contexts. Waldman's
political poetry, for instance, often employs figures of pathos to reinforce
positions and attitudes regarding social and environmental issues. Amiri
Baraka's work likewise directs controversial critical performances to bring
attention to racial and social practices, while Eshleman's persistent inquiries
into the events associated with 9/11 draw attention to complex political
and social motives behind wars in the Middle East. These poets have am-
plified some of Levertov's poetic strategies to increase pressures in public
contexts as a way to draw attention to shared attitudes and beliefs.[81] By
accepting a new role as a public figure, Levertov was able to bring poetry
to new contexts and to perform in public as a committed orator, leaving a
record of public action for future generations of writers.

Together, Levertov and Duncan reveal the possibilities and limitations
to public engagement through poetry. The record of their correspondence
provides insights to writing strategies in a world where private and public issues interpenetrate, and the role of the poet begins to shift beyond the
page to account for the larger contexts of experience in a global economy.
The writing of Lorenzo Thomas and Edward Dorn also will address controversial public issues in the following chapter, but their interventions
focus more on the circulation of public images in broadcast media; their
particular subversions offer not so much a plan of protest as ways of acting
out against the commodification of cultural narratives.

3
Public Witness/Public Mind
Media, Citizenship, and Dissent in the Poetry of Lorenzo Thomas and Edward Dorn

> There is no such thing as Art and Politics, there is only life.
> —Amiri Baraka quoted in Lorenzo Thomas, *Extraordinary Measures: Afrocentric Modernism and Twentieth-Century American Poetry,* 2000

Just as print media in the eighteenth century influenced the rise of a public sphere (as Jürgen Habermas has shown), television and other media in the middle decades of the twentieth century similarly shaped attitudes and beliefs about public and cultural life in the United States.[1] But television did more than this: it complicated perceptions of public and private space, introducing a steady stream of advertising, journalism, dramatic and comedic entertainment, and other genres into the complex sensorium of domestic experience.[2] With the Vietnam War, images of Cold War containment circulated in the private sphere, bringing a violent and abhorrent reality from Southeast Asia into the idealized calm and suburban bucolic of the American middle class—a social and economic foundation in postwar society that was increasingly informed by televised images for public consumption and emulation. Likewise, images of violence from civil rights protests brought the urgency of racial segregation to "middle America," whose false consciousness and indifference to global conflict was addressed in the writing of Robert Duncan and Denise Levertov. The discordance between the circulation of war and racial strife reported by the evening news and the familial comfort of the evening meal introduced a strange public dissonance to that abstractly conjured, postwar entity: the American home.[3] Within that domestic space, sociocultural claims addressed viewers through the images and performances of public dialogue. Unlike the eighteenth century when patrons gathered in coffee houses to read printed material and to debate the significance of the news, the more complex, at times passive, and uncoordinated reception of televised images during the Vietnam War blurred the relation between the state and individual, between the public and private spaces that continued to morph, merge, and, increasingly, to interact. The rambunctious and provocative social spaces provided by coffee houses became in postwar America havens for artists, poets, and other figures of countercultural revolt, whereas the majority of public opinion was generated increasingly at home by the interpersonal exchanges of family and friends. If the public sphere for Habermas had been that space where bourgeois spectators met to discuss issues of social, political, and economic relevance, then the television restricted meetings to smaller familial units, in many ways fragmenting and distorting public definition. The need to go out in public for news had been radically altered: the news came into the home. And so did advertising, drama, sitcoms, and other genres of communication that attempted to reinforce cultural values in a climate of Cold War.

This chapter is concerned with the circulation of public images generated after 1960 and looks at the rhetorical and textual interventions of two poets whose writing brings attention to exchanges of commonplace imagery. Their responses reveal how a rhetorically engaged poetry can use the broadcast of public images to increase possibilities of public understanding. Their poetry talks back to dominant forms of media by accommodating public voices aloud and in print that challenge and critique hegemonic public views. By creating a critical commentary that addresses significant public events, the poets I turn to in this chapter compose political and social offerings for a literary public. Beginning with the Vietnam War and continuing through the Reagan-era conflicts in Central America, the burden of reconciliation and resistance to mediated images of various public phenomena increasingly concerned poets who wondered how the invasion of images of statecraft, ceremony, war, and public drama circulated through the domestic hearth. For Lorenzo Thomas and Edward Dorn the intrusion of televised images into the privacy of the home also influenced the social imaginary.[4] If social legibility is constructed in part by shared circulating images that modally sharpen or increase possible attitudes or positions in cultural situations, how might a poet intervene to give shape to capacities that develop or rework commonplace cultural phenomena?[5] How, for instance, might a poet embody a response to the televised images she encounters? If the image-life of a people is sustained in some ways through intimate experiences of televised light, how should a poet intervene through written and spoken words to sustain practices of citizenship and dissent?[6] As Thomas and Dorn tried to shape social space, they developed rhetorical strategies that let them act out against publicly mediated images. They appropriated the texts and images generated by the "talking heads" of news networks who validated a public sphere even as other modal possibilities were being expressed by less visible actors to create other civic contexts. Since their rhetorical approaches to the poem during this period differed significantly (Thomas employed surrealist lyricism to sustain his writing while Dorn turned to brief satire and moralistic epigrams), their work provides useful entry points for seeing how poetic voices in print and speech invite reflection over contested public topics.

Black Arts and Spoken Word

Lorenzo Thomas was born in Panama and grew up in New York City. He served in the Vietnam War, moved to Houston in 1973, teaching first at Texas Southern University, where he edited the magazine *Roots,* and then later joining the University of Houston–Downtown as a professor of English.[7] His participation in the Umbra Workshop, a collective of writers associated with the Black Arts movement[8] in New York City in the 1960s, significantly influenced his poetics and established a firm sense of personal and cultural history that was, in many ways, alien to the official cultural narratives mediated during the 1960s and '70s. With David Henderson, Askia Muhammad Touré, Larry Neal, Tom Dent, and others, he began a study of poetry that was inspired by the racial, political, and cultural movements of the period. For Thomas, whose family came from the Caribbean via Central America, poets of the Négritude movement like Léopold Senghor and Aimé Césaire appealed to his sense of identity as a black writer. African poets writing in Portuguese—people like Francisco-José Tenreiro and Marcelino dos Santos—also motivated his work, along with Harlem Renaissance figures, to a lesser degree.

In a study of twentieth-century African American literature, music, and popular culture, he presented an alternative tradition to a Eurocentric modernist heritage. While Maria Damon has related Afrocentric poetry to historiography, claiming, "Afrocentric literary historiography is a form of ★social★ witnessing,"[9] in *Extraordinary Measures,* Thomas also describes rhetorical strategies that open Afrocentric approaches to nonliterary contexts and voices that compose poetic history.[10] Indeed, Thomas's sympathies are described in detail in this critical volume. Through his association of the Black Arts movement with the Beat and Black Mountain traditions of writing, Thomas links the rhetorical function of an Afrocentric poetics to popular, speech-based approaches to public writing. Poetry for him is politically and socially motivated, providing a perspective of "witness" to the social injustice that motivates much of North American culture. In "Neon Griot," a chapter that discusses the "Functional Role of Poetry Readings," Thomas examines the history of poetry readings in white and African American communities, considering the public situations these construct.

His concern with the public contexts and presentations of readers brings Thomas to acknowledge how the "dynamic interactive relationships—formal and informal—between artist and audience define the heritage of the poetry reading; yet to the extent that poetry readings have been perceived as entirely secondary to the existence of poems as printed texts, very little attention has been directed to the possible impact of performance contexts on poetic composition."[11] While Thomas also observes that public readings can be tiresome and fall short of an audience's expectations, he looks specifically at the "coffeehouse poetry readings" of the 1950s as a model that inspired the Black Arts movement's more radical attempt to bring poetry into broader social and cultural contexts. Such public contexts influenced his own approach to poetry, for he associated poetic speech with performance, the written word being a score that guides the more important performative voice.

He considers other aspects of Afrocentric poetry in relation to the Beat movement of the 1950s, claiming that many Beat poets at midcentury "did not regard their work as 'high art.'"[12] He links this impulse to "Emerson's rejection of European 'cultivation' in favor of an indigenous and energetic American inventiveness,"[13] but associates this also with African American "interest in jazz." Thomas, echoing Amiri Baraka, who had been a tremendous force in establishing social and artistic projects in New York City in the 1960s, observes how "one of the goals of the Black Arts movement was the creation of a mass art," and he distinguishes between popular, street-level public readings and "poetry reading as 'cultural event,'" finding a more socially rewarding potential in the former.[14] If poetry recitations failed to achieve the same public approval as jazz for a popular audience, some performers such as Bob Kaufman managed to fully use their poetry to achieve a public presence in the live performances of their work.[15] For Thomas, the theory behind public engagement came from Charles Olson's 1950 essay, "Projective Verse," which was promoted to Black Arts writers by Amiri Baraka.[16] Like Olson, he prized speech over the written word, and the public context of poetry's delivery was valued over anthologized textual atmospheres. For Thomas and others in the Black Arts movement, "art was—and should be—a political act."[17]

If Black Arts poets "extended the venues for their performances beyond storefront theaters to neighborhood community centers, church basements, taverns, and the street," Thomas argues, it was because such work "drew upon the rhetorical conventions of the black church."[18] The Black Arts poetry that Thomas identified with was built on a rhetorical model of social and cultural engagement. Its performative nature was derived from traditions in African American music, an African American vernacular speech that was based specifically in the oratorical traditions of the black church, and "the material and physical context of Black Arts poetry readings."[19] While Thomas describes a Black Arts–based context for a rhetorical poetics that engaged with audiences in diverse public settings to enact political change, his own poetry can be read as an extension of this practice. It is important, then, to keep in mind the primacy of the spoken word when discussing Thomas's writing. "All poetry is incomplete until it is read aloud," he writes. "The idea that sophisticated readers can simulate this experience mentally is, of course, a long-standing article of faith that has been systematically assaulted by subsequent technological efforts to construct 'virtual' realities. Nevertheless, the poem printed on the page is effective when it (1) functions as a memorandum to excite the reader's recall of a previous performance or (2) serves as a score for future vocal reproduction. If the poet has done the job of preparing that alphabetic transcription well, she can be sure that the poem will live."[20]

With this oral sense of poetry in mind, and with the cultural and historical interest in social contexts, Thomas's own writing achieves what Damon sees as a form of social witnessing, though the oratorical background suggests also a greater persuasive and active commitment to social change.[21] In the scenes that follow, specific social situations are encountered through a poetics that can address traumatic public events in ways that contemporary media fail to achieve. By writing poems that are meant for public readings, Thomas creates scripts that can later be documented in books, but the primary impulse is to make social works that are based in speech and that anticipate an audience in need of reconciliation to traumatic events. By addressing issues of race and civil rights, Thomas recasts potent public images in poetry, and in the epideictic mode he enables new perspectives and resolutions for audiences who seek to understand the violence and contradictions of American life. As an orator-poet, his persuasive appeal enables new perspectives on current events and brings the possibility of social transformation to his audience.

"The Bathers"

A poem of the same title as Lorenzo Thomas's 1981 book-length collection, *The Bathers,*[22] looks at the alienation of African American culture from the more pervasive media narratives that circulated for public consumption. The poem reads contemporary social events with the vernacular cadences and imagery of African American church traditions as a way to repossess officially mediated narratives and to intervene in their making. Here as in much of his work, Thomas was compelled to investigate points of contact where individual and communal perspectives collided with larger public agendas that attempted to contain cultural dissent, mark racial and social classes, and create neat, narrative selvages to manage the social reinforcements of cultural and public life. By taking Martin Luther King Jr.'s Birmingham campaign of 1963 as the topic of his poem, Thomas integrated public events with concerns over cultural identity in an attempt to reclaim public narratives and to increase actions and capacities in his audience. By investing the public narratives he experienced in the news with his own sense of social and racial identity, Thomas reshaped the story of racial conflict for an African American public. This reclamation of public narrative allowed him to comment on crucial social events, and through them he submitted his perspective as a witness to the management of public images as they were disseminated through photography, television, and other media. By revising these images he retells the story of protest against racial segregation for a black audience as well as for nonblacks who may benefit from the new perspectives of Thomas's writing. His poems then work in a double sense, for by investing an understanding of African social and political struggle in the narrative of protest, Thomas reinforces the cultural beliefs and desires of his community of black readers and auditors.[23] Others outside this community, who do not identify with the Africanized experience Thomas proposes, nevertheless are challenged to integrate the biblical narrative of Exodus as a way to more fully understand the historical and public significance of the Birmingham, Alabama, conflict. His poems in certain ways pose sociopsychic studies of everyday life in the racially subdivided contexts of North America.

As a published artifact, the book form of *The Bathers* rhetorically prepares readers for the poems to come. Cover art by Cess Thomas depicts four nude white women (see figure 1). The collage satirically references Édouard Manet's *Le déjeuner sur l'herbe* (1863), incorporating images of nude women lunching in a bucolic setting along with modern objects, such as a motorcycle and suntan lotion. The women lounge near water, celebrating the warmth of summer like mock river nymphs, one supposes, who are isolated from the cares of the world that follow in the pages of Thomas's book. Images on the frontispiece, however, depict a scene from the Birmingham campaign, the figures of young black men and women intensely burdened by the pressure of water sprayed at them from a fire hose (see figure 2). One figure attempts to cover his face as another receives a blast of water from a high-pressure hose. Another illustration also is based on the iconic *Life* magazine photographs taken by Charles Moore on May 3,

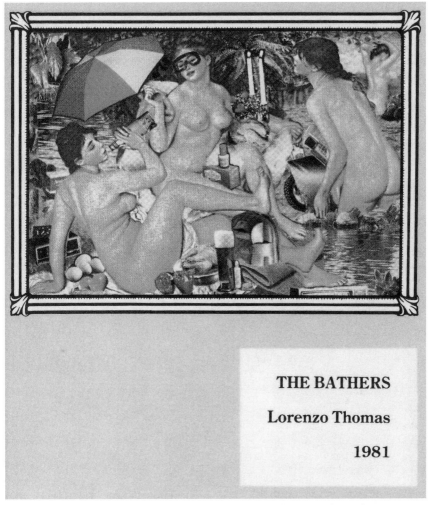

THE BATHERS

Lorenzo Thomas

1981

Figure 1. Book cover with collage artwork by Cess Thomas, *The Bathers* (New York: I. Reed Books, 1981).

1963 (see figure 3). By representing the images in the context of Thomas's poems, and in relation to the cover collage, the writing is presented in a charged contextual atmosphere of racial prejudice, social change, and public mediation. The book's ironic title uses these images to prepare readers for the social and historical confrontation of the poems. These illustrations also suggest the discordant racial perspectives generated by mass media. The oblivious "river nymphs" enjoy the privilege of their situation while the children attacked by workers for the city of Birmingham, Alabama, pre-

Figure 2. "The Bathers" title page with illustration by Cess Thomas, *The Bathers* (New York: I. Reed Books, 1981).

Figure 3. "The Bathers" frontispiece collage by Cess Thomas, *The Bathers* (New York: I. Reed Books, 1981).

sent another sickening aspect of American life. The book therefore engages and broadens W. E. B. Du Bois's notion of "double consciousness," for the bathers of the book's title indicate not only the children of Montgomery and the jailed civil rights protestors but also other white witnesses of the event. The book's cover also challenges the privilege of such witness, suggesting that white culture quickly attempts to categorize racial strife in easy-to-consume narratives of cultural discord. The distance created by a circulation of public forms in distinction to the violent acts that occurred on actual bodies in Birmingham spins violence into narratives that are reconciled according to the privileges of perspective. A white public will consume the circulated forms of the event through an understanding that at the time was segregated culturally from the African American bodies represented in the broadcast and print imagery. The social imaginary of bodies and race produce conflicting narratives in the circulatory field. Cultural attitudes and ideologies, the book suggests, are reinforced by the public consumption of such imagery. Thomas's poems in this context, then, propose strategies that reveal how double consciousness is emergent in racially oriented perspectives, and he writes poetry that can speak back to racial indifference as it has been allowed to circulate. Such efforts reclaim the "self-as-other" in the direct engagement of the terms by which crucial events can be organized as oppressive cultural forms in the social imaginary.

Birmingham

Birmingham, Alabama, was one of the most segregated cities in the nation when the Southern Christian Leadership Conference (SCLC) led by Martin Luther King Jr., organized a campaign in the spring of 1963 to desegregate the city.[24] Despite the group's nonviolent methods of resistance, police arrested and jailed protestors early in the campaign, including King. As a response, SCLC nonviolent strategies of resistance began to exert pressure on the local government by filling jails with arrested protestors as a way to exhaust city resources and management and as a way of intensifying the growing media spectacle. On May 2, local children were organized to protest segregation, and nearly one thousand were arrested. The next day, Sheriff Eugene "Bull" Connor ordered the fire department to spray high-pressure fire hoses at protestors while police dogs were used to intimidate black participants in the protest. The images captured by Charles Moore and Bill Hudson of the Associate Press were in part credited for turning public opinion against the city of Birmingham. President John F. Kennedy called the photographs "shameful."[25] Several senators and representatives brought civil rights legislation to the Senate and House floors, while Kennedy sent Assistant Attorney General Burke Marshall to negotiate a truce. With more than two thousand protestors jailed, images of children brutally attacked by fire hoses and dogs, and the city virtually collapsing, the conflict slowly resolved in favor of the civil rights movement. Prior to resolution, however, a bomb destroyed the Gaston Motel where King was staying. The violence and drawn-out intensity of the Birmingham campaign circulated for public consumption, and it complicated issues of black identity and action, particularly as Malcolm X and others criticized King's nonviolent methods of protest.

Given this volatile context, "The Bathers" engages public, private, and communal aspects of events that circulated globally. Although Thomas was not in Birmingham, the reception of the spectacle haunted his imagination and he was, of course, as an African American Black Arts writer, intimately concerned with the public displays of violence and humiliation. As a writer confronting the notion of the "self-as-other," Thomas's modernist strategies of poetry were based on social and political commitments adopted by the Black Arts movement to bring about social change. One strategy Thomas developed is what Damon calls an "Afrocentric literary historiography," or, "a form of social witnessing." By circulating Afrocentric narratives that recast public events for African American public spaces, Thomas contributed to a rhetorical poetics that engaged public events. The sense of history Thomas advocated offers contexts of identity for audiences, and his methods of writing integrate with this historical consciousness and the values of black communities. If the larger, nameless "mass" public is the recipient of televised images, Thomas reinvests these images with historical contexts of slavery, a cultural lineage to Egypt, and the oratorical traditions of the black church in order to appeal to specific communities that overlap with other public identities. As Damon observes, "social and subjective witnessing are not separate events." In this way, "social trauma" is common to both the writer and the audience. "To write history through poetry and a poetic historiography is to knit oneself even more closely to community."[26] The historical narratives shared by African American audiences provide Thomas with a common point of departure for making sense of the larger cultural narratives generated for public consumption. As a social witness, therefore, Thomas's work persuades an audience of potential strategies for understanding and acting on the "double consciousness" that in part constructs black identity in the complicated terms of national power and history.

Afrocentric Rhetorical Poetics

As a social witness who is also distant from the scenes of action, Thomas negotiates the tropes of historical consciousness that he identifies with an Afrocentric modernism—a rhetorical poetics based in cultural and social advancement. In "The Bathers," the dramatic and violent events of Birmingham, Alabama, are narrated and reflected on from within an Africanized context that reclaims the publicly mediated images for the needs of a specific community. As Aldon Lynn Nielsen observes, "Thomas portrayed this as a possibly redemptive rebirth of a nation," discovering in the events at Birmingham a "historical text when an African spirit was reborn among his lost North American children."[27] For Thomas, the irony of the fire hoses gave him an opportunity to transform the situation by extending a strong sense of identification with the "bathers," those children newly baptized in the city waters of Birmingham:

> We turned to fire when the water hit
> Us. Something
> Berserk regained
> An outmoded regard for sanity

> While in the fire station
> No one thought of flame
> Fame or fortune did them
>
> We did them a fortune. We did
> Them a favor just being
> Ourselves inside of them
>
> Holy day children
>
> In the nation coming your children will learn all about that
>
> But the water creep about us
> Water hit us with force.[28]

The understatement of these lines lends tremendous force to the voice reconstructing a narrative of baptism. Drawing on religious imagery significant to African American identity, Thomas's lines describe the rebirth of these "Holy day children" into lions:

> We saw a boy transformed into a lion
> His tail is vau the syllable of love
> A master before fellow craft
> The summit of the Royal Arch
>
> Lotus. Mover on the face of the waters . . .[29]

While this baptismal imagery draws on church sources, the poem quickly shifts to accommodate an Egyptian and magical religious narrative with roots in Africa, too, as seen in the Egyptian script above. While Nielsen sees in these symbols "living glyphs, transformative signs" that reclaimed the experience for a black audience by associating the contemporary within an ancient Afrocentric tradition of script and mythic substance, the Africanized narrative reinforces black identity and complicates the public presentation of the images projected from Birmingham.[30] Rather than offering a version of the "self-as-other" in relation to public circulations of imagery from the Birmingham protests, Thomas relates African American cultural identity through his own intervention of Africanized cultural forms. This allows the experience of African Americans in the New World to overlay onto the narrative of exile in Genesis, extending cultural identity through an oratorical trope of religious and spiritual familiarity. Thomas continues:

Sleepless Horus, watch me as I lie
Curtained with stars when ye arise
And part the skies. And mount the Royal
Bark

They said the ancient words in shameful English
Their hearts rose up like feathers
In the hidden place

And Horus step into the flood of noon
Shedding his light upon the worlds

It was in Birmingham. It happened.

Week after week in the papers
The proof appeared in their faces

Week after week seeing the same moment grow clearer. . . .[31]

In Egyptian mythology Horus is a solar deity that also, in the form of a falcon, associates with war. By projecting African myth as a narrative conceit for the poem, Thomas identifies Horus with the solar "light" cult of American culture and its mediation of images through televised screens and photographs.[32] In an oblique way, the poem comments on the uses of such images as Charles Moore's iconographic photo. By recasting such images into a scene of baptism, Thomas reclaims the potency of the image for an African American experience rather than for a secular and public determination of meanings. Thomas's poem then argues against the "electromagnetic light" images recorded on camera and announces instead the negative and opaque motives of spiritual revival:

O electromagnetic Light shadûf!

Ancient hands bearing water
Ha

    The star broke
Over the tub

    All righteousness

Not deceived by sunshine nor the light
From a man's desire

Deceived by desire
So that in the moment
The people cast light from their bodies
"Light" being the white premeditation
The simplest fashion
What they want is light

Another source to equip
Their dry want

Want fire light. Space light
Discretions of neon. . . . [33]

The Arabic word "shadûf," a tool for moving water, here puns with "shut off," as though demanding that the "electromagnetic light" by which images are televised be turned out while a more ancient narrative relation is improvised. As an instrument that bears water, a shadûf correlates with the Big Dipper constellation, thus extending a cosmic relation to this segment of the poem. The distinction between "them" and us moves the issues in Birmingham onto a larger spiritual stage, too. The children of Israel—slaves to Egypt—are to confront a master narrative in a solar cult of domination and war. While on one hand this poeticized narrative may speak to the communal imagination of a shared Christian narrative, Thomas appeals to a black audience through these collective images with the cadences of a black minister. He hopes to persuade them to stand up to Egypt in order to abandon a figurative enslavement that replaced an actual experience of slavery. If, too, the tension between Martin Luther King's nonviolent resistance and Malcolm X's more aggressive call to arms remained unresolved as the Birmingham campaign intensified, we may hear in Lorenzo Thomas's poem a persuasive appeal to resist with force if necessary, though this is ambiguously stated. For the hatred expressed in it can be read as the hatred of the bigoted South for civil rights, but it can also be heard as a black confrontation with the solar cult of Horus—the American social and political reality. Or, of course, we can read both:

Bathing in the dark
The water glowing
In the plastic curtain
Suddenly heated

As another expels past satisfactions.
cold as she washes gas tears
From her man's eyes. We hate you.

Hot on her soft thigh
Like the dog's breath at noon by the Courthouse

We hate you for that

   But ancient hands raised
This water

As the street's preachers
Have a good understanding hear them

      O israel this O israel that

Down here in this place
Crying for common privilege
In a comfortable land

Their anger is drawing the water
Their daughters is drawing the water.

Their kindness is laving and
Oiling its patients.

   That day
  The figures on the trucks inspired no one

Some threw the water
On their heads.
They was Baptists

And that day Horus bathed him in the water
Again

And orisha walked amid the waters with hatchets
Where Allah's useful white men
Came there bearing the water
And made our street Jordan
And we stepped into our new land

Praise God. As it been since the first time

The tear of a mother.[34]

While these lines assert African American cultural identity through rhythmic cadences and intonations of voice, as well as in imagery that recasts the slave trade from Africa in spiritualized or mythic terms, the speaker calls directly for social change. "Crying for common privilege / in a comfortable land," as Thomas writes, invites anger, too. As a poem of social commentary built from the communal narratives of a brutally repressed people, Thomas is able to recast Moore's public image for communal reflection. He is able also to speak to an African American audience about their origin in slavery and their struggle to attain equality with whites. By identifying "the bathers" in Birmingham as "Baptists" who "cry for common privilege / In a comfortable land," Thomas transforms Moore's image by restating it in a context of the black church, and by appealing to an audience that identifies not with the mediated stream of events, but with a terse understanding of the larger historical forces that created the situation of slavery and segregation in America in the 1960s. By using the cadences of a black oratory tradition, and by basing the language in spoken-word, free-verse forms rather than in metrics, Thomas creates a text that appeals to the cultural situation of his listeners and readers. He reminds them of the stakes in Birmingham by speaking to a communal situation that has been denied representation through larger media outlets. In this way he presents a historical context that gives another spin to the meaning of Moore's images and to the significance of events in Birmingham in May 1963.

Warhol's *Race Riot*

Consider, by contrast, Andy Warhol's 1963 silk-screen paintings, *Race Riot,* displayed in his first European solo exhibition in Paris, 1964.[35] Originally intending to call the show *Death in America,* Warhol displayed various images of deceased individuals. *Race Riot* was the exception to this, though images of black youths rounded up by police dogs suggested a context in which the threat of death was present. Basing these images on photos also by Charles Moore from the May 3 Birmingham protests, Warhol creates a quite different perspective of the events for a European audience and for a potential public concerned with contemporary art, popular culture, and communication. As a public artifact, Warhol's images and Moore's photographs helped create the popular imagination of events in the South, and such illustrations take on iconic significance. The images stand in also for other narrative possibilities. They conduct representations of race where blacks are victims of white violence rather than subjects of national identity and tension. The traces of spiritual identification that Thomas's poems bring forward are absent on the flat surfaces of canvas and in the mechanical precision of the camera. The contexts are secular, shaped by racial prejudice and fear. While a political urgency motivates the subjects of the camera's lens as well as Warhol's silk-screen duplication, the submission of nonviolent protestors to the force of the hose and police batons portrays African Americans as weak and ineffectual actors in public events. Such perceptions of public narrative reinforce racist perspectives of white superiority. While these images can produce disgust and outrage over the events in Birmingham, they are the product of a white racial perspective and do not represent the views of the stakeholders there. The "objective" views of journalism and their reproductions as art can be seen as objectifying forces that circulate images of African Americans without black consent.

Thomas's version of these images in "The Bathers" submits another perspective and situates it as a call to action. To act in this case could mean, to an African American, going to Birmingham and participating in events. A call to action might inspire others to act locally within specific communities to demand common rights. Such attention could also inspire action that reinforces cultural and communal ideals and identities, strengthening bonds that can be negotiated publicly in response to the events in Birmingham as well as to the reification of those events through visual media. Thomas's rich document engages not only the Birmingham "Children's Crusade" but also the images created by others for new public purposes. King needed mediated images to help gather support for his nonviolent protests.[36] Yet as those images became historicized and associated with the civil rights movement, their iconographic placement in the pantheon of pop culture froze in time the events of May 3 rather than inviting more crucial reflection on the identity of the participants or offering greater critical arguments about the injustice of American political life and social attitudes in the South and beyond. By associating those iconographic images with a particular moment and event, the arguments latent in such imagery are ambiguous in terms of moving beyond a merely representative function to include greater argumentative roles in the ongoing process of cultural awareness and change. By isolating the images from the events, Warhol contributed in an erasure of the complex social ground that originally gave the images such stirring power. Recontextualized as art in a museum, the "Race Riot" scenes enter a conversation centered on iconography and cultural representation, the terms of which have little to do with the rhetorical situation of Birmingham and its stakes.[37]

The distance between these cultural symbols and their original public situation is important to understand. Thomas's response in "The Bathers" engages not only a specific cultural moment but also an entire symbolic system that erupts through visual media. By including a representation of Charles Moore's photographs in the frontispiece of the book, Thomas also extends the visual frame of events into the performative space of the poem. He asks readers therefore to reconsider the implications of the photograph for different audiences. Certainly, Warhol's Parisian audience responded in dismay to the "Race Riot" images (just as Charles Moore's photographs stirred strong responses globally to the events in Birmingham). But the publics engaged by these competing uses of imagery invite different possibilities of response, thereby shaping contexts in complex ways. While Warhol's images may have contributed to creating international sympathy for civil rights, they preserved a sense of black otherness, for the narrative of struggle against hegemonic Western power tends to override the claims and identifications of cultural and personal history involved in the situation. By reclaiming the image of "the bathers" in a specific context in his book, the poem becomes a rhetorical artifact that describes the events within a context of African American cultural history. For Thomas, other issues in addition to civil rights were involved: Birmingham released the pent-up forces that haunted the legacy of slavery and emancipation through violence, fear, and segregation. It is one thing to receive a televised image, or a photo, or to attend a gallery exhibit with representations of powerful cultural events, and another to reinforce those images with meaningful detail for a particular public audience. Thomas reinforced not only the crucial social values at stake in Birmingham for a broad audience, but he also used the occasion to orient his readers to larger historical contexts that made Birmingham possible.[38]

"Framing the Sunrise"

In "Framing the Sunrise" (1975) Thomas documents more explicitly the postwar years of US social and political hostility to modes of life that conflicted with narratives mediated by large national broadcast companies. The opening line—"Satellite countries"—offers a double take on the pun "satellite," for this could reference other smaller nations open to US-led democracy, or it could signify those Western nations whose satellites deflect televised images around the globe for public consumption. Whatever the case may be, these images can be seen "with anachronistic pomp or tragedy / in living rooms // where a magazine is thrown carelessly / by the sofa / Family Circle." Thomas observes "solemn middle American words /

about mortars and dyings," and ironically notes how "[the] state of the art is improving."[39] For instance, he writes:

remember the technical shakedown
Elizabeth Two's coronation
the excellent march on Lam Son

surplus camouflaged maimed
          ARVN vets
the colorful Beefeaters
         Grant Park mounted police
Caroline's jumper remember Selma
               the bridge
colorful b&w 8mm teargas clouds
             from Budapest
  by satellite relay
bullets from Kent State Ohio[40]

The "memory" related here is also technologically produced by "satellite relay," to enter the "solemn middle American" home. "Remember," he writes, "the festive gold knobs / on the Magnavox of live assassinations,"[41] here collapsing the distance between private space and public events. He wonders how this mediation of state ceremony and violence filters through domestic experience. "We lived with this shit twenty years," he says, "and each became monsters / lazy unfeeling / brutally corrupted by our senses."[42] The argument that these images habituate a public to accept representations of social and political events that have been selected for global consumption reveals an anxiety about the nature of public participation. If the rational-critical discourse of the public sphere has been reduced to private viewing habits that numb the personal reception of global events, then a public space where decisions are made becomes a spectacle for domestic consumption.[43] The productive actions of public experience, Thomas argues, are to be found outside of the mediating forces that not only interrupt domestic life but also invade it, shaping it with cultural expectations and ideological values that may even contradict the beliefs and attitudes of viewers like Thomas.

Responses to televised images here and in "The Bathers" let Thomas model strategies of public participation. By bringing attention to the distances between publicly mediated narratives and personal or domestic receptions of them, he can show how cultural events like the National Guard shootings at Kent State reduce public "news" to "memes" over time that numb public feeling.[44] At a certain level, Thomas's poem suggests an indifference to world events as they are presented on TV, and yet behind the mediated surface lie real events that form the fabric of national identity, too. As an African American who learned in the Black Arts movement to collapse the distance between art and politics by bringing poetry to specific communities with controversial social and racial issues at stake, Thomas's sense of rhetorical action is rooted in performative engagement. Since the circulation of imagery and events can form commonplaces that support and deny various ideological forces, Thomas was able in "Framing the Sunrise" to show readers strategies of integrating these seemingly disparate events into new cultural contexts, readings, and print presentations. His interventions prepare audiences for future deliberative engagements by equipping them with new insights and resources of knowledge and belief. By recontextualizing public images in a poem he challenges the assertions of traditional broadcast media by showing how seemingly isolated events conjure, through imagistic presentations, passive attitudes toward larger national issues such as war, protest, and race. An audience that hears a poem aloud will experience public events through a different order of intertextual relationships. Even on the page "Framing the Sunrise" intervenes to collapse the original contexts of these events, reorienting and carefully registering critical perspectives that challenge the passive consumption of public events through broadcast media. Thomas's actions on the page or in the register of the spoken word insist on shaping capacities to resist and reanimate cultural events through incongruent textual arrangements.

Amadou Diallo

A more recent poem looks at an event that circulated in the national news for several weeks in 1999. "Dirge for Amadou Diallo" addresses the police killing of a twenty-three-year-old immigrant from Guinea who was shot with forty-one rounds of ammunition in front of his home in the Bronx. The four officers involved in the shooting were later acquitted. The horrific event inspired numerous public protests against racial profiling and police brutality, with African American leaders like Al Sharpton and Jesse Jackson, along with other political and entertainment celebrities, contributing to the protests. As a public event, the shooting brought attention to issues of race and the complicated cultural interactions between law enforcement officers and residents in minority neighborhoods. Thomas, however, contextualizes the shooting within a narrative of familial grief. As an immigrant from Panama, he sympathized with Diallo's family, and recast the events as a poem about the loss of a son. "We could blame chance / Or curse our earthbound ignorance," Thomas writes. "Vow to concoct new mythologies / That wouldn't / Forge us such raw cruelties / Marching our hope / In coffles toward the grave."[45] "Coffles"—a group of slaves chained together for transport—casts a historical shadow over the more contemporary "incident," relating the violence between owner and owned, European and African. "It is hard to have your son die / In a distant land," echoes the poem's refrain. "And harder still / When we can't understand."[46] These stanzas seek reader sympathy, taking the narrative out of its mediated contexts and humanizing the situation for public knowledge. "Questions will fill / That churning emptiness / Shaped like a boy / Grown beautifully into a man," Thomas writes. "There'll be no answers / Still, we understand."[47] The final line provides a crucial argument that unites a minority audience with the personalized narrative of familial grief. With "coffles" figured as the historical signifier that casts the context under the atrocities of slavery, the knowing nod to the absent answers reveals a public attitude of doubt, paranoia, and indifference to mediated outcries for justice. Indeed, the injustice of the murder is situated in Thomas's poem within a context of ongoing human travesty. By humanizing Diallo, Thomas removes him as an image for public circulation and reforms the event as a personal tragedy in an ongoing transmission of violence directed at people of color. This reinforcement of ethnic identity may not speak out for public change in the same manner as the cries for justice offered by Al Sharpton. But it reaffirms cultural knowledge and condemns the too-easy distortions of facts in the taking of human life. For Thomas, the killing of Diallo did not offer another opportunity to protest racial inequity; it provided instead a path for reflection on the loss of a young man who also happened to be clutched by cultural and ideological circumstances that far outpaced him. By identifying with Diallo as an immigrant located within the cultural history of racist oppression, Thomas engages readers with a historical and personal interaction.

While "Psalm," dated "Waco, Texas, 1993" (in reference to the government standoff with a separatist religious group in April of that year in Waco, Texas), might not relieve the suffering of the Diallo family, it intervenes with sad mockery against the ideological reinforcements that certain media narratives illustrate for viewers in contemporary culture. As in "Framing the Sunrise," the poem here registers, though more passively and sarcastically, the overwhelming failure of meaning generated by the images of evening news. "We're in the tube, my friends," Thomas writes, acknowledging how understanding of public events arrives through televised images constructed for particular uses. But the accumulation of images of suffering has changed for Thomas since the civil rights clashes of 1963. Appealing to his audience through the voice of the southern church, much as he did in "The Bathers," the voice in "Psalms" is more confused, ironically distant and frequently submissive to the flow of horrific global imagery. In response to images of "Kampuchea and South Africa" and "Somalia" where "Boys are initiated into death / Before they learn the skill that brought them here," and where "Children [are] completely dipped in numbing pain / Conduct[ing] slaughter in the streets," Thomas provides the following refrain: "I don't know what to do / Lord, I don't know what to do."[48] Ambiguously stated, the paralysis of the speaker indicates a sense of overwhelming saturation in the proliferation of circulated imagery. And while he protests the claims of "Psychotic prophets," the final movement of the poem culminates in arguments of sardonic irony and contempt for the advancement of endless, unresolved narratives of public doubt, immobility, and anticathartic social stress:

Thank you O Lord
For the comfort of minute awareness
Our journalists have not forsaken us
Return to tell in microwave Homerics
A vigil that disrupts
The Price Is Right each morning
Just before the Showcase Showdown
But cuts away
Before we miss the end
Who wins the game.[49]

This critical response to journalism and broadcast media suggests that the presentation of news along with game shows interferes with an audience's ability to reflect on the meaning of these intensely coded textures of public life. Without further breaking down the content in greater ways and reinforcing shared cultural values and beliefs, public space will further dissolve. Rather than providing a strong narrative of national and broad public identity, Thomas argues that broadcast media largely confuses audiences with its profoundly disorienting bandwidth of imagery, and particularly it isolates the most radical and nonstable public groups where images are:

Reflected in the dark, round
Always and forever open eyes
Of those made homeless, hopeless
By bombs and guns made in the USA
Properly taxed
Or smuggled by collusion of the law
And slushfund patriots. . . .[50]

While Thomas speaks out with sympathy for those who see in these public narratives contradictions of justice and inconsistent behavior, he also concludes with a mockingly ironic awareness of their danger: "O Lord, I don't know what to do / I don't like watching what comes into view / I will narrow my eyelids / Till there is nothing in the world but You."[51] The supplicative closure offers a claim of dark and consistent value: without a commitment to rhetoric in the evaluation of cultural events, the risk of isolated and potentially totalitarian claims of truth take the place of a functioning democracy. The ironic ending of the poem, referencing Waco, Texas, 1993, provides substance to this claim. The American public, Thomas argues, is not inherently unstable, but without a strong sense of possible values to guide understanding of the circulation of cultural phenomena, there is risk in an ongoing fragmentation and isolation by those who will seek religion or other agencies with claims to truth over the contingent choices of right and wrong.

Tom Dent has observed that Thomas's "sense of irony, absurdity, and his social awareness are very much a part of the shared concerns of contemporary black literature, despite his surreal influences." Dent argues moreover that Thomas is "a critic of the Western world writing from the perspective of Afro-America, with inherited and acquired attitudes of an Afro-Caribbean. His sympathies are with 'the people,' the folk, the poor, the oppressed, of which people of African descent happen to be card-carrying members in the Western world."[52] This understanding of his work puts Thomas, partly, in the company of Edward Dorn, another critic of the Western world. Their perspectives were informed by different social, historical, and cultural contexts, but they both used poetry to address their locations in Western culture. While Dorn turned to satire and the eighteenth-century Enlightenment to help in his understanding of the West, Lorenzo Thomas's use of the surrealist lyric dealt with the absurdity and irony he experienced as a black American living in large urban spaces. Both poets offer ironic visions of American culture, but Thomas's poems, charged with images of the social fabric, comment more on the suffering and voice-lessness of individuals. Laughter frequently results from the poetry of both men, but in Thomas's case, the work is accompanied also with a sadness grounded in the perspective of his race.

Edward Dorn

Like Thomas, Edward Dorn often addressed the conflicting public interests of American democracy with a rhetorical poetics immersed in the practices of the historical avant-garde.[53] Whether he wrote with passionate lyricism or scathing satire, he frequently argued for the local and personal perspectives of democratic public values against the advancement of social and political institutions that limited human rights. In his earliest work, poetry was written to address public situations many of us have experienced, such as Fourth of July festivities, political election, and other customary civic events. But he also praised the weak and exploited laborers of the American West and its native inhabitants while critiquing with satirical invective institutional claims of authority over public and personal rights. He made himself accountable to his experience of the American West, relating it through his public and private uses of the poem.[54]

Prior to this prolific period of early writing, Dorn had begun attending Black Mountain College in North Carolina where he studied with Charles Olson, Robert Creeley, and Robert Duncan. In "A Bibliography on America for Ed Dorn," Olson outlined a course of study that would occupy Dorn's attention. Besides figures of literary modernism, Olson suggested readings from the philosophy of Alfred North Whitehead, the cultural geography of Carl O. Sauer, and the historical studies of the American West by Bernard DeVoto and Frederick Merk. By shifting stress from literature to the intersecting vectors of historical and geographic "fact," Olson insisted, "it is not how much one knows but in what field of context it is retained."[55] Such approaches to knowledge are in many ways rhetorical, for these strategies alter attention to particular environments and argue for new perspectives of history, social values, and political positions. Dorn's investigation of this bibliography led him to use poetry as a method for discovery and judgment that is not based on aesthetic principles but on the organization of a field poetics, a mode of creative composition based in large part on Olson's "Projective Verse" essay. In "The Problem of the Poem For My Daughter, Left Unsolved," he notes how "the oblivious process / of a brutal economic calculus" shifted his attention from "superficial . . . quality in other poems." He discusses this notion of a "field":

> In the chronically vast complex
> explanation, a field true,
> but a field
> no field hand knows
> beyond the produce of it
>   on some citizen's land. . . ."[56]

The measure of his poetic "field" against that of the "field hand" shows a tenuous link between poet and laborer. Dorn searched for a more permanent change in the process of how we think about the places we inhabit, and through the agency of the poem he arrived at arguments he hoped would persuade readers of the technological forces that distance human activity and life from meaningful labor and production.

Gunslinger (1975) marked a radical departure in Dorn's work from lyricism to satiric commentary on publicly mediated images and events. While the poem focused on the internal compositions and extensions of psychic forces at work behind American social life, Dorn took into account the agonistic public situation that had risen through the advancement of the Vietnam War. The "Elizabethan ear" Charles Olson admired in Dorn's early writing began tuning in on popular culture to elements such as comic books, westerns, drug slang, and slapstick to relate the more serious political and philosophical orientations of the West.[57] *Gunslinger,* staged as road trip, featured a number of existential figures, such as the Gunslinger "of impeccable personal smoothness," Dr. Flamboyant, and The Stoned Horse who rolls bomber joints.[58] An ironic and complex work that integrates humor and puns into its pre-Socratic revision of the Western psyche, *Gunslinger* proposed a kind of study of Western culture through many of its mediated images.

After the success of *Gunslinger,* Dorn turned increasingly to the epigram as the prime literary form for his satirical interventions into public sensibility and the conservative social and political climates of the 1980s and '90s, and I will largely look at these satiric works for the remainder of this chapter. In *Hello, La Jolla* (1978) and *Abhorrences* (1990), for instance, Dorn aimed his sardonic invective against European and American culture and its economic stranglehold on world resources by commenting frequently on publicly mediated images and events. He continued to view social problems, political greed, and national aggression in technological terms, but he examined cultural manifestations in print and broadcast media as a way to be "always road-testing the language for a particular form of speech."[59] Unlike the epic-length *Gunslinger,* the brief poems of *Hello, La Jolla* and

Abhorrences have been stripped to a central message. Rhetorically, these poems work differently from Thomas's insofar as the audience is not always so specifically defined, and because Dorn's goals as a writer are to comment broadly on cultural manifestations through the construction of an authoritative ethos that reaffirms the commitments of certain readers while attacking the broadly accepted values and ideologies of others. If the "double consciousness" Thomas exploited brought his audience to identify with new cultural and historical possibilities in publicly mediated events, Dorn pointed out the contradictions and inconsistencies of public narratives that reinforced social and political ideologies.

John Hinckley Jr. and the 1980s

One way to approach Dorn's writing from the 1980s is to look at how such work generates reflection through suasive commentary on particular social and political situations. Reprinted in *Abhorrences,* for instance, the following found poem "from the 2nd floor toilet" of Hellems, a building on the campus of the University of Colorado, states:

> "Why is wanting to kill Ronald Reagan
> and fuck Jody Foster
> considered insane?
> Makes sense to me."[60]

As an example of the epideictic mode of rhetoric, this satiric epigram works in a number of surprising ways to address a "public mind,"[61] Dorn's shorthand term for his audience, whom he saw as constituting a rather vaguely drawn, but commonly held, system of public values or beliefs. For one thing, this poem offers none of the aesthetic pleasantries usually associated with poetry, such as elements of verbal richness, complex rhythmic variation, or closely monitored contours of a crafted "voice." If Thomas could draw on the cadences of the African American church, Dorn, by contrast, flattened his speech to a kind of antipoetic voice composed of flat one-liners and terse understatements that signaled a position of judgment more akin to stand-up comedy than poetry. In this way an anonymously written message from a campus toilet is ironically transposed into a poem that works by a kind of quasi-logical association of public event with sexual desire and political protest. By publishing it in a book he makes the claim that this, however, is a poem. And yet as an example of the art, it does something different from what an audience typically expects from poetry. In company with other satiric verses, however, this poem makes sense, and it argues for a perspective on 1980s sociopolitical life in a surprising and unexpected way. By pausing to look more closely at Dorn's argument, we can observe an instance of modernist inquiry where "rhetorical habits of entertaining possibilities, extensions, [and] disbelief" play out through poetic gestures and actions.[62]

The March 30, 1981, assassination attempt on the life of Ronald Reagan shocked the nation. John Hinckley Jr., now a marginal figure in the national narrative of the Reagan era, had hoped to impress the actress Jodie Foster by gunning down a powerful head of state. Although he wounded Reagan, press secretary James Brady, and two others with a .22 caliber revolver outside the Hilton Hotel in Washington, DC, Hinckley's legal defense won his case on a plea of insanity. He was subsequently instituted at St. Elizabeths in Washington, DC, the same asylum, coincidentally, that housed the poet Ezra Pound for nine years.

Dorn's epigram, however, flips this public narrative in order to comment on the socially conservative triumph of the New Right, the economic rise of the yuppie, and other social indulgences that had come to be associated with the era. Without deliberating on the benefits and drawbacks of the Reagan presidency, the poem provides a space for a public audience to orient attention to the troubling years of that administration. For the poem to work, certain assumptions may be made, such as: Ronald Reagan is bad and the country would have been better off without him; masculinist desire recognizes girlish screen stars as sexually attractive figures; Hinckley *got away* with an assassination attempt on *the* leader of the free world, a beloved actor, "The Gipper," no less. In the forensic debate, a pledge of love to a screen actress, extraordinarily, persuaded a court to spare Hinckley from criminal punishment, declaring such love to be "insane." And this is the key rhetorical turn of the poem, for it confronts us with a division in the national narrative that rests on a crucial definitional argument of sanity.

Dorn is not alone in his fascination with the assassination attempt. Cultural references to the event are everywhere, from an episode of *The Seinfeld Show* to the 1980s new wave band, Devo, who put some of Hinckley's lyrics to music (John Hinckley Jr., had been an aspiring songwriter before giving his obsessive attention to Foster). At some level in popular consciousness, Hinckley's relationship to the assassination-attempt narrative is filtered through his legally observed insanity. By flipping this narrative in the poem, Dorn provides a space for an audience to recognize the deep resentment that may be harbored against Reagan by those who identify with the Left. For many, the poem, of course, would be offensive. A nonpartisan reading, on the other hand, could introduce other considerations in the mind of an audience. Why was Reagan loved? Why was he hated? What does it mean for an individual to risk life for love in our society? What can be risked in an act and how will that risk and act be evaluated through different perspectives and in different contexts?

Depending upon the perspective of his public audience, Dorn's work complicates the epigrammatic form. For the informed literary insider who identifies with Dorn's satiric mask, the poems reinforce existing political beliefs that oppose Reagan's New Right. For others, values are challenged by the reflective aims of the satirist. Readers may share committed political views but find the assertion of desire for Jodie Foster to be an expression of sexist determination. Such social attitudes can be seen operating in conflict with the political identifications in the poem. While Dorn's epigrams can build capacities in an audience by producing reflection on sociopolitical issues, they also question the social capacities of his audience to identify too easily with the target of his satiric poem. While in some sense he may be seen extending capacities for certain audiences through arguments that brought awareness of the self-interests of American geopolitical economic expansion during the Reagan era, Dorn used satirical epigrams also to quickly disorient commonly held beliefs in order to create agonistic environments in which social values and political commitments could be engaged. In Kenneth Burke's useful terms, he challenged an audience's "strategies for living" in a democratic situation whose Enlightenment ideals had been corrupted by the interests of global capital.[63] By looking at these poems we can learn how epideictic suasion can be used to expand the reflective capacity of readers in a modernist literary context.

The Public Mind

In *Abhorrences,* Dorn presents satiric and largely epigrammatic verses that had been inspired by his study of eighteenth-century rhetoric and satiric poetry.[64] Committed in his work to a reading of democratic Enlightenment ideals and, like Jürgen Habermas, to a critical mode of its practice,[65] he challenged the beliefs and desires of his audience by arguing for a renewed understanding of key democratic terms. He did so through carefully crafted and compact arguments that relied on a quasi-logical appeal to a reader's sense of value. As a dispassionate "chronicle of the eighties" these epigrams present social and political news taken "from the air" of radio, television, and other media to organize arguments that may help "correct" the "public mind."[66] As an audience, this "public mind" is of particular concern to Dorn. His focus is not on their emotions—the heart of the public, say. This "public mind" is a projected construction of Dorn's imagination. There is no way, obviously, to chart by statistics an accurate description of a public mind—at least not the one Dorn valued. In terms of an audience, we might think of this mind as a formal body of intelligence that for him requires correction for its moral failings. This correction, however, should be measured in the kind of reflective potential Dorn offered an audience. These controversial poems remain significant today as a body of work that attempted to provoke reflection through satiric argumentation in order to restore a space for reflective reasoning. While he often had agonistic purposes in mind, the poems complicate responses to mediated cultural phenomena.

A poem, for instance, early in the book argues with a succinctly constructed claim that states: "one bullet / is worth / a thousand bulletins."[67] While some critics of the last decade have recoiled at a "masculinist" persona extended in these crisply rendered epigrams, this poem can be understood also as an argument for rhetoric over physical violence.[68] Indeed, the poem operates effectively by exposing the etymological implication between bullet and bulletin to make a number of claims. First, bullets are final. Their violent power operates to silence opposition and is symbolic of the kinds of postwar political strife Dorn accuses US administrations of causing abroad in the 1980s. We need only to remember conflicts in Granada, Nicaragua, El Salvador, and Libya, to name a few places where US foreign policy under Reagan undermined diplomatic solutions with violence. Conversely, bulletins can multiply ineffectively in bureaucratic contexts. A bulletin's value is diminished as others accumulate. The tension comes through Dorn's recognition of an innate contradiction in American foreign policy and in domestic understandings of it. By pitching the symbol of violent solutions—the bullet—next to a symbol of bureaucratic obfuscation and clutter—the bulletin—Dorn suggests that neither solution is adequate. Instead, we remain in a rhetorical situation in which neither truth (the violent finality of death) nor the extension of relative positions can negotiate policy effectively. While the solution to this problem is not offered by the poem, Dorn may be suggesting that other methods of confrontation, rhetorical negotiation, and political action are necessary to break this deadlock. At any rate, he values modalities of possibility, and he intervenes to ensure that multiple perspectives are at play in moments of cultural conflict.

The image of the bullet returns, moreover, in the final poem of the book, appropriately titled "The End."

Did you know that
when they execute you in China
they send your next of kin
a bill for 1 Yang (28¢)
to cover the cost of the bullet?
This is the very definition
of frugal management.
Maybe Bush can learn something
from Deng after all, maybe
there's a pow-wow under the kow-tow.

It's a good thing Reagan
didn't know about this practise.
He'd have considered it tax relief.[69]

As with the previous bullet poem, the argument centers on an object of violence and its administration in Chinese execution. The violence, however, shifts from the principle object of death to an administered agency that seeks financial accountability. Again, the argument against bureaucratic violence is created through an incongruent relation of symbolic actions. The bullet as an agent of death is reduced by the broader administrative concerns for the financing of systems of execution. The joking second stanza argues for a perspective on American capital punishment and its administered support by looking at execution through the Chinese model. The claims offered through a satiric mode do not address the death penalty nor do they seek to make cultural evaluations of regional customs. Instead, bureaucratic management is targeted for ridicule because it provides an agency in which bullets contribute to deadly human designs. Here, as in other poems, Dorn argues that key terms or symbolic values are meaningful only within the broader contexts that give them meaning. He places value on the motives and circumstances that provide purpose for the bullet. Indeed, bullets are more effective at ending life, but bulletins determine whose life shall be terminated.

While Dorn's poems are relatively brief, we can see how many possible perspectives they provoke through reflection on the terms and conditions of the arguments. His claims maintain a formal relation between author and reader, even when the joke stems from the demotic scene of a campus toilet. These poems create desire to work through the implications of the reasoned assumptions. Readers must reflect, additionally, on their own positions regarding gender, capital punishment, Ronald Reagan, or, more broadly, the meaning of cultural life in the 1980s. By inserting satiric arguments into the more accepted national narratives of the period, Dorn addresses an audience's belief and desire. What happens with that reflective potential is quite interesting, and again, it comes down to a perspective on how we read our social milieu. Dorn could be strengthening our capacities to deal with confusing social and political situations. His poems show how the agonistic forms of argument are essential to democratic institutions, and yet he understood how agonistic values erode under the ongoing demands of capital. Or he could be preparing us for a more radical form of dissent in order to more firmly reestablish claims for democracy, which, however, would introduce schism into our late corporate global enterprises. What is important to recognize is that whatever this intervention accomplishes in readers, Dorn does not call for a restoration of social institutions. At best his arguments maintain uneasy awareness of how compromised democracy is under our current geopolitical corporate regimes.

While belief and desire remain key elements in constructing social possibilities and inquiry through modal rhetoric, faith in social institutions, in our era, is shaky, for many good reasons. Dorn's poems keep us alert to the uncertainty we inhabit in our social situations. For him the "public mind" was infinitely "correctible," a hopeful, if satirically arrogant, claim. By focusing on this "public mind," however, Dorn situated his arguments in a nonpartisan attempt to point out ideological biases that interfered with ideal notions of democracy. The ideal, perhaps, is unattainable, but worth striving for given capitalism's global commitments. What these poems point out in their satiric urgency is that "existing ideology" is beyond confirmation. The poems argue for a kind of reflexive resistance to ideologies that get in the way of democratic purposes. The reflection in a "public mind" brought about through modal inquiry into cultural possibilities keeps readers focused on the contradictions and upheavals of our social and political moment in late capitalism. This valuable art contributes to a more flexible and reflective "public mind."

Dorn's Ethos

Dorn's ethos in *Abhorrences* is created through an aggressive and authoritative presence in the poem. By trying to write political poetry that responds often to mediated events, he relies on his perspective as a poet and cultural observer to create agonistic situations that persuade readers of particular views, or that push others away by offending them while encouraging factional debate and controversy. Although Dorn cautioned against creating "axiomatic" poems, he offered his position as the authority on contemporary social topics. "You can't reduce everything to a maxim," he said in an interview with Kevin Bezner in 1992. "Another thing, one of the overriding attitudes and pervasive methods [in *Abhorrences*] was to take as much exception as possible. Whether this is true or not, and it's arguable, it's good for the method. You have to have a similarity of concentration over an extremely long period of time, and you have to trust that it's correct." While the author may "trust" in his responses being "correct," he must persuade readers of this authority, too. The poems in *Abhorrences* are often funny, intelligent, and rigorous in their pursuit of circulated imagery and events, but much of their success for an audience requires a certain submission to Dorn's claims to cultural authority. In the interest of those claims, he says:

> One of the basic propositions of *Abhorrences* is that the only poetry that really matters and the only poetry that anybody might want to pay attention to is the poetry that exhibits a certain kind of aggression towards the readers. I don't see any reason to write any other kind of poetry at this moment and by this moment, I mean from now to whatever happens at the end of the second millennium. It's not that far off.
>
> Given where we're at, nobody is going to be aesthetically enlightening, certainly not if you look back over the last 150 years.[70]

While this preference for an aggressive poetics rather than one motivated by aesthetics provides Dorn with an approach to cultural and social phenomena, he imagines a public audience in need of correction rather than entertainment or instruction, say (falling back on Horace's ancient quip). While Dorn can be both entertaining and instructive, the assumption of authority in taking on a role of correction for an audience can damage his constructed ethos. The questions of trust and identification are necessary to address when reading a work that pledges, like Dorn's, to be so thoroughly aggressive in the service of political ideas. Lorenzo Thomas, by contrast, drew on the shared cultural cadences and imagery of the African American church to establish bonds with his readers. While both men aggressively oriented social and political images and events for readers to help them better comprehend the cultural situations facing them, Dorn's satire threatens to alienate a larger potential audience. Thomas, by contrast, gives his readers purpose and identity through the historical circumstances of his work.

Confronting the Circulation of Public Events

While the circulation of images and texts can contribute national narratives that reinforce cultural identities and make claims about the kinds of publics we inhabit through narrative, Lorenzo Thomas and Edward Dorn addressed the expressions of US national culture after 1960. Their commitments to show readers and auditors how they might receive and approach events such as the Birmingham civil rights marches or the assassination attempt of Ronald Reagan helped reclaim public events for new forms of circulation in literary public spaces. While it could be claimed that only a tiny fraction of the American public would have encountered the works of either, it can be argued that through public readings, magazine publications, and finally in book form (not to mention the efforts of critics, reviewers, and other advocates), the public issues they engaged did reach a significant audience, one that could motivate others to revise assumptions about public events and their mediation to the home via satellite. It is important also, particularly in Thomas's case, to think of both writers as activists in some sense. Dorn constructed a public persona that inspired debate, and he published magazines that included poetry, political commentary, and social analysis of significant social issues in the political and literary journals *Bean News* and *Rolling Stock*.[71] Thomas, by contrast, worked as a young activist in New York in the 1960s. As Nielsen notes, "Thomas was also accruing early experience as a public speaker that would stand him in good stead when he joined in Umbra's legendary public readings. A member of the National Conference of Christians and Jews, the teen-aged Thomas 'went around to schools, synagogues and churches giving . . . little speeches about brotherhood and equality.' "[72] Through the Umbra writing workshops and the Black Arts movements' socially committed public agenda that brought theater and poetry to the streets of Harlem in the late 1960s, Thomas developed a lifelong appreciation of poetry as public event.

More importantly, as both men were compelled to confront the circulation of public events that intruded on the private sphere of the home, they worked to understand what it meant to no longer live in a world where public and private life remained easily separated. The distance between public and private spheres narrowed considerably in postwar America, and yet for them poetry provided a way to negotiate that new experience. If Robert Duncan and Denise Levertov provided ways to understand the uses of poetry in responses to war in a new era of televised conflict abroad, then Thomas and Dorn employed rhetorical modes of critical inquiry that increased possibilities of public awareness and understanding of significant public images. They increased social possibilities by acting as citizens engaged with the actualities of cultural experience rather than as passive recipients of public projections or attitudes constructed from legitimately recognized media. By engaging the circulation of events through broadcast media, both writers encouraged new social possibilities in the reconstructed narratives of public culture their work represents. Their writing also looks forward to the strategies of public engagement poets decades later will introduce as they protest American foreign policy in the Middle East.

4
Poets Against War

Inquiries and engagements in public poetry have grown in recent years out of opposition to the wars in Iraq and Afghanistan.[1] While forms of social protest continued in poetry during the decades following the public outcry to war in Vietnam, the Iraq War has challenged poets to develop strategies of social engagement in ideological situations that differ considerably from the 1960s-era environments of cultural change. Although poets like Duncan and Levertov voiced their positions on war within a context of popular resistance, others who sought to bring attention to the war in Iraq have done so, until more recently, without broader ideological support. This chapter looks at how public poetries have emerged in opposition to Bush-era policies in Iraq and other regions of the Middle East, and how such writing is being used by some to address social and political issues of global conflict and its domestic consequences.

To understand how some poets work to speak about the contemporary situation of war, we should recall how American foreign policy has changed since the fall of communism in 1989, and resulting from that we can begin to understand how the ability of nation-states to influence global policy has considerably weakened. With the era-defining events of September 11, 2001, and the subsequent invasions of Afghanistan and Iraq, poets have been challenged to find rhetorically significant methods of public address that differ from earlier approaches taken by Duncan and Levertov.[2] While the Bush administration justified an ideology of retaliation and aggression in the Middle East after the World Trade Center attacks, many poets, horrified by the violence of the event, nonetheless initiated alternative inquiries in American public spaces to address readers (and viewers) by expressing calm, concern, reasonable evaluation, and other modal possibilities of social response than those claimed necessary by the government and military. The urgency to respond in unity as a nation to the attacks, however, made it difficult to sustain dialogues that proposed more reflective and measured considerations within legitimate print, broadcast, and digital spaces. Even as the justification to go to war against Iraq defied evidence to the contrary that Saddam Hussein was in any way connected to Osama bin Laden, a majority of Americans were willing to suspend critical judgment in order to support the political objectives of the Bush administration. The situation facing oppositional thinkers and poets, then, was drastically different from the contexts offered by the Vietnam War era, where a broad and popular resistance movement provided support to perspectives that opposed US policy.

Parallel to the official narrative that was presented to the American people after the 9/11 attacks, some poets brought forward alternative positions in public, forming temporary public alliances in opposition to war. Such alliances are provisory and often limited to specific instances of protest or public engagement. They are composed of loose networks of actors who share ideological values, and these can shape alliances to bring alternative beliefs into public settings. The efforts of such groups to use poetry to alter public space raise important questions. For instance, is it enough to voice opposition to government policy—even if few listen or respond? Or should rhetors expect their work to be recognized and rewarded with specific actions in these instances? More importantly, how do subaltern claims that run counter to a larger ideological environment reach a legitimate and powerful audience? One problem faced by politically motivated poets is that their work, while potentially persuasive, is simply far outnumbered by others motivated within the dominant ideological environment: a rhetoric of advantage will have a difficult time playing out in such a field of discourse. One thing necessary, given this predicament, is for protesters to reconsider their objectives and to imagine new audiences in times of war. Poetry, indeed, is a potentially powerful and subversive art for an era where deliberative speech is compromised by market necessity and the conservative political infrastructure that supports it. Instead, the epideictic mode can be more fully exploited to increase social awareness by addressing broadly imagined communities within the larger global markets that more and more define how we think about public space.[3]

I have hastily sketched out this post-9/11 situation because it is important to understand how poets have come to adapt their work in an era of increased national security informed by conservative ideological pressures. Of course, many do not adapt to the new conditions: numerous writers who protest the war in Iraq frequently resort to models of confrontation that operate under 1960s assumptions of public space, assuming that ideologically they possess enough popular support to successfully share their oppositional views through significant real-world and online sites. Others, however, reflect differently on their potential for influencing public opinion. They contribute through poems, performances, commentary, and documentation in intimate public settings new perspectives and arguments that can lead an audience to understand better the conditions of war that occupy official public narratives. While these poets do not provide definitive answers to social and political problems, they offer apertures through which situations can become better known, thereby helping to shape cultural beliefs and attitudes. Although there are numerous theories of the public sphere—notably Habermas's model, as well as municipal, state, and federal legal definitions that govern public spaces—some contemporary poets enter these contested spaces legally or illegally, informed or not by public sphere theory, to influence the environments around them. In the sections that follow, I will look at several approaches to recent wars through the perspectives of poets invested, at varying degrees, in shaping messages within public spaces. First, Sam Hamill's Poets Against War web archive provides a public, online resource that has collected thousands of poems to protest the Iraq War. Next, I look at the documentation by Kristin Prevallet and her contribution (with many others) to the Poetry Is Public Art (PIPA) and Debunker Mentality projects, based in New York City. Finally, Kent Johnson's Iraq War poems provide a new perspective on American attitudes toward the Abu Ghraib torture scandal. Unlike the previous public poets studied here, his work runs parallel, though with obvious differences, to the strategies of Robert Duncan, who asked that we imagine evil rather than protest it.

Poets Against War

Sam Hamill's Poets Against War (PAW) website makes use of rhetorical strategies similar to those practiced by Denise Levertov during the Vietnam War. While it is impossible to provide a profile for the 30,000 poets who have given work to this site since its inception in January 2003, the newsletters, statements, and other supporting material endorsed by Hamill shows how the site's mission works to address human suffering in the current context of the Iraq War.[4] Poets Against War's purpose, for instance, is to continue "the tradition of socially engaged poetry by creating venues for poetry as a voice against war, tyranny and oppression."[5] A key term— "against"—echoes Duncan's disagreement with Levertov. While we do not have to accept Duncan's argument that poets explore evil rather than oppose it, we can ask, rhetorically, how such opposition plays out in a public poetics. And since the thousands of poems gathered on Hamill's site provide a wide and varied range of responses to war—and certainly not a homogenized address—the context given by the organization's newsletter and editorial statements introduce arguments that can help us better understand the potential modal values of such a public poetics. We must read these arguments within the context of the public space of the web, however, and therefore try to evaluate the aims of the executors of the organization and then look at the resulting consequences of their arguments.

Sam Hamill in many ways is an extraordinarily committed poet and publisher whose tremendous efforts have furthered poetry as a public force for several decades. Besides the publication of his many books and the reception of numerous awards and recognitions, including a Guggenheim, he is the founding editor of Copper Canyon Press, one of the nation's most prominent literary publishers. As a Vietnam veteran, his commitment to the social movements that protest war has inspired numerous public responses, and with the advent of Poets Against War, he has been a committed activist, providing a space for poets to register their dissent against Bush administration policy in Iraq since 2003.

According to Hamill, Poets Against War was first conceived when he declined an invitation in January 2003 to attend a symposium in Washington, DC, sponsored by First Lady Laura Bush, that proposed to celebrate "Poetry and the American Voice." Instead of attending the function, he asked poets to submit work in the spirit of the Vietnam War–era protests "to speak up for the conscience of [their] country and [to] lend [their] names to petition against this war."[6] These responses grew and were subsequently entered into the PAW website. Although by March 2003, PAW had received more than 13,000 poems from writers around the world, US troops began a ground invasion of Iraq. Since then, Hamill has published a smaller print anthology,[7] and he has presented the poems gathered on the site to congressional representatives, with much of the work being entered into the *Congressional Record*. Hamill writes: "Today, although the attack wasn't prevented, poets continue to speak out for a world in which nonviolence and international cooperation will ultimately prevail over a single administration's philosophy that the most horrendous crimes are justified in the service of foreign policy. Today it is more important than ever to lift our voices in support of respectful explorations of alternatives to war. Please join us. Organize a reading. Keep joining protests. Teach compassion. Participate. In all of America's history, poets have never made such a difference."[8]

The events generated by the White House invitation helped the public launch of PAW and immediately drew widespread support from around the world. Hamill's compelling claims also provided ways to think about the nature of public space and poetry's potential use in it—particularly as it exists on the web. One problem, however, is that with the invasion of Iraq already in commencement, the platform created by Hamill could only function as a site of protest and opposition to an act of war that received wider ideological and political support at the time.[9] While poetry certainly can influence attitudes and beliefs—and the Poets Against War site reveals a striking record of beliefs anthologized in poetry—Hamill's understanding of public space leads him to assume much on behalf of his audience. The first thing we as readers may ask is how do we navigate a site that contains nearly 30,000 poems? If each expresses some view opposing war, how are we in turn to respond? Do we contribute our own view? Or perhaps we should be inspired to create new contexts for the reading and publication of antiwar poetry. To what extent do such values need to be reinforced for compassionate readers? Also, since the digital environment is accessible from many public and private locations, how can sympathetic readers actively work to oppose policy via the web? Perhaps the site, more realistically, provides a space for an audience to reflect on its attitudes and beliefs toward the government's invasion of Iraq, but with so many poems, and with an agenda that supports an active, oppositional role, how should readers begin to navigate the oppositional space of the site?

These questions can in part be addressed through current theoretical and technological discussions taking place about how the Internet's architecture changes the nature of public engagement. If, as Michael Warner has argued, circulation in many ways defined how publics were addressed through broadcast and print media, how do publics change when centralized forms of circulation are replaced by Internet protocological distributions of information?[10] Alexander Galloway, for instance, sees the Internet as both liberating and restrictive in how the possibilities of communication are determined by structural conflicts between the family of protocols known as TCP/IP and the more decentralized DNS database "that maps network addresses to network names." According to Galloway, "all DNS information is controlled in a hierarchical, inverted-tree structure. Ironically, then, nearly all Web traffic must submit to a hierarchical structure (DNS) to gain access to the anarchic and radically horizontal structure of the Internet. . . . [T]his contradictory logic is rampant throughout the apparatus of protocol."[11] What this means is that the Internet not only moves data and information horizontally from node to node, it also creates an archival layer that complicates user access. This is important to understand because two contradictory forces in part define the Internet. Data move horizontally from node to node while simultaneously exerting top-down, vertical control over information. Those theorizing the Internet do not often acknowledge this, but Galloway's theory of protocological control lets us see how the Internet is defined by an essential ambivalence. Internet protocol also provides a way of understanding the distribution of texts online. The horizontal movement of information is aligned with the documentation of events that attract public attention, while the vertical ordering of information is best understood in the extensive archives created by websites and databases. Hamill's site, for instance, initially functioned at an upper level of public awareness when the war in Iraq had just been declared, providing a space for writers to engage a public with views that contradicted official US policy. Over the years, however, the project became more of an archival source. PAW's contribution to war resistance efforts, then, continued most successfully by creating horizontal movements through news updates and by inviting new voices into an established conversation that intervened originally, in 2003, in the affairs of state. It has since become an archival presence of potential validation and support for those who persist in activist efforts, and the site's vertical control of documents preserves the initial efforts of protest. Such documentation may inspire others to conduct similar interventions, thus increasing potential civil engagements online. While many of the poems spotlighted by PAW may resort to figures of pathos, and through them speak largely to like-minded activists, the extensive archive (closed only as of 2010) provides an array of work that presents conflicting viewpoints and poetic strategies of critical engagement. While it is far easier to access the horizontal news and updates on the site, the vertical archive provides a foundation of navigable responses to the war that documents a history of opposition to US foreign policy after 2003.

The poem I submitted to the site in 2003 is clearly ambivalent.[12] I often wonder about that ambivalence, and the motives for my submission to the anthology. My prose poem made little attempt at "protest," and yet as a poet I felt compelled to include my voice with the others in, what at the time even, felt like a hollow and futile public engagement. Looking back now, I see that difficulty even more clearly, for the site, as I understood it at the time, provided a complex space of opposition in a digital environment where whatever leverage such protests offered quickly dissipated behind the viewing habits and search queries provided by viewers motivated in advance to support the perspectives expressed by PAW. But I was not prepared in 2003 to understand how radically the Internet had begun to change notions of public engagement and activist possibilities in it. My assumption of a public relied on circulatory strategies of intervention. Such modes of circulation anticipate an even flow of information from centralized sources. And yet the hardwired system of Internet protocol makes this impossible in a node-to-node distribution of data. The sudden emergence and quick disappearance of arguments in online public spaces clash with the assumptions and experiences I previously held about the dissemination of news and public perspectives in traditional media spaces. An online archive interacts in new ways with publics by expanding possible access, in one sense, and by putting the advancement of social possibilities into the hands of many committed users who share links to others via blogs, social networking sites, or Listservs.

Rhetorically, the Poets Against War website has generated a popular space for poets to contribute perspectives on the Iraq War and on other political and social issues. It may be argued that by successfully preparing a space for democratic exchange, PAW has contributed a successful forum on important political issues. The basic premise, which recalls Levertov's agit-prop protests of the 1960s, is one that many identify with and are eager to expand through poetry.[13] Through newsletters, e-mails, special features by guest poets, op-eds by Hamill, and other horizontal forms of news documentation relevant to the interests and concerns of its participants, PAW provides a space of online social exchange wherein attitudes and positions against the Iraq War find a public forum for ongoing development and exchange.

While the site may serve to reinforce the values of its participants, and to exert mild, and limited, pressure on what became eventually an unpopular presidential administration, the definitions of public space PAW encountered are in conflict, for the technological structures that allow rhetorical perspectives to be shared in many contexts had changed dramatically since the 1960s. Forms of protest that were successful during the Vietnam era no longer succeeded because the protocological distribution of messages, poems, news, and other media online now conflicts with the centralized forms of broadcast circulation that defined public address in the 1960s. While New Media scholars have only more recently begun to discuss how Internet activism works to address social injustice, Hamill's 2003 project of protest initiated an early confrontation through web technology that contradicted previous modes of public engagement.[14] PAW's innovative use of the web to bring like-minded authors and activists together led to new possibilities of public intervention through the web. It also used this platform with expectations partially based on prior models of circulation. The rhetorical strategies used by some poets, in the context of the horizontal and vertical forces of the web, provided an experiment with online political intervention that corresponds to other public forms of confrontation. Some poets who are "against" war thus began to adapt rhetorical strategies and definitions of public space that relied on performance, street-level engagements with urban commuters, and elements of documentation that relayed localized public interventions to other larger reading publics.

Guerrilla Poetry

Jules Boykoff and Kaia Sand argue that certain poet-activists use poetry to broaden awareness of public spaces by physically inhabiting particular environments. In *Landscapes of Dissent,* they summarize some of the key issues in public sphere theory, discussing Jürgen Habermas's foundational critique of the public sphere along with Nancy Fraser's claims on behalf of subaltern counterpublics. In addition, Boykoff and Sand review significant legal definitions of what constitute public spaces. They argue that although streets and other public places have been traditionally perceived as a privilege of citizenship, what is known as the "public forum doctrine" allowed the Supreme Court to create "three categories of public space, each with different levels of scrutiny and regulation."[15] One significant result of this "doctrine" is that "in traditional public forums—such as streets, sidewalks, and parks—the state may not restrict speech because of its content unless the state can show that such regulation is necessary to achieve a compelling state interest and is narrowly tailored to achieve that interest." But such restrictions, Boykoff and Sand argue, "impose 'legibility' on society." "Guerrilla poets," they claim, "regardless of whether they are aware of this hierarchy of restriction and the state's efforts toward legibility, operate within a matrix of legal stricture and easement. Laws regarding public space are inherently exclusionary, even if, on the surface, they appear designed toward inclusion."[16] Many guerrilla poets use "locational conflict" or "interventionary practices" to reclaim public spaces as sites of social production. "Such poetic intervention," argue Boykoff and Sand, "poaches public space in innovative and sometimes antagonistic ways, seizing democratic rights, rather than stuffing them silently into pocket."[17] These uses of public space also challenge state definitions of it by actors motivated by other ideological interests.

So rather than relying on the rhetorical strategies of actors who operate within the parameters of shared ideological values, such as sites of opposition like Poets Against War, guerrilla poets adapt resilient methods that require social networks, reduced spatial scales of action, temporal codes optimized to target transient auditors, and unpredictable and adaptable modes of composition. Although these strategies are similar to practices of nonstate actors in other fields, such as agents in third-world countries operating against global market interests—often with violence or the threat of violence—guerrilla poets frequently bring messages of peace, or introduce epigrammatic commentary to generate greater reflection on social events. What these poets hold in common with "terrorists" is an explicitly rhetorical sense of strategic timing and target selection. Their understanding of *kairos* provides maximum effect for potential auditors with a minimum of investment in the textual environment. Instead, attention is often drawn to physical spaces, the texts and images used by artists often encoding these spaces with quick commentary, deliberately gnomic statements, and provocative images designed to confront passersby.

Along these lines, PIPA (Poetry Is Public Art), a collective of poet-activists based in New York City, uses "interventionary practices" in public spaces and documents their efforts to address diverse audiences. Based on Robert Duncan and Charles Olson's claims of an open field poetics, "Brooklyn-based PIPA poet Kristin Prevallet" has come "to think of poetry in public space in the context of ongoing conversations about the relationship between poetry and politics."[18] During the 2004 Republican National Convention and anti–Iraq War demonstrations, Prevallet, Anne Waldman, and others made signs with slogans such as: "'Permanent Cultural Vibration'; 'Lose the Illusion of Your Exemption'; 'Dear World Bank: Free People, Not Markets'; and 'Ask not what you can do for your country; ask what Bush is doing to your country.'"[19] Besides these signs, posters and business cards have been used also to "challenge the narrow bandwidth of acceptable language practices" in certain public settings. Prevallet, Rodrigo Toscano, and others, moreover, increasingly turn to public performances to comment on political issues. These public interventions correspond to the ludic moments of protest observed at People's Park, where the "People's Prick" confronted Denise Levertov over interventions in Vietnam; the sardonic textual performances of Lorenzo Thomas and Edward Dorn also relate, as we will see, to the attempts in print and on the street by PIPA to address controversial public topics.

Prevallet documents many of these public strategies in her book, *Shadow Evidence Intelligence,* where she describes PIPA as "a conceptual collaborative endeavor based on the site-specific potential of poetry projects to intersect with public spaces. What this means is that poetry can happen anywhere, at any time. It can intersect with space and time not as random wordplay but as covert reflective commentary."[20] Before further describing some of PIPA's public interventions, I want to direct attention more closely to the main theoretical platform rendered through Prevallet's PIPA manifesto; besides the compelling practical strategies it engages, the arguments correlate in ways similar to the activist strategies documented by Denise Levertov in *To Stay Alive:*

> PIPA has no members except for those who, intentionally or non-intentionally, choose to break poetry out of the frame of the page and test its assimilation and/or intrusion into public spaces. Although the archive implies organization, there is no organizing principle behind PIPA, except for the organizing principles at work in the mind of any poet who, at any time, chooses to design, orate, sloganize, decorate, or sculpturally infiltrate public space. (*See disclaimer.*)[21] PIPA is not a container for the minds of poets, but rather is a convergence of minds working independently or in groups to infiltrate public spaces at the level of poetry. PIPA activities will include and/or have included:
>
> - any poetry activity that causes passersby to pause
> - handing out poems on busy avenues (the haughtier the better)
> - slapping poetry stickers on advertisements that "talk back" to the advertisement
> - leaving poems behind on park or subway benches (which brings up the problematic poetics of littering)
> - leaving poems in the form of messages on phone booths or public toilets that cause passersby to pause and think: that language looks quite strange
> - writing responses on subway and bus advertisements (after all, they are trying to talk to you.)
> - proclaiming poetry from soapboxes
> - using poets' condensers-of-language skills to create witty and provocative slogans for political rallies
> - designing poetry signs to blend in with the surrounding signage

- spray-painting the sidewalk through the ingenious method of stenciling and cutting out slogans at the base of a cardboard box
- etc.

This list from the PIPA archives is not the work of one, but rather many publicly minded poets. And it is quite possible and even likely that the numerous people involved in the above projects do not know that the PIPA archives are chronicling their activities. PIPA hopes that the poetry practitioners alluded to in this document know the spirit of camaraderie and generosity that is at the heart of PIPA. The PIPA of possibility is equally the PIPA of hazard. The PIPA of enthusiasm is also the PIPA of failure.[22]

A number of provocative arguments stand out in this enthusiastic manifesto, particularly the modal rhetoric of possibility that underscores Prevallet's key claims. For the purposes of this study, I want to bring attention primarily to how this document both correlates with and departs from a Levertovian understanding of political poetry. My secondary intent is to argue that such a shift from 1960s-era rhetorical strategies, developed from within popular oppositional communities, has radically altered in today's post-9/11 ideological context. PIPA, therefore, is organized along different temporal and spatial scales in order to engage public spaces that are striated with local and diverse global interests and ideologies. Although state or municipal laws administer local spaces, public practices and social commitments also are influenced by the economic necessities of a global economy, and by humanist-based cultural and moral values that transcend the expressed interests of statecraft and markets. By using poetic language in public spaces to confront "passersby"—an anonymous public audience—PIPA shifts the values of opposition away from representative state players in order to expand capacities in local audiences to recognize discord between local life and global political agendas. While Levertov and other peace movement protesters organized rallies and prepared public events in which poetry, song, and oratory were used to address an immediate and definable national audience, PIPA's strategy integrates more fully into urban environments. Its efforts are organized to confront ideological narratives with creative wordplay through slogans, handbills, and songs. The swarm-like objectives of PIPA recall, too, the descriptions of nonstate entities working against global market initiatives detailed by political theorists like Michael Hardt and Antonio Negri.[23] These approaches to poetry as an art of rhetorical intervention are scaled down from the 1960s' larger popular reinforcements of values in peace movement protests. Many PIPA attempts to bring poetry into public spaces, moreover, are only recognized ephemerally, and the audience is broad and indefinite. So how does this work as a public art with real value for those who seek to challenge the established public narratives we live with every day?

PIPA in Public Environments

Unlike the Poets Against War website and its address through digital space, PIPA enters controversial urban environments, and the expectations of an audience have not been prepared in advance through invitation to a particular rhetorical site of exchange. Instead, these public auditors are limited to particular situations, and the poet enters an exchange that is fostered by individual scale. In other words, the dissemination of texts in these contexts is much more intimate, if numerically limited. While Poets Against War and other protest groups identify goals they hope to achieve through their rhetorical site of intervention (such as the end to the conflict in Iraq), PIPA's more modest goal is to "cause passersby to pause and think."[24] To establish caesura within the nominal narratives of daily life, PIPA poets provide moments of introspection for some. By refusing to measure their achievements by the number of successfully transformed attitudes, they provide strategies for entering diverse public sites in order to reach flexible and realistic success through a mutable public audience. This kind of rhetorical use of poetry in many ways resembles word-of-mouth marketing and communication strategies. Basing his claims on models of contagion, Malcolm Gladwell argues, "sometimes big changes follow from small events, and that sometimes these changes can happen very quickly."[25] By preparing a situation wherein conflicting ideological perspectives enter public environments, PIPA activist-poetics engages at a grassroots level to influence how auditors begin to think about the received opinions and ideas that compose dominant ideologies.

While these transient public strategies are much different from the more traditional model of site-formation strategies, efforts to document PIPA projects extend the life of these public interventions, too. In a sense, two or more audiences can exist: the first audience is composed of those passersby who encounter PIPA texts within specifically targeted public environments, while the second audience includes readers either within the extended domain of the collective who receive word-of-mouth documentation of individual poetic efforts or, if printed in a book, readers who compose a much broader potential audience that exists in diverse public locations. These documentation projects increase public perspective by inviting readers to compare PIPA efforts in particular locations with their own sense of public space. Moreover, as dominant national narratives are extensive across North American public spaces, PIPA's goal of disrupting market-influenced ideologies returns attention to a public space that is influenced by contrasting social vectors. Public space, in this context, no longer serves the expressed needs of states, markets, or ideological or theoretical agencies. Instead, public space becomes a controversial ground for a potential discourse in which texts operate to direct attention to political issues, though without the desire to determine the outcomes of such public confrontation beyond the hopes that beliefs and attitudes may be changed in preparation for future debate. While it may be argued that the limited persuasive potential of these interventionist practices will reduce the value of projects like PIPA, such arguments may be countered by pointing out how the intimate space of contact between author and audience, the poetics of surprise in this kind of public engagement, and the mobile and adaptable goals of PIPA participants maximize possibilities of successful intervention. These engagements take place in a suasive realm where attention is drawn, however briefly, to issues that stand out against the everyday ideologies that frame public life.

In September of 2000, for instance, Prevallet was a member of the Real-Po Listserv, an online space that "facilitated the flow of PIPA."[26] Correspondence during the final week of that month focused on strategies of public engagement, documenting ideas such as "handing out 'Poetry Cards,'" poetry leaflets, poetry stamps, bumper stickers, and other media resources to be used in public confrontations. Prevallet has documented the results of this online strategy session:

> Small poetry cards were indeed printed and distributed on subways, left on benches (to be cleaned up by MTA janitors), stuck in phone booths, and inserted into advertisements. Magnets with anti-SUV slogans were printed and stuck on SUVs in California and New York. The only effect (but it's not really about the effect, is it?) was one PIPA enfacer [*enfacer* (noun) = a person who leaves behind propaganda, but doesn't deface property] getting yelled at by a SUV owner. But, although the gesture remains a gesture (not a movement) some good PIPA slogans were generated and did appear on signs at several political rallies, including the Republican convention, the (un)inauguration, and two IMF/World Bank protests.[27]

Prevallet's documentation of how these small poems were used in public contexts can inspire others to conduct similar poetic operations. And the playful but serious nature of the poetic acts documented here provides relief to the page-based poems that attract attention in more traditional poetry formats. One moment for pause, however, is when she asks about the "effect" of these acts, claiming that such is not the point. With further reflection through Prevallet's documentation, we might, however, find an effect or effects that are significant. For one thing, these gestures generate excitement and enthusiasm among sympathetic poets and artists, thereby increasing the movement's presence in public. Other effects are difficult to measure, yet, plausibly, we might recognize even the most indifferent shrug by a passerby as a response—a denial of the possibility of reception, though encountered bodily. Compared to Poets Against War's broad digital archive, the slogan-poems distributed by PIPA perform in urban space to address specific audiences. Public space, moreover, is, briefly, infiltrated by the agenda and desires of PIPA, thereby transforming public environments through an initial encounter and its subsequent documentation.

Responding to 9/11

After the attacks on the World Trade Center on September 11, 2001, poets in New York City met to discuss strategies of poetic intervention in public, forming "Debunker Mentality," "a group," like PIPA, "who met weekly and on email to sloganize, design flyers, lexicons, and otherwise discuss the potential for language in the midst of language's co-option."[28] In this regard, Prevallet describes her reaction to the official narrative delivered by the Bush administration, which encouraged the nation to "return to normal." As a response, she writes, "we decided that instead we needed to wheatpaste poems all over the city, to remind people of their primary HUMAN reaction to the Fallen Towers Atrocity."[29] The poems PIPA distributed included: "Tree of Fire" by the Palestinian poet Adonis; a selection from objectivist poet George Oppen's *Of Being Numerous;* "Conclusivity" by Fanny Howe; "My Time" by Osip Mandelshtam; and "The Angel of History" passage from Walter Benjamin's "Theses on the Philosophy of History."[30] These works share a sense of the futility and horror of war without forming a specific sense of protest to a particular situation. Instead, these authors expand capacities that help audiences realize the complications of state violence in the lives and deaths of nonstate participants who are inadvertently involved. Debunker Mentality's goal with posting these texts around New York City was to engage the narrative of retaliation and economic prosperity (a return to "normal"), by showing that such normalcy is a rhetorically constructed event purchased with state-sponsored violence abroad.

A poem by Robert Hayden shows an example of the kind of work distributed across the city by activists at this time. It brings attention to the contradictory purchase of normalcy at home through violence against others:

Oh, what a world we make.
oppressor and oppressed.

Our world—
this violent ghetto, slum
of the spirit raging against
itself.

We hate kill destroy
in the name of human good
our killing and our hate
destroy.[31]

Accompanying the poem in the left-hand column are texts written by Debunker Mentality. The questions provide a rhetorical context for Hayden's poem that makes it relevant to New York City passersby during the emotionally confusing aftermath of 9/11. The accompanying texts read:

THIS IS A
MESSAGE OF
GRIEF.

CAN WAR BE
MOURNED?

IS IT RIGHT
TO MAKE AN
ENTIRE
COUNTRY
PAY FOR THE
CRIMES OF
EXTREME
INDIVIDUALS?

IS THERE A
DIFFERENCE BETWEEN AN
INDIVIDUAL
AND HIS
COUNTRY?

WHY IS THE
MEDIA NOT
TALKING
ABOUT OIL?

WHY IS IT
UNPATRIOTIC
TO DISSENT?

THIS IS A
MESSAGE OF
GRIEF.[32]

By posing these questions within a context of grief rather than revenge, the Debunker Mentality project attempts to shift the rhetorical situation identified by the dominant narrative supported by mainstream media and the government in the aftermath of 9/11. By placing the event within a situation that these activists identify as an ongoing failure of human organization to prevent war and acts of catastrophic violence, passersby are asked to consider alternative responses to an invasion of Afghanistan. They are asked, too, to consider the meaning of terms like *patriotism, dissent,* and *national identity.* By bringing poems such as Hayden's into public spaces, Debunker Mentality introduced epideictic suasion as a tool of public influence. For these poet-activists, public address had to be constructed through reflective texts designed to bring an audience into sympathy with a broad human struggle between "oppressor and oppressed." While not condoning the acts of terrorists, Debunker Mentality sought to bring awareness to the conditions that may generate terrorism as a seemingly viable option for certain groups. These activists wanted to bring attention to how violence results from a breakdown of conversation between groups, noting how certain ideological conditions can prevent successful dissent through peaceful channels. One key question—"Why is the / media not / talking / about oil?"—implicates US policy in the Middle East as a potential source of conflict over global resources. So by shifting the perspectives beyond the dominant ideological narratives of the period, Debunker Mentality constructed alternative textual environments in public spaces that could generate reflection in the aftermath of the attacks.

Challenging Normative Narratives

Echoing the investigation of key terminology introduced by Edward Dorn in *Abhorrences,* Prevallet explains how a lexicon project, developed by Frances Richard and *Cabinet* magazine, "reclaim[ed] words being used in the mass media by writing through their surface and into their deeper meanings."[33] Rather than thinking of these as containing "deeper meanings," however, we might look at how, through the playful etymology around the word "Normalcy," Richard shifts perspectives through an over-used term employed after 9/11 to help restore a sense of order and national narrative. She writes: "NORM from *norma* meaning 'the carpenter's square' meaning 'a perpendicular line' meaning 'knowing the time by looking at the sundial.' What is the other side of the norm? The moondial which is witches time. Or: 'The wish for normality is the other side of indifference' (*Yitzhak Laor*). So the other side of indifference is from the Greek word gnomon meaning 'column or pin on a sundial that casts a shadow indicating time of day.'"[34] Richard goes on in this way by offering a kind of grammatical discovery around the term in order to complicate it and reclaim it. The recovery becomes poignant when a quote from Hermann Goering is used to show how constructions of "normalcy" are politically motivated. "Voice or no voice," writes Goering (through Richard), "the people can always be brought to the bidding of the leaders. All you have to do is tell them they are being attacked, and denounce the pacifists for lack of patriotism and exposing the country to danger." Richard follows this by saying, "All you have to do is change people's conception of time as no longer secure. Any minute (YOU COULD BE SHOPPING) you will be attacked."[35] By stressing the regulation of time in the construction of normalcy, Richard attempts to broaden perspectives on how audiences relate to the Bush administration's request to return to normal. Like Dorn, Richard takes a key term and employs it within new contexts in order to generate diverse perspectives on how an audience receives public narratives.

This ability to expand possible perspective is one of the most significant contributions offered by a publicly motivated poetics. The sense of surprise and intrusion into the daily routine can radically alter perceptions in public space, suasively, for particular audiences. Such acts do not prevent events like the Iraq War or the invasion of Afghanistan. But with the recent election of the first African American president, who ran on a strong antiwar message, it could be argued that poets who perform this kind of public-oriented work prepare audiences slowly to engage the world differently. It is difficult to measure the direct influence of these actions, but it is plausible that they are influential in proposing new ways of observing the social and political narratives that in part shape public spaces and public reactions in them.

"As technicians of the word," Prevallet writes (with Rodrigo Toscano): "we very much can and should enter into this burgeoning peace (justice) movement, to help shape it, and transform it. As living preceptors of now twisted truths, we must keep the political dialogue going, even though the politics of the moment seemingly lack the urgency of the politics of the past. There is always a-politics, a-language, a-idea that is on the waning side of articulation, unintelligible until dared to come into language."[36] This sense that poetry can facilitate difficult or oppositional messages is important because it keeps vital perspectives available within the leading narrative paradigm. Significant, too, is the understanding of how new ideas are generated over time as they come to inhabit diverse situations and contexts. PIPA and Debunker Mentality's contributions to the theory and practice of public engagement offer ways to think rhetorically about how social and political ideas form, mutate, and arrive, finally to larger audiences as the scales continue to shift for greater and greater public reception.

Such work is appealing because it is based in political activism—something not always associated with poetry, though clearly poets such as Milton, Blake, Shelley, and others produced work in the past that was motivated politically. Without worrying too much over legal or theoretical definitions of public space, the poets here simply find ways to enter the public realm in order to generate common awareness of how we interact in shared locations. Through documentation of these public interventions, moreover, we can begin to see how immediate acts of public confrontation are then further transformed through written and visual archives, thus converting the notion of public space through print and online media to include other public settings. Through these documents others can learn how to engage their own locales in provocative ways. Such documentation also brings with it a critical sense of self-reflection, helping to ground activist poetic works in a context of social strategies others have applied elsewhere. What I find most appealing about guerrilla poetry is that it asks us to think of the poem as something that has life both "on and off the page."[37] More importantly, its rhetorical strategies bring poetry closer to an actual public dialogue that can reinforce the objectives of certain communities rather than only speaking to more ideologically legitimate ones.

More than anything, such guerrilla tactics are determined by actual situations in physical locales that bring their own sets of problems and concerns. Our understanding of poetry is broadened, too, when writers like Prevallet, Richard, Toscano, and others associated with activist groups like Debunker Mentality engage in the unglamorous activity of building resilient communities.[38]

"Lyric Poetry after Auschwitz"?

Many recall Theodor Adorno's claim that following the atrocities at Auschwitz, it had become impossible, in the West, to write lyric poetry.[39] Of course, that has not stopped anyone from trying. We have seen in this study, however, that most of the poets who desire to engage with issues of public relevance have abandoned the lyric in favor of satire, social documentation, modernist assemblage, and other strategies of poetic engagement. Groups of activists like PIPA, moreover, combine a skillful use of poetic language with social commentary that can be adapted to specific public environments, creating textual spaces that transform the area in which readers pass. The roots of this sort of direct public engagement can be seen in the personal documentary and expressivist lyrics of Denise Levertov, with others following her lead in this regard, adapting urgent social or political messages to fit the requirements of place and time.[40] Those still practicing lyric poetry, however, frequently do not engage the public sphere with the same kind of conscious desire to change perceptions of social issues in it. Although the ethical portent of Adorno's statement remains challenging to anyone who works within the romantic lyric mode, for the purposes of this study it might be enough to say that the lyric's value can be found outside of public contexts. Its audiences are composed, more frequently, of creative writing students and professors who distribute their work within the fairly confined social spaces of the university and other legitimizing institutions. While certainly lyric poetry might still be used to make large public statements, its success as rhetorical discourse that engages a public audience on diverse social issues is achieved with greater difficulty. Adorno explains this as a result of social transactions in an environment that since World War II implicate the "innocent" activities of poets (and everyone else) within a larger frame of political and cultural submission to Western economic objectives.[41] More self-conscious rhetorical strategies and poetic modes are required to effectively comment on issues relevant to public concern.

While this is not the place to consider Adorno's claims more fully, it is important to acknowledge this divide between lyric practice and public engagement when turning to the work of Kent Johnson, a poet based in a small town in northern Illinois, where he teaches Spanish and English at a local community college. Despite this geographically remote location, his reputation and presence online and in print have grown dramatically over the last decade. Importantly, his political satire comments on a number of issues that allow readers to reflect on the role of poetry as an art of social change for communities of authors as well as the diverse public spaces they inhabit. Particularly, Johnson aims his arguments at contemporary avant-garde poetry audiences,[42] challenging them to look at the rhetorical contexts in which aesthetic forms operate and how social situations and ideologies have changed radically since the inception of Italian Futurism, Dadaism, and other avant-garde movements of the last century. By doing this, he moves attention from the aesthetic object to the rhetorical contexts that give meaning to poetic practice. For Johnson, writing can be used to challenge existing ideological paradigms, and in many ways he relies on the agonistic and even nihilistic tendencies found in early twentieth-century avant-garde work.[43] His critique of ideology, power, coterie formation, and aesthetic practice within contemporary poetry communities attends the discordant relations between much contemporary avant-garde theory and practice, too. Although Johnson shares a predominantly leftist ideology with some members of contemporary avant-garde poetry communities, he wants to bring attention to the rhetorical failure of many contemporary writers to fully exploit their poetry within situations that give meaning and shape to public life.[44] Since the US government exerts so much power globally, he reminds those involved in forms of North American–based poetry that their art should advance social awareness rather than perform aesthetic values appreciated only within the more limited communal spaces of contemporary poetics.[45] Rather than performing the correct ideological values in a particular poem or avant-garde performance, Johnson wants to find more rhetorically effective and persuasive means to speak out about dissonant social realities that exist in contemporary ideologies and artistic practices. In order to show how Johnson's satire persuades readers to reflect more carefully on their ideological commitments, I want to look at a few poems that address the ongoing wars in the Middle East. I will show how they work not only to bring attention to those wars in Iraq and Afghanistan, but also to challenge readers to evaluate their roles within contemporary avant-garde communities.[46]

In *Homage to the Last Avant-Garde* (2008),[47] Johnson reflects critically on the political and social contexts in which poetry is written. One way he does this is by bringing attention to how contemporary avant-garde communities privilege particular textual canons and aesthetic practices over addressing situations of public crisis and social value. In "The New York School (Or: I Grew Ever More Intense)," the first-person persona he creates describes a morning toilet routine, interspersed with voices that recount horrific scenes of loss and terror in certain Asian, African, and Arab nations. He achieves incongruent juxtapositions in the poem by placing satirical commentary on modern American poetry next to scenes of violence in the contemporary Middle East. For instance, he writes: "I turned over the bottle of shampoo and Frank O'Hara came out. I rubbed him all into my head, letting the foam rise, knowing I was just warming myself up, excited by the excess of what was to come."[48] Later on, New York school poet Barbara Guest squirts out of a shaving cream can and James Schuyler is squeezed from a tube of toothpaste. Images of Ted Berrigan aftershave and Kenneth Koch mouthwash also are directed at readers familiar with New York school poetry. Between these satiric paragraphs, however, we find narratives such as this: "a young girl . . . climbed out of the burning car in which her mother, father, and sister sat dead, their open-eyed bodies on slow fire. In shock she walked around in tight circles, her fingers hanging by nerves and skin from her hands. . . . She simply walked in circles for about five minutes, an impassive look on her face, until she slowly knelt and curled up in apparent sleep on the street, the shooting continuing above her body for another twenty minutes or so. During that time, she bled to death."[49]

Readers, then, must confront these prosaic frames, alternating between poetic satire and horrific narrative. This incongruent presentation never explicitly states an argument, and it is possible that some might find the satire to be directly aimed at those poets of the New York school whom Johnson so enthusiastically absorbs into his body. But really, the satire is directed at contemporary poets who are too preoccupied with their investments in particular schools of thought or practice to apprehend how their reception of particular historic practices of writing may not work rhetorically under new social and political contexts. For instance, the New York school poets featured in this poem all came into public view during the 1950s and '60s as the Cold, Korean, and Vietnam Wars informed the political agendas and ideology of the period. Using Adorno's argument that implicates Western complacency as a kind of shadow agency making possible global economic and political policies for disadvantaged nations, Johnson suggests that the time and social space made available to these New York school poets was bought through the suffering of others in faraway places. The American practice of poetry is paid for in blood insofar as the freedom from economic stress purchased through US policy abroad allowed certain poets to pursue their art in all its complex dimensions and avant-garde formal possibilities.[50] While contemporary avant-garde aesthetic practice is often linked historically to Italian Futurism and, especially, Dadaism, with an emphasis on "a revolt against art, morality, and society,"[51] Johnson points out that since the conditions of society have altered significantly—particularly in the decade since 9/11—the rhetorical-poetic strategies of these earlier movements are no longer useful. After witnessing an initial campaign in Iraq, for instance, that promised "shock and awe," Johnson suggests that other strategies contesting American foreign policy and domestic ideology are required for poets who must stop living in the past with avant-garde formal techniques that now even the US military employs to reinforce its own message of change.[52] Johnson, by contrast, asks readers to examine their situations as American citizens and what that means within the smaller communities and public spaces they inhabit. Doing this, his discordant or incongruent prose segments destabilize expectations, and his work asks that reflection on social practice extend to other global communities and not just to a contemporary lineage composed of avant-garde formal strategies. In this way, public spaces can be addressed by poetry to make diverse communities more aware of the interaction of global politics and economic systems with the social and moral values in our daily experience.

If an avant-garde—governed, etymologically, by a metaphor of militarization—is supposed to be situated at the front lines of culture, showing others new perspectives of the world and how to live in it—as well as promoting, among other things, social change and demonstrating responses to potentially dangerous ideologies—then Johnson's critique asks for a greater rhetorical role for poetry, and not just a formal and historical acceptance of strategies developed in the past for other situations. His work questions relationships of imagination to poetic practice, personal experience, and political power. He insists, too, that poets are not innocent of the political forces they may critique, and that rhetorical strategies that bring awareness to diverse global and cultural situations are preferable to the less persuasive formal performances of in-groups reinforcing their own limited cultural beliefs. By bringing this kind of awareness of the various social strata that exist in public situations composed of US poets and their audiences, Johnson challenges contemporary public narratives that associate poetry with aesthetic pleasure. His work, therefore, shows that American conflict abroad requires poetic inquiry because such address differs significantly from mediated forms that deliver a legitimized public debate. Johnson's use of poetry to make sociopolitical messages influences belief and desire, so that in effect he prepares readers in advance of their participation in other forums of public deliberation.

"Lyric Poetry after Auschwitz, or: 'Get the Hood Back On,'" a poem that examines American ideological values in correspondence with the Abu Ghraib prison abuse scandal, also challenges readers to consider the rhetorical atmosphere in which poetry is produced and read. While this long poem works through a number of cultural perspectives and public narratives that juxtapose American ideological values with physical acts of torture in Iraq, I want to focus on the final performative section. In it, Johnson explicitly argues for more effective social and political witness from contemporary poets. "Hi there, Madid," he writes in this controversial stanza:

I'm an American poet, twentyish, early to mid-thirtyish, fortyish to seventyish, I've had poems on the *Poets Against the War* website, and in *American Poetry Review* and *Chain,* among other magazines, and I have a blog, and I really dig Arab music, and I read Adorno and Spivak, and I'm really progressive, I voted for Clinton and Gore, even though I know they bombed you a lot, too, sorry about that, and I know I live quite nicely off the fruits of a dying imperium, which include anti-war poetry readings at the Lincoln Center and the Poetry Project, with appetizers and wine and New World Music and lots of pot. And because nothing is simple in this world, and because no one gets out unscathed, I'm going to just be completely candid with you: I'm going to box your ears with two big books of poems, one of them experimental and the other more plain speech-like, both of them hardbound and by leading academic presses, and I'm going to do it until your brain swells to the size of a basketball and you die like the fucking lion for real. You'll never make it to MI because that's the breaks; poetry is hard, and people go up in flames for lack of it everyday. By the time any investigation gets to you, your grandchildren will have been dead over one thousand years, and poetry will be inhabiting regions you can't even begin to imagine. Well, we did our best; sorry we couldn't have done better . . . I want you to take this self-righteous poem, soak it in this bedpan of crude oil, and shove it down your pleading, screaming throat.
Now, get the hood back on.[53]

Here the rhetorical voice begins as a kind of left-leaning stereotype of what a contemporary poet might be. Such a person makes their political commitments known through the Poets Against War website, or by writing for other recognized journals. She is culturally sophisticated, embracing "Arab music" and reflects with critical acumen on "progressive" issues through the cultural criticism of "Adorno and Spivak." This liberal individual "voted for Clinton and Gore" in what is meant to suggest a tepid form of sociopolitical commitment. Although he is creating a "straw man" caricature of left-leaning poets, these images suggest how some stereotypical narratives remain viable in contemporary culture. The critique is not solely against the scandal of abuse at Abu Ghraib; it is directed at conflicting moral and social values in American ideology that officially or unofficially create environments for actions as extreme as torture. Although we like to tell stories of ourselves as good people who bring freedom and democracy to other nations, western ideologies also validate aggressive social behavior in many situations. The images from Abu Ghraib shocked and confused viewers because of the intense conflict the prison scandal raised about official ideologies and American narratives. Identification with the side of righteousness was submerged in images of prisoners reduced to the level of animals at the hands of the US military. By using these volatile images of prison torture to construct his poetic narrative, Johnson rhetorically engages American cultural values and military law by arranging satiric narrative through the perspectives of different US citizen types, including poets who like to identify socially and politically with the Left and its culturally legitimizing institutions. By doing so Johnson suggests that actions and attitudes performed within diverse public modes are implicated in global events, too. And in his work he addresses those beliefs in order to make persuasive commentary on perspectives that are in conflict with our own.

Preparing Publics with Poetry

How, as Charles Bernstein once asked, should poets "pursue our own forms of ethical and aesthetic response" in the face of "the sort of pronouncement by fiat and moral presumption of President Bush and his partisans"?[54] This dilemma has challenged poets and artists of the last decade to evaluate rhetorical strategies, determining what may work from the past and what needs to be reinvigorated. One noticeable change in the present is that the formal obligations of poetry are beginning to give way to a more thoughtful understanding of the contexts in which forms contribute to arguments that can persuade public audiences on issues of social significance. Although the Bush administration contributed to an era of ideological fear and uncertainty, sending troops to war on one hand while call-ing, on the other, for Americans to "participat[e] [with] confidence in the American economy" after the attacks of 9/11, many poets, artists, activists, and intellectuals found other ways to conduct life. And in response to wars in Iraq and Afghanistan, many took their views into diverse public spaces where speculation on the nature of contemporary life in democratic so-ciety could be renewed, or could be shaped in opposition to official con-sensus and ideology.

While poets and activists during the Vietnam War could address audi-ences who shared similar social and cultural claims about war, domestic policy, and other issues that would include gender and race in the 1960s and '70s, poets who shared positions against war and the Bush adminis-tration's retaliatory strikes after 9/11 confronted greater ideological chal-lenges. While large rallies and oratorical practices that addressed activists were useful in the past, the post-9/11 situation required new rhetorical strategies that could speak to an audience, often by word of mouth, through direct exchange of printed texts and performative engagement, or through the digital possibilities offered by the web.

Although there are similarities in these strategies, there are numerous differences, too. Poets Against War, PIPA, Debunker Mentality, and Kent Johnson all share similar ideological perspectives that would associate their social and political views with the Left, and yet their strategies of engage-ment with an audience are radically different.[55] Sam Hamill's promotion of Poets Against War as a digital site of protest provides thousands of textual responses to war. While many of the site's poems rely on expressivist ap-peals to reach readers, the node-to-node transmission of textual possibili-ties online enabled a quick response that displayed broad public resistance to the invasion of Iraq in 2003. The representation of the voices on the site, then, is not so much concerned with particular arguments, but about quickly organizing a public response en masse to reinforce opposition to official policy. While public models based on circulation and node-to-node distribution create conflicting expectations in online viewers, PAW pre-sented an intertextual forum for diverse voices, and Hamill supported the antiwar poets gathered on his site through commentary, public events, po-etry spotlights, and other types of engagement that helped maintain the site's visible status as a public entity.

PIPA, by contrast, as we see in the representative work of Kristin Pre-vallet, offers interactive, if limited, strategies, aimed at a local audience. By developing a plan of action and then assembling as a group to bring po-etic messages directly into diverse public settings, PIPA and other groups like Debunker Mentality engage in strategies that can be persuasive in local contexts. By taking poetry directly to others, PIPA leaves open the possibility of belief in shared communication. One drawback to this, however, might be the limited range of engagement. If your message or poem only reaches a few people in a day, it is difficult to see how this can be considered rhetorically successful when all around there are messages being broadcast with much greater frequency to larger audiences that reinforce dominant ideologies. And yet for poets involved in PIPA, numbers are not as significant as the ethical acts involved in bringing oppositional messages into public spaces. Besides, as many marketers understand, word-of-mouth communication remains an effective, if difficult-to-measure, strategy for communication. And if epideictic rhetoric affects beliefs and desires, the intimate contact on the street between poet, text, and reader or observer creates a potentially more radical bond. Chances are good that a passerby will leave the unexpected engagement with poetry to reflect on the transaction of that experience.

Kent Johnson's satiric stance finally brings critical attention to the role of contemporary poetry insofar as his arguments question the values held by communities of writers and their willingness to contribute to important public issues. While his work is often seen as controversial, and his critiques against his peers are received frequently with hostility, he continues an avant-garde project that values "a revolt against art, morality, and society." Such a "revolt" for Johnson is centered predominantly on how collective ideologies and national narratives shape artistic, moral, and social values. By bringing new perspectives in his satire into collision with received poetic practices, Johnson challenges contemporary poets to consider more carefully their commitments to audiences in diverse public situations. He asks also that they adapt their words and images to the particular requirements of social and political life. The mobile public scenarios where national narratives and ideologies are processed by observers of foreign and domestic policy become significant staging grounds where poetry can be used to exert pressure on existing civil discourse to increase possibilities and actions in a great variety of contexts.

Afterword
Poetry as a Modality of Rhetoric in Modernist Inquiry

Consider, again, Nancy S. Struever's engagement with modality, and her urgency "in defining not Modernity as epoch, but the nature of Modernist inquiry."[1] In her argument, systemic political philosophy accounts for actualities at the expense of possible actions and capacities, new inroads of thought and engagements that can transform public situations. Categorical models of civil structures may help us better understand certain factual relations, but these formal elements neglect a more dynamic account through rhetoric of how new procedures come into being, or how alternative actions arrive to change attitudes and beliefs about public issues. Poetry as a modality of rhetoric contributes significantly to modernist inquiry, for it produces shifts of attention that give new ways of understanding current predicaments of social and political action.[2] For Struever, modality "extend[s] the pertinent range of application to 'any possible' agent or action, an extension which is, at the same time, a questioning of previous limits, previous certainties, necessities. Possibility as change of register promotes inquiry as not simply investigation of what might, or could happen, but as an engagement with the tone and temper of a fully explored life, intricating, indeed, aesthetic with social parameters."[3]

Literature in this context enables modernist inquiry because "one is required to consider not simply the 'actual' in the sense of what transpired, or transpires, but alternates, extensions, extensions invoking fullness, freedom, in some puzzling way."[4] While Struever is concerned with civil discourse and political philosophy, and the ways rhetorical modality expands, complicates, and shifts the possibilities of engagement and intervention in these disciplines, her model of Walter Benjamin as modernist rhetor invites poetic strategies and critical perspicacity that can enliven and mobilize variant discourses from within the more rigid structures of communication that so often define social and political contexts. Whether it is Charles Olson asking the citizens of Gloucester to consider the agencies that inform urban transformation, or Denise Levertov insisting that attitudes composed toward Vietnam be examined in light of larger American imperialistic motives, or Lorenzo Thomas intervening on popular media images to reclaim their potency for an African American audience, the inquiries these poets perform register through modalities that are composed in opposition to rigid disciplinary fields.

If "Benjamin's mastery is mastery of the essential fluidity of forms, of the modes, procedures, traditions of practice and recognition in the creation of literature and art," then literature, when used attentively to affect public discourse, likewise can produce essential interventions that contribute to the fluency of rhetorical practices.[5] As a rhetorical strategy, poetry and art, when brought to public contexts, expand issues and explore responses to a whole range of possible actions. The intervening gestures employed by PIPA, for instance, are productive not only as aesthetic experience, but as enlargements of basic inquiries into the nature of conflict and war, social space and public action. "By defining rhetoric *as* inquiry, engaged, from the beginning in the rescue of topics from, and in opposition to, philosophy, an opposition that is functional, specifying, essential," poetry, when used rhetorically, enacts basic premises of civil discourse through an insistence on the values of the contributions of an engaged citizenry. As Struever argues, "a primary and significant element in [rhetoric's] opposition is its primitive, early devotion, asserted in Aristotle's *Rhetoric,* to possibility as mode, rather than to the necessity intricated with philosophical systematizing. The engagement with describing the 'general space of possibility' is fundamental to rhetorical inquiry."[6] Olson, Duncan, Levertov, Prevallet, and others considered in the preceding pages bring attention to the situated conditions of public experience; they intervene in spaces that often are considered inflexible, structured as irrevocable dimensions of civic life. These interventions recall in the public observer or reader the mutable conditions that underscore civil conventions, and these poets ask that others look at events in the world not through some preexisting lens of legibility, but through potential variations and imaginings of the kinds of actions available through reflexive discourse. "For John Dewey it is 'pathological' to forget our rootedness in an experience of qualitative interaction," while "for Adorno the pertinence and quality of our conceptual thought depends on consciousness of its original 'pulsion'."[7] The poets in this book contribute to contemporary social and public discourse by an insistence on the force of their gestures and inquiries within specific contexts. The incongruent engagements these inquiries can lead to produce variances and new potentials in what are otherwise evenly prescribed constructions of public culture and the many civic facades that compose contemporary life.

This notion of inquiry empowers the poets examined in this book to "negotiat[e] clarification."[8] Modal registers of possibility produce new perspectives and invite examinations of motives. Those authors and actors who take it upon themselves to initiate strategies of public engagement provide essential examples of public ethics, and they demonstrate civil participation. Their risks as public actors (rather than speaking among peers in a much smaller coterie situation), provide examples of how future inquiries may be modeled while the specific forms of their actions suggest the complex pressures that shape and make demands on social interactions and discourse. As Struever observes, "*reflexivity*" of modality is "unavoidable; one can't observe it without using it. The reflexivity of the operation of the mode is primitive; it invests one of the major inquiry strategies: consideration in their instance requires consideration in ours; to consider remote possibility involves specifying near."[9]

Inquiry, finally, is intrusive. It slides into impacted formations of social and public experience that will seek to divert or receive the intruding gesture, but such spaces do not accept the critical gesture easily. Perhaps this is why poetry provides an opportune genre of linguistic inventiveness and moral certitude. Poetry plays into a contradictory public imagination of the art's power to produce revolution or voiced dissent. Poetry can put forward the affective possibilities that motivate existing situations.

This is not to put too happy a face on things. Terrence Des Pres, writing near the end of the Cold War, observed how "in the Age of the Bomb, it's not hard to see that between them the superpowers have recolonized the globe; that they have carved the planet into spheres of influence, forcing smaller nations to toe the new alignment, and that now they proceed with the standoff they've locked themselves into."[10] Now, some twenty years later, and despite the official end of the Cold War in 1989, there appears to be no relief from the global predicament he describes; there are only new formations of influence and power divided among wealthy nations, corporations, and those whose violent resistance in the various troubled spots of the globe persist with varying degrees of success and failure. The War on Terror presents a new predicament, however, in that revolutionary hope is in decline just as the legitimacy of nation-states wanes under the influence of transglobal banks, resource markets, and shadow bazaars of arms and drugs. The idealism that shaped so much of the last century has been damaged by the cold and permissive logic of markets, the self-sustaining drives and libidos of technoculture, the repressive and violent reinforcements of religious fundamentalism in the West and East, the narrowing of privacy through the medical and surveillance industries, and the "down-

turn" of the global economy. And in an age of virtual reality, social networks, YouTube entertainments, and more, it isn't hard to see why poetry,
at a glance, hardly matters given its conservative legacy, coterie isolation,
and intimate and dogged persistence as cultural practice and artifact.

Duncan, perhaps, in the purity of his vision, is right: art sustains perspectives beyond individual longing and can reveal the pressures, conflicts, and
contradictions that are otherwise incredibly difficult to realize in a culture
that values the political meme, the slogan, the ad, the brief sound bite, headline, tweet, or blog post. There are more powerful forms of communication as well as more practical media that reinforce existing platforms of social and public engagement. Yet poets persist, against all common sense, to
demand human dignity, reflection, and understanding of the present condition of things, as Olson would have said. But while poetry won't change
the world directly, it does challenge individuals. It can lead to better visions of what is possible in the world, and it can initiate inquiries and re-
visions of civil and global practices.

When I began writing this book, George W. Bush had been reelected
for a second term of office as president of the United States. Soon after,
disturbing images of Abu Ghraib entered public discourse; charges of false
documentation over weapons of mass destruction in Iraq were filed in a
US court; the failure of the Bush administration to respond promptly to
Hurricane Katrina, and its support of monetary policies that enabled the
2008 financial crisis, all collided with Barack Obama's 2008 White House
victory. A change had taken place in the imagination of the electorate.
The poets discussed here, however peripheral, or seemingly tangential in
their efforts or effects, found ways to reinforce bodies of feeling that ran
counter to dominant civil narratives. Whether their works are propaedeu-
tic or inventive of strategies that produce actions—actions that include reflexive considerations within highly concentrated realms of disciplinary
legibility—poetry since the Vietnam War intrudes upon contemporary life
with multiple possibilities to remind us that definitive notions of reality
are at best provisory and subject to constant revision. If democracy in the
United States persists, then a committed notion of how civil discourse is
furthered in specific contexts must include the inquiries and incongruencies
of art and poetry. These aerate disciplinary procedures with possible outcomes that bear a weight of permanence in their virtuosic and deliberate
intrusions. A poem may not change the world, but collective efforts in poetry to engage the realities facing us can lead to a future we are otherwise
unlikely to imagine.

Notes

Introduction

Nancy S. Struever, *Rhetoric, Modality, Modernity* (Chicago: University of Chicago Press, 2009), 6.

1. Literary critics frequently acknowledge the revolutionary possibilities of early modernism in the opening decades of the twentieth century, though the postwar poetry of the Beats or Black Mountain is usually not considered in the same revolutionary context. Marjorie Perloff, for instance, argues, "The first thing to understand is that in the early avant-gardes, the aesthetic and political were inseparable. Especially the Russian avant-garde was politically AND aesthetically revolutionary, marking a sharp break with the past." Postwar modernist writing for Perloff, however, no longer retains the same vital revolutionary promise. "Poetry today," she argues, "must be understood in terms of the modernist revolution, a revolution much more dramatic than that of Charles Olson in 'Projective verse' or Allen Ginsberg in 'Howl'." By dropping revolution as a requirement for modern art, however, the features of today's writing can be better understood within contemporary social realities that determine specific actions in poetry. See Jeffrey Side's interview with Perloff in the *Poetry Salzburg Review*, no. 10, Autumn 2006 (available at *The Argotist Online*, http://www.argotistonline.co.uk/Perloff%20interview %202.htm/); and for recent social, political, and philosophical commentary on revolution and global capitalism, see Slavoj Žižek, *Living in the End Times* (New York: Verso, 2010).

2. For recent cultural histories of postwar formations of US poetry communities, see Joseph Harrington, "Poetry and Its Publics in the 1990s," in *Poetry and the Public: The Social Form of Modern U.S. Poetics* (Middletown, CT: Wesleyan University Press, 2002), 159–86; Daniel Kane, *All Poets Welcome: The Lower East Side Poetry Scene in the 1960s* (Berkeley: University of California Press, 2004); for backgrounds to the more recent cultural significance of slam poetry, see Susan B. A. Somers-Willett, *The Cultural Politics of Slam Poetry: Race, Identity, and the Performance of Popular Verse in America* (Ann Arbor: University of Michigan Press, 2009); and for a discussion of how literature is discussed by public audiences in contemporary

culture, see Rosa A. Eberly, *Citizen Critics: Literary Public Spheres* (Champaign: University of Illinois Press, 2000).

3. This institutional success is most recently seen with the publicity surrounding Rae Armantrout's *Versed* (Middletown, CT: Wesleyan University Press, 2009), winner of the 2010 Pulitzer Prize. Usually associated with a group of writers known for their relationship to experimental formalist practices as well as Marxist political commitments, Armantrout, through her prize-winning book, has helped establish Language Poetry in the ongoing canon formation of contemporary literary history.

4. Part of this problem has to do with traditional rhetorical views of literature. For instance, Christopher Burnham, discussing James Britton's theoretical approach to expressivist rhetoric, reveals a common attitude: "Poetic writing is language used as an art medium, as a verbal icon whose purpose is to be an object that pleases or satisfies the writer. The reader's response is to share that satisfaction. In traditional terms poetic writing is literary discourse, language that 'exists for *its own sake* and not as a means of achieving something else' (Britton et al., 91)" (26). Michael Warner similarly regards lyric poetry "not as communication but as our silent insertion in the self-communion of the speaker, constructing both an ideal self-presence for the speaking voice and an ideal intimacy between that voice and ourselves" (81). While this traditional view of poetry, as Warner shows, can be found at least as early as 1833 in an essay by John Stuart Mill, who says, "Eloquence is *heard,* poetry is *overheard*" (quoted in Warner, 81), my goal is to go beyond these "traditional terms" to show ways that poetry can be used for "achieving something else." See Christopher Burnham, "Expressive Pedagogy: Practice/Theory, Theory/Practice," in *A Guide to Composition Pedagogies,* ed. Gary Tate, Amy Rupiper, and Kurt Schick (Oxford: Oxford University Press, 2001); and Michael Warner, *Publics and Counterpublics* (New York: Zone Books, 2002).

5. It is true, however, that the darker side of certain modernist revolutionary agendas, such as Italian Futurism, was explicitly fascist. See, for instance, Robert Casillo's discussion of Ezra Pound in *The Genealogy of Demons: Anti-Semitism, Fascism, and the Myths of Ezra Pound* (Evanston, IL: Northwestern University Press, 1988).

6. Many, of course, continue to protest events at state and federal capitols: numerous examples of recent marches in Washington, DC, include, for instance, a "Tea Party" march "promising to mobilize conservative voters on election day to take back the country." See Kathleen Hennessey, "'Tea Party' Activists March on Capitol Hill," *Los Angeles Times,* September 13, 2010, available at http://articles .latimes.com/2010/sep/13/nation/la-na-tea-party-rally-20100913, accessed October 30, 2010; Glenn Beck's August 28, 2010, rally drew an estimated crowd of 87,000 demonstrators; and the Million Man March of October 16, 1995, attracted more than a half million supporters of awareness of racial and economic strife among African American men. While it is true that many activists continue to organize demonstrations over important political and social issues, the goals are usu-

ally not to accomplish the sort of revolutionary changes in divisions of labor seen in Seattle in 1919 or after in workers' strikes and activism that resulted in the chartering of unions by the CIO in the 1930s. And since the 1989 collapse of the Soviet Union, socialist revolution is arguably dead in the United States.

7. Rita Raley, *Tactical Media* (Minneapolis: University of Minnesota Press, 2009), 28–29.

8. Of course, public culture is composed of discourses, too, that never come to deliberation. Many kinds of utterances are used instead to reinforce belief and desire, prejudices and attitudes, rather than inviting more sustained judgments and debates.

9. Theodor Adorno, *Aesthetic Theory,* trans. C. Lenhardt (1970; London: Routledge and Kegan Paul, 1984), 1.

10. Amiri Baraka (a.k.a. LeRoi Jones), for instance, relates the following anecdote from a revolutionary moment in the 1950s or early '60s with joking self-awareness: "One Story told to me by a friend of [Frank] O'Hara's had this poet rushing in to tell Frank, 'Leroi Jones has said he wants to kill all white people.[']' O'Hara's rejoinder (probably without putting down his drink) [']Well he won't start with us![']" In another instance of the same text, Baraka discusses how established poetry communities began to lose direction and come apart in the 1960s: "That the big Greenwich Village of our younger days which stretched from Black Mountain to San Francisco and the well advertised bongo playing Road of the Kerouacs had become dysfunctional. The era of Good Feeling, Ginsberg called it, had passed. My own move uptown and then back home was my own way of co-signing this occurrence." See Amiri Baraka, *Ed Dorn & the Western World* (Austin: Skanky Possum and Effing Press, 2009), 15–17.

11. Michel Foucault defines biopolitics as an "attempt, starting from the eighteenth century, to rationalize the problems posed to governmental practice by phenomena characteristic of a set of living beings forming a population: health, hygiene, birthrate, life expectancy, race . . . We know the increasing importance of these problems since the nineteenth century, and the political and economic issues they have raised up to the present." See Michel Foucault, *The Birth of Biopolitics: Lectures at the Collège de France, 1978–1979,* ed. Michel Senellart (New York: Picador, 2008), 317; and see Walter Benn Michaels, "Empires of the Senseless: (The Response to) Terror and (the End of) History," *Radical History Review* 85 (Winter 2003): 108, 112.

12. Gilles Deleuze, "Postscript on Control Societies," in *Negotiations, 1972–1990* (New York: Columbia University Press, 1995), 177–82.

13. For more on technocapitalism and publicity, see Jodi Dean's *Publicity's Secret: How Technoculture Capitalizes on Democracy* (Ithaca, NY: Cornell University Press, 2002).

14. See Ed Sanders, *Tales of Beatnik Glory* (New York: Stonehill Publishing, 1975).

15. For instance, Jodi Dean's arguments on behalf of "civil society" as opposed to "public sphere" as a term of political and social action aligns well with how I

understand "public culture." I retain the latter term, however, because it is more suggestive of the ways in which poets after 1960 theorize and practice their particular communicative actions. See Jodi Dean, "Cyber Salons and Civil Society: Rethinking the Public Sphere in Transnational Technoculture," *Public Culture* 13, no. 2 (2002): 243–65.

16. A theory of motives also applies to how poetry can be understood in a rhetorical context. To this end, in chapter 2 I consider Kenneth Burke's advancement of rhetorical possibilities in literature, particularly by way of his discussions of the "rhetoric of advantage" and the "rhetoric of pure persuasion" in *A Rhetoric of Motives* (Berkeley: University of California Press, 1969).

17. Daniel C. Brouwer and Robert Asen have used "modality" recently as a metaphor to replace "sphere" in Jürgen Habermas's term "public sphere." Similar in some ways to Struever's arguments, Brouwer and Asen argue that "modality illuminates the diverse range of processes through which individuals and groups engage each other, institutions, and their environment in creating, reformulating, and understanding social worlds." See *Public Modalities: Rhetoric, Culture, Media, and the Shape of Public Life,* ed. Daniel C. Brouwer and Robert Asen (Tuscaloosa: The University of Alabama Press, 2010), 16.

18. Struever, *Rhetoric, Modality, Modernity,* 1.

19. Ibid., 81–82.

20. Ibid., 81.

21. Ibid.

22. Ibid.

23. Ibid., 82.

24. Ibid.

25. Ibid., 83.

26. Ibid., 83, 87.

27. Ibid., 88.

28. For an excellent account of ancient rhetoric and poetics, see Jeffrey Walker, *Rhetoric and Poetics in Antiquity* (Oxford: Oxford University Press, 2000).

29. As Wayne A. Rebhorn explains, literature "presents a direct modeling of rhetorical situations." It "is a privileged discourse, in a sense, for it opens up the equivalent of a liminal space, a site adjacent to but separate from the space of the real world, in which authors can represent that world in such a way that while often merely rehearsing conventional ideas and arrangements, they also have the freedom to analyze, refine, and critique them." See Wayne A. Rebhorn, *The Emperor of Men's Minds: Literature and the Renaissance Discourse of Rhetoric* (Ithaca, NY: Cornell University Press, 1995), 17–18.

30. Brian Vickers, writing of the Renaissance, also observes "that rhetoric was *the* important discipline for a writer; all would have known how to treat a theme, how to divide up the parts of a speech, what to do with rhetorical figures such as *isocolon, polyptoton, paronomasia, gradatio,* and their schooling was that of Virgil, Dante, Milton; Rabelais, Montaigne, Bacon; Marlowe, Ben Jonson, Racine; Pe-

trarch, Du Bellay, Pope." See Brian Vickers, *Classical Rhetoric in English Poetry* (Carbondale: Southern Illinois University Press, 1970), 15–16.

31. Barbara Warnick, *The Sixth Canon: Belletristic Rhetorical Theory and Its French Antecedents* (Columbia: University of South Carolina Press, 1993), 5.

32. Warnick, *Sixth Canon,* 5.

33. Ibid.

34. Ibid.

35. Matthew Arnold, "Culture and Anarchy: An Essay in Political and Social Criticism (1867–69)," in *Culture and Anarchy and Other Writings,* ed. Stefan Collini (Cambridge: Cambridge University Press, 1993).

36. Jeffrey Walker, *Bardic Ethos and the American Epic Poem: Whitman, Pound, Crane, Williams, Olson* (Baton Rouge: Louisiana State University Press, 1989), 18.

37. Walker, *Bardic Ethos,* 19.

38. Andrei Codrescu gives a vivid sense of this opening night, writing: "Suddenly, nonsense noises, whistling, and shrieks were heard behind the curtain, and the lights went out. A green spotlight revealed four masked figures on stilts, each hissing a different sound: sssssss, prrrrr, muuuuh, ayayayayayay. The figures alternated their sounds and began a crazy dance. While the grotesques flailed and stomped, one of them tore open his coat to reveal a cuckoo clock on his chest. The audience stomped and shouted, and soon got into the act, rhythmically joining in by making the sounds, too. At a frenzied point when the shouting reached its most feverish pitch, Tzara reappeared onstage dressed in tails and white spats, shooed away the dancers, and started to recite nonsense in French. The performance ended with Tzara unrolling a roll of toilet paper with the word 'merde' written on it." See Andrei Codrescu, *The Posthuman Dada Guide: Tzara and Lenin Play Chess* (Princeton, NJ: Princeton University Press, 2009), 29–30; see also Tom Sandqvist, *Dada East: The Romanians of Cabaret Voltaire* (Cambridge, MA: MIT Press, 2005).

39. Codrescu also observes how "the revolutionary avantgarde of the 20th century was in large measure the work of provincial East-European Jews." While it is beyond the current focus of this study, the influence of Jewish cultural participation based on a "centuries-long experience of directed study and self-directed humor" should not be overlooked in the development of a European avant-garde. See Codrescu, *Posthuman Dada Guide,* 170, 173.

40. Latin American modernists like José Martí, Cesar Vallejo, Vicente Huidobro, Gabriela Mistral, and Pablo Neruda present yet another politicized tradition of poetic engagement that differs significantly from Anglo-American modernist commitments. Colonization, imperialism, Catholicism, and race are often addressed through a complex aesthetic that draws inspiration from local cultural identities, social and political revolution, and European literary traditions.

41. Cary Nelson, *Repression and Recovery: Modern American Poetry and the Politics of Cultural Memory, 1910–1945* (Madison: University of Wisconsin Press, 1989), 11.

42. Nelson, *Repression and Recovery,* 19.

43. Harrington, *Poetry and the Public,* 13.

44. Ibid.

45. See, for instance, Maria Damon's *Dark End of the Street: Margins in American Vanguard Poetry* (Minneapolis: University of Minnesota Press, 1993).

46. Some key texts in studies of the public sphere include Habermas's *The Structural Transformation of the Public Sphere: An Inquiry into a Category of Bourgeois Society,* trans. Thomas Burger, Studies in Contemporary German Social Thought (Cambridge, MA: MIT Press, 1991); Hannah Arendt's *The Human Condition* (Chicago: University of Chicago Press, 1998); Charles Taylor's presentation of the public sphere as an element of contemporary social formations in *Modern Social Imaginaries* (Durham, NC: Duke University Press, 2004); Gerard A. Hauser's emphasis on discursive practices in *Vernacular Voices: The Rhetoric of Publics and Public Spheres* (Columbia: University of South Carolina Press, 1999); and the collection of essays edited by Craig Calhoun, *Habermas and the Public Sphere* (Cambridge, MA: MIT Press, 1993).

47. For Jeffrey Walker, "'epideictic' appears as that which shapes and cultivates the basic codes of value and belief by which a society or culture lives; it shapes the ideologies and imageries with which, and by which, the individual members of a community identify themselves; and, perhaps most significantly, it shapes the fundamental grounds, the 'deep' commitments and presuppositions, that will underlie and ultimately determine decision and debate in particular pragmatic forums." See Walker, *Rhetoric and Poetics in Antiquity,* 9; see also Sharon Crowley, *Toward a Civil Discourse: Rhetoric and Fundamentalism* (Pittsburgh: University of Pittsburgh Press, 2006), 73.

48. See Kenneth Burke, "Definition of Man," in *Language as Symbolic Action: Essays on Life, Literature, and Method* (Berkeley: University of California Press, 1966), 3–24. Burke has christened "man . . . the symbol-using animal," and looks at human capacities to narrate motives, translating them into "symbolic action." Many narratives, in this sense, compete on the symbolic marketplace, too, for our identification: historical and patriotic narratives often are used during periods of international conflict; the narrative that America brings democracy to the world also has played an important role in recent years; the narrative of American innocence after the September 11, 2001, attacks has captivated attention, too. Popular music, film, television, print, and online opinion spaces all contribute narratives that enhance certain ideological threads.

49. See Lester Faigley, "Rhetorics Fast and Slow," in *Rhetorical Agendas: Political, Ethical, Spiritual,* ed. Patricia Bizzell (Mahwah, NJ: Erlbaum, 2005), 3–9.

50. See Terrence Des Pres's pursuit of poetry and politics that begins with an account of how the political is an intrusion into the subjective experience of the poet. For more of his insightful analysis on modernist poetry, see *Praises and Dispraises: Poetry and Politics, the Twentieth Century* (New York: Viking Penguin, 1988).

51. While he is largely critical of Nancy Fraser's discussions of subaltern counterpublics, Michael Warner argues convincingly that a "counterpublic maintains at

some level, conscious or not, an awareness of its subordinate status. The cultural horizon against which it marks itself off is not just a general or wider public but a dominant one." Moreover, he maintains that "the discourse that constitutes [the subaltern counterpublic] is not merely a different or alternative idiom but one that in other contexts would be regarded with hostility or with a sense of indecorousness" (119). The emphasis on community and coterie in the formation of postwar American "schools" of poetry often creates arguments that appeal to in-group positions on art and culture, but that rarely invent possibilities to shape those appeals for other public alternatives. The Language School arguably provides one of the most recent examples. Insofar as Ron Silliman, Charles Bernstein, and others confront "Official Verse Culture" from their subaltern positions, little opportunity exists for a broader public understanding of their arguments. And while Language Poetry has received greater institutional acceptance in the last decade, Bernstein and others still maintain a subaltern stance in their claims against mainstream American literature. For more see Warner, *Publics and Counterpublics,* 114–24; Bernstein's "State of the Art," in *A Poetics* (Cambridge, MA: Harvard University Press, 1992), 1–8; Ron Silliman's *The New Sentence* (New York: Roof Books, 1987); and Marjorie Perloff, "A Conversation with Charles Bernstein," at the Electronic Poetry Center, hosted by SUNY-Buffalo, available at http://epc.buffalo.edu/authors/perloff/articles/mp_cb.html, accessed September 13, 2010.

52. Malcolm Gladwell has made a career in popular culture by showing how individual enthusiasms and interests compel large-scale "contagions" that spread products, ideas, and events from small communities to larger groups. See *The Tipping Point: How Little Things Can Make a Big Difference* (New York: Back Bay Books, 2002).

53. *Scale shifts* or *scale jumps* are terms used by cultural geographers to describe spatial and temporal shifts of scale in social space. Jules Boykoff, for example, looks at how Martin Luther King Jr., jumped scales to increase awareness of civil rights issues from a congregational space to a larger national arena. He also discusses how the FBI actively worked to reduce King's ability to shift scale. For more on scale shifts, see Jules Boykoff, "Surveillance, Spatial Compression, and Scale: The FBI and Martin Luther King Jr," *Antipode: A Radical Journal of Geography* 39 (September 2007), available at http://www.blackwellsynergy.com.ezproxy.lib.utexas.edu/action/showFullText?submitFullText=Full+Text+HTML&doi=10.1111%2Fj.1467-8330.2007.00549.x, accessed April 7, 2008; and Neil Brenner, *New State Spaces: Urban Governance and the Rescaling of Statehood* (Oxford: Oxford University Press, 2004).

54. Robert Duncan and Denise Levertov, *The Letters of Robert Duncan and Denise Levertov,* ed. Robert J. Bertholf and Albert Gelpi (Stanford, CA: Stanford University Press, 2004), 669.

55. For the importance of "circulation" in the categorical constitution of a public sphere, see Warner, *Publics and Counterpublics,* 90–114.

56. William Carlos Williams first uses "field of action" to denote a rhetorical poetry in "The Poem as a Field of Action" (1948). In *Selected Essays* (New York: New Directions, 1969).

Chapter 1

1. Olson's presence continues to influence civic reflection in Gloucester, as a recent article indicates. See Gail McCarthy, "Charles Olson Today: 20th-Century Gloucester Poet Remains Relevant into the 21st Century," *Gloucester Daily Times*, December 31, 2008, at http://www.gloucestertimes.com/pulife/local_story_366210543 .html, accessed August 29, 2009; see also *Polis Is This: Charles Olson and the Persistence of Place*, 2008, DVD, directed by Henry Ferrini; and finally, the celebration of the centenary of Olson's birth was held in Gloucester October 3–10, 2010, with many poets, including Diane di Prima, and town citizens in attendance at readings, panels, and lectures dedicated to the poet's civic and literary contributions.

2. Olson's public example, moreover, shows how poetry can contribute to civic discourse in ways unanticipated by Jürgen Habermas in his critiques of the public sphere: rational-critical discourse, as I hope Olson's case illustrates, rests on interventions and performative encounters by communal actors who shape deliberative debate. Modality especially provides values, coloration, and potentiality to deepen descriptions of deliberative situations. Modality also requires interventions of gesture and surprise that can quicken the sensitive process of reason, making critical engagement flexible while reorienting reason away from adherences to formal procedures. For Nancy S. Struever, "there is a deep compatibility between the very specific analytic techniques rhetoric must develop to fulfill the demands of persuasion, the core political functions, and the very general commitment to the modality of possibility as the domain of rhetorical duty. There is a beneficial interactivity of modal proclivity and analytic habits that energises; it is profoundly non-dismissive." Olson fulfills this sense of "rhetorical duty" by flexing certain civic potentials through nonprogrammatic strategies of poetic encounter. See Struever, *Rhetoric, Modality, Modernity*, 7.

3. See Struever, "From Early to Late Modernity," in *Rhetoric, Modality, Modernity*, 82.

4. Charles Olson, "The Song and Dance of," in *The Maximus Poems* (Berkeley: University of California Press, 1985), 58.

5. Edward Dorn, "Dismissal," in *Way More West: New and Selected Poems* (New York: Penguin Books, 2007), 292.

6. Michael Davidson, *Guys Like Us: Citing Masculinity in Cold War Poetics* (Chicago: University of Chicago Press, 2004), 20.

7. Davidson, *Guys Like Us*, 20.

8. Ibid., 21–22.

9. In "A Lustrum for You, E. P.," Olson writes: "There is a court / where order, traitor / —you stood with the lovers of ORDER" (5). This correlates with

Catherine Seelye's editorial presentation of Olson who, at the time of his meeting with Pound, "had been actively involved in public life for several years," taking on roles as chief of the Foreign Language Information Service of the Common Council for American Unity in New York, as assistant chief, Foreign Language Division, Office of War Information (OWI) in Washington, DC (1942), and as foreign nationalities director of the Democratic National Committee (1944). Seelye argues that "Olson's own inherent sympathies and understanding of the problems encountered by ethnic groups were strengthened by his work in Washington." His "identification of himself with minorities made impossible any lasting bond between Pound and himself" (xviii–xix). For more on Olson's political disagreements with Pound, see both the collection of responses to his visits with the elder poet and Catherine Seelye's introduction in *Charles Olson & Ezra Pound: An Encounter at St. Elizabeths,* ed. Catherine Seelye (New York: Paragon House, 1991); for a literary comparison, see also Robert von Hallberg, "Olson's Relation to Pound and Williams," *Contemporary Literature* 15 (Winter 1974): 15–48, available at http://www.jstor.org/stable/1207708, accessed September 14, 2010.

10. See Boykoff, "Surveillance," for ways in which rhetors shift the scale of their influence from small groups to larger communication platforms in postwar society.

11. Olson turned this offer down in a February 5, 1963, letter to Weld, saying that "it is wholly attractive, and valuable to me . . . but the terrible fact is that I am like a creature swimming in bloody water and haven't been able for some time to catch up with what I have to do (even what I must do) and until something happens I don't dare commit myself or involve myself." Weld responded, saying that he "in no way" wants "to add blood to your water," and left the offer open to Olson for future consideration. It is indeed interesting that Weld sought Olson's presence for his paper, and equally compelling that Olson desired to remain focused on his literary pursuits. See David Rich, ed., *Charles Olson: Letters Home, 1949–1969* (Gloucester: Cape Ann Museum, 2010), 94–95.

12. By contrast to Olson, other editorials of the period expressed concerns over the fishing industry, religion, alcoholism, and the arts, usually occupying no more than a half page of print space or less. See *Gloucester Daily Times,* editorial section, December 1965.

13. See a reprint of the November 30, 1965, article announcing the destruction of the house in Charles Olson, *Maximus to Gloucester: The Letters and Poems of Charles Olson to the Editor of the Gloucester Daily Times, 1962–1969,* ed. Peter Anastas (Gloucester: Ten Pound Island Book Company, 1992), 90.

14. Olson, *Maximus to Gloucester,* 87.

15. Ibid., 88.

16. Ibid., 91.

17. Ibid., 88–89.

18. Peter Anastas, writing in a December 7, 1965, letter to Charles Olson about his "scream," claims: "This is a far cry from the sonnets of the *Tribune* and the

flower poems of the little old ladies the *Herald* used to run. And I wonder if any paper in the country would do what the *Times* has done. . . . It would seem to me that you have space for the asking there and that this is more valuable in a way than attending Council meetings and making the usual, small, half-assed protests the Historical Soc. people make against the Grant Circle shopping center. Maximus must say SOMETHING about *that*." Significantly, Anastas also responds to Olson as an engaged town citizen, not as a literary figure, and writes: "I come . . . not as a reader to a poet in the sanctuary of HIS book, his ground which I have to accept and gain admission to (if not as a votary at least as, what, initiate). Instead I open the pages of a newspaper and suddenly Maximus is in the public stream, among the clothing ads and the Viet cong [*sic*] and the cake recipes and dear abbey and the movie bill. And Maximus not only commands attention by the force of his language but BELONGS in there with all the rest, is not, it seems to me, out of place but rather very immediate, generating the tension of the news or actuality, yet *not*—and this I really believe—ephemeral as news or the newspaper which you read quickly one day and wrap a fish in the next." For Anastas, the experience of reading Olson in the paper transformed the poem: "it was not poetry at all—not verse: it was news." Anastas's enthusiastic response provides some insight to the effect of reading Olson at the time, and the excitement his words could generate for some readers. See Rich, *Letters Home,* 115.

19. Olson, *Maximus to Gloucester,* 89.

20. Ibid., 88–90.

21. Ibid., 90.

22. Ibid., 91.

23. Ibid.

24. See Olson's essay, "Projective Verse" (1950), in *Collected Prose,* ed. Donald Allen and Benjamin Friedlander (Berkeley: University of California Press, 1997), 15–26.

25. Cape Ann historian Joseph E. Garland (b. 1922) frequently corresponded with Olson in the 1960s and both competed, as David Rich notes, "over the same set of Gloucester-based source materials" in their extensive research. At one point both men considered working together on the republication of John J. Babson's 1860 *History of the Town of Gloucester.* Significantly, in the *Gloucester Daily Times,* Garland contributed reflections about Olson after his death, reminiscing on the poet's public presence: "A year has passed since Charles Olson passed from among us, but I see him now in my mind's eye, stalking the streets in his odd raiment of capes and shawls and sweaters, throwing his huge arm over my shoulder, all rambling talk and rumbling laughter." He adds, "Olson was too big for us. Gloucester was too big for him." See Rich, *Letters Home,* 121–39.

26. Books available by Garland include *Down to the Sea: The Fishing Schooners of Gloucester* (Boston: David R. Godine, 2000); *Gloucester on the Wind: America's Greatest Fishing Port in the Days of Sail* (Mount Pleasant, SC: Arcadia Publishing, 1995); *Lone Voyager: The Extraordinary Adventures of Howard Blackburn Hero Fisherman of Glou-*

cester (New York: Touchstone, 1998); and others. For more on Garland's relationship to Olson and Gloucester, see Rich, *Letters Home*, 121–23.

27. Olson, *Maximus to Gloucester*, 93.

28. Ibid. 96.

29. Ibid.

30. Ibid.

31. Ibid.

32. Ibid., 93–94.

33. Ibid., 94.

34. Ibid.

35. See *Longinus*, "'Longinus' on the Sublime," trans. W. Hamilton Fyfe (1927), Loeb Classical Library (Cambridge, MA: Harvard University Press, 1982), 121–256.

36. Olson, *Maximus to Gloucester*, 103.

37. Olson, *Collected Prose*, 246.

38. Ibid., 17. Note also that for Olson "geography" replaces Pound's "culture" as the motivation for public engagement.

39. Anne Day Dewey provides a genealogy of "field poetics," looking particularly at ways in which Olson, Dorn, Levertov, Duncan, and others interpreted social agency. She traces their shift from a sense of value in individual agency toward a more environmental and cultural construction of agency through the writings of Henry and Brooks Adams. The former, in particular, in the essay, "The Virgin and the Dynamo," introduces a notion of agency originating in the material world. This essay, Dewey claims, significantly influenced the modernist tradition. See Anne Dewey, *Beyond Maximus: The Construction of Public Voice in Black Mountain Poetry* (Stanford, CA: Stanford University Press, 2007), 17–43.

40. Jeffrey Walker discusses traditions of an American literary sublime that begins with Emerson and Whitman, and that influences the development of modernist verse through Williams, Pound, Olson, and others. See "Prospects" and "The Rhetoric of 1855" in *Bardic Ethos*, 1–33.

41. Olson, *Maximus to Gloucester*, 94.

42. Ibid.

43. Ibid., 95.

44. Ibid.

45. Ibid.

46. Ibid., 96.

47. Ibid., 99–100.

48. Ibid., 68.

49. Ibid., 100.

50. Michael Davidson discusses Olson's masculinist rhetoric in relation to Cold War literary communities in "Compulsory Homosociality: Charles Olson, Jack Spicer, and the Gender of Poetics," *Guys Like Us*, 28–48.

51. Olson, *Maximus to Gloucester*, 110.

52. Ibid., 109.

53. Ibid., 109–10.

54. Ibid., 110.

55. Ibid., 103.

56. Peter Anastas, April 7, 2008, e-mail correspondence with Dale M. Smith.

57. Olson, *Maximus to Gloucester,* 105–6.

58. For more on this civic debate, see Anastas's editorial comments in Olson, *Maximus to Gloucester,* 106–7.

59. Olson, *Maximus to Gloucester,* 113–14.

60. Ibid., 114.

61. Ibid., 115.

62. Olson, however, was careful in how he imagined his civic engagement as something quite distinct from other literary endeavors. In a February 27, 1966, letter to Weld, he withdrew a poem he had previously submitted, stating: "I am trying to figure out how to act, now that I am back in Gloucester, in terms of the existence of *The Times,* and it seems to me that a pure poem, such as that one is, imposes rather than contributes to that use." See Rich, *Letters Home,* 103.

63. See Walker, *Bardic Ethos,* 203–35.

64. Olson's student, George F. Butterick, edited the final book of *Maximus* after Olson's death in 1970. While he chose not to include the poems and letters to the *Gloucester Daily Times* in his edition of the *Maximus Poems,* doing so would significantly change the context for understanding the final years of Olson's writing, revealing an active public side that complements the inward address of the other poems.

65. Olson, *The Maximus Poems,* 559.

66. See Richard Murphy, *Theorizing the Avant-Garde: Modernism, Expressionism, and the Problem of Postmodernity* (Cambridge: Cambridge University Press, 1998), 11.

67. Olson, *The Maximus Poems,* 628.

Chapter 2

1. Burke, *A Rhetoric of Motives,* 60 (Burke's emphasis). While agonism often produces negative connotations that associate with aggression and hostility, Burke uses the term as a necessary component of civic engagement. As Patricia Roberts-Miller also points out, "Advocates of agonism" like Hannah Arendt, "insist that a confrontational method of public discourse may be the best way to prevent tyranny and totalitarianism, to ensure that injustices are discussed." For Roberts-Miller (and Arendt), democracies thrive best under agonistic models of argumentation: totalitarian societies, by contrast, greatly discourage confrontations in agonistic discourse. See Patricia Roberts-Miller, *Deliberate Conflict: Argument, Political Theory, and Composition Classes* (Carbondale: Southern Illinois University Press), 121–25.

2. Burke, *Rhetoric of Motives,* 60.

3. Ibid.

4. Ibid., 269.

5. Ibid.

6. Ibid., 270.

7. Ibid.

8. This will be especially relevant in chapter 4 when looking at the poets involved with Poetry Is Public Art (PIPA), but there is also a strong resonance between Duncan and Levertov's Vietnam War protests and the sardonic textual engagements over race, civil rights, and social values addressed by Lorenzo Thomas and Edward Dorn in chapter 3.

9. For an evaluation of the literary strategies and significance of the correspondence, see Marjorie Perloff, "Poetry in Time of War," in *Poetry On and Off the Page: Essays for Emergent Occasions* (Evanston: Northwestern University Press, 1998), 210; and for a discussion of agency in the poetics of Duncan and Levertov, see Anne Day Dewey, *Beyond Maximus: The Construction of Public Voice in Black Mountain Poetry* (Stanford, CA: Stanford University Press, 2007), 113–54.

10. Denise Levertov, "Politics and the Poet: An Interview with Denise Levertov," conducted by E. G. Burrows (1968), in *Conversations with Denise Levertov,* ed. Jewel Spears Brooker (Oxford: University Press of Mississippi, 1998), 30–31.

11. See Michael S. Foley, *Confronting the War Machine: Draft Resistance during the Vietnam War* (Chapel Hill: University of North Carolina Press, 2003), 194–249.

12. See "The Draft: Doctor's Dilemma," *Time* magazine, January 12, 1968, at http://www.time.com/time/magazine/article/0,9171,837647,00.html, accessed August 16, 2009.

13. See Boykoff, "Surveillance."

14. Perloff, *Poetry On and Off the Page,* 210.

15. Denise Levertov, *To Stay Alive* (New York: New Directions, 1971), viii (Levertov's emphasis).

16. Levertov, *To Stay Alive,* viii–ix.

17. Ibid., 13–14 (Levertov's emphasis).

18. Ibid., 17.

19. Ibid., 17–18.

20. Ibid., 14.

21. Anne Dewey, by contrast, argues that such appeal by pathos establishes a "distinction between private and public spheres." See "Poetic Authority and the Public Sphere of Politics in the Activist 1960s: The Duncan-Levertov Debate," in *Robert Duncan and Denise Levertov: The Poetry of Politics, the Politics of Poetry* (Stanford, CA: Stanford University Press, 2006), 118: "Although the collage notebook form of 'Staying Alive' implies Levertov's belief in a liberal democratic public form, the development of the poem's narrative and imagery expresses her growing difficulty in embracing such a conception of the public sphere. In setting her own memories, letters, and poetry in dialogue with those of other specifically named protesters and politicians, Levertov represents political advocacy as a debate among autonomous individuals on the model of face-to-face community. Even as the poem records her increasing exhaustion and despair in dedication to long-term

activism, it continues to assert the distinction between private and public spheres, 'daily life' and 'history,' and to project their ideal 'meshing' in 'song.'" The point I wish to add, however, is that Levertov's representation of political advocacy runs into rhetorical problems that can subvert her political will. By speaking to activists and reinforcing their agenda at the expense of a tuned-out middle America, it's unlikely that Levertov's arguments will reach beyond the activist community to invite further public possibilities.

22. Levertov, *To Stay Alive,* 45.

23. Ibid., 46. This list also corresponds with certain public goals of PIPA that will be examined in chapter 4.

24. See Perloff, *Poetry On and Off the Page,* 212, for her discussion of revolution, the avant-garde, and community.

25. Duncan and Levertov, *Letters,* 530.

26. Ibid., 532.

27. Ibid.

28. Ibid., 563.

29. Ibid.

30. Ibid.

31. Ibid., 607.

32. Ibid., 740–41.

33. See Michael Davidson's examination of Cold War communities, cultural values, and masculinity in "Compulsory Homosociality," in *Guys Like Us,* 28–48. My consideration of the rhetorical and cultural contexts for Duncan's response to Levertov is in part derived from Davidson's work, as well as from Judith Butler's arguments regarding the performativity of gender in social and cultural contexts in *Gender Trouble: Feminism and the Subversion of Identity* (New York: Routledge, 1999).

34. The long association of rhetoric with witchcraft is seen early in the Sophist Gorgias's relation of rhetoric and incantation: "Sacred incantations sung with words are bearers of pleasure and banishers of pain, for, merging with opinion in the soul, the power for the incantation is wont to beguile it and persuade it and alter it by witchcraft." In the Socratic dialogue, *Gorgias,* Socrates observes that oratory appears as "something supernatural in scope." As Plato relates it, rhetoric is "a knack" and "a shameful thing." For more on Plato's debate between rhetoric and philosophy, see "Gorgias," 456a; 462c; and 463d. See also "Gorgias' Encomium of Helen," in *The Older Sophists,* ed. Rosamond Kent Sprague (Indianapolis: Hackett Publishing, 2001), 10.

35. See Robert J. Bertholf, "Decision at the Apogee," in Gelpi and Bertholf, eds., *Poetry of Politics,* 1–17, on Duncan's experience with anarchist movements and political philosophies.

36. See Dewey, *Beyond Maximus,* 147–54, for a discussion of the relation of public voice to poetic agency in Duncan and Levertov's poetry.

37. See Davidson, "Compulsory Homosociality," 28–48.

38. Duncan and Levertov, *Letters,* 610 (Duncan's emphasis).

39. Ibid., 611.

40. Aaron Shurin, "The People's P★★★k," in Gelpi and Bertholf, eds., *Poetry of Politics,* 74.

41. For instance, Students for a Democratic Society first used the slogan in the early 1960s, though it became more important to the feminist movement after the publication of Carol Hanisch's 1969 essay, "The Personal Is Political," originally presented in *Notes from the Second Year: Women's Liberation: Major Writings of the Radical Feminists,* edited and published by Shulamith Firestone and Anne Koedt (New York: Pamphlet, 1970). Hanisch, in a 2006 reflection on the influential essay, observes that it "was written in reply . . . to Dottie Zellner, who contended that consciousness-raising was just therapy and questioned whether the new independent WLM [women's liberation movement] was really 'political.'" Moreover, "this was not an unusual reaction to radical feminist ideas in early 1969. WLM groups had been springing up all over the country—and the world. The radical movements of Civil Rights, Anti-Vietnam War, and Old and New Left groups from which many of us sprang were male dominated and very nervous about women's liberation in general, but especially the spectre of the mushrooming independent women's liberation movement, of which I was a staunch advocate." Hanisch notes too that the term "'political' was used here in the broad sense of the word as having to do with power relationships, not the narrow sense of electorial [*sic*] politics." While the main arguments of the essay respond to the internal political organization and claims among leftist activists and feminists, Hanisch's insistence that consciousness raising is an important political tool correlates with the possibilities enacted by modal rhetorics. "Consciousness raising," reinforcements of images, claims, and feelings, along with performances, gestures, and forms of acting out can contribute to new perspectives and political realizations. See Carol Hanisch, "The Personal Is Political: The Women's Liberation Movement Classic with a New Explanatory Introduction," available at http://www.carolhanisch.org/CHwritings/PIP.html, accessed September 26, 2010. Alice Echols also observes how "the notion that the 'personal is political' owes a lot to the radical sociologist C. Wright Mills and the New Leftist Tom Hayden, who popularized Mills's insight. If women's liberation was preoccupied with the psychological dimensions of power, this was to some extent because the early New Left was as well. Even consciousness-raising, feminism's most effective organizing tool, was imported into the women's movement by left-wing veterans of the civil rights movement. And the New Left's antipathy toward capitalism was built into the DNA of socialist feminism and early radical feminism." See Echols's review of *The Feminist Promise: 1792 to the Present,* by Christine Stansell, in *Women's Review of Books* 27 (September/October 2010): 8.

42. See Mikhail Bakhtin, *Rabelais and His World,* trans. Helene Iswolsky (Bloomington: Indiana University Press, 1984).

43. Shurin, "People's P★★★k," 74–75 (Shurin's emphasis).

44. The "People's Prick" situation resembles ways, also in public sphere literature, in which the perspectives of women can be dismissed too readily. I am thinking specifically of Michael Warner's response to Nancy Fraser's arguments on behalf of the notion of subaltern counterpublics, and how the queering of the public sphere can produce its own alienation of feminist subaltern perspectives. See Warner, *Publics and Counterpublics,* 118–19.

45. Michael Davidson, *The San Francisco Renaissance: Poetics and Community at Mid-Century* (Cambridge: Cambridge University Press, 1989), 172.

46. Jack Spicer, "For Joe," in *The Collected Books of Jack Spicer,* ed. Robin Blaser (Los Angeles: Black Sparrow Press, 1975), 62.

47. Denise Levertov, "Hypocrite Women," in *O Taste and See* (New York: New Directions, 1964), 70.

48. See Davidson, *Guys Like Us;* also see his description of Spicer's offensive reading to Levertov in *San Francisco Renaissance,* 172–73. For a response to male attempts to limit feminist actions in activist communities, see Hanisch, "The Personal Is Political."

49. Duncan and Levertov, *Letters,* 666.

50. Ibid.

51. See Graça Capinha, "Robert Duncan and the Question of Law," in Gelpi and Bertholf, eds., *Poetry of Politics,* 18–31, for insight to how Duncan's study of medieval jurisprudence led him to understand that "the social is religious." For him, Capinha argues, "the process of social construction is ritualistic, and thus sacred in that it means the survival of community."

52. Duncan and Levertov, *Letters,* 673.

53. Ibid., 672–73.

54. Ibid., 667.

55. Ibid., 661.

56. Ibid., 668.

57. Ibid., 669.

58. Ibid.

59. Ibid., 670.

60. Ibid.

61. Ibid.

62. Ibid., 699, 715.

63. Ibid., 675.

64. In Letter 453 Levertov's frustration with Duncan comes to a head, and her angry response seems justified. She writes: "*Taste:* You object to the word, the concept; yet you (to a degree you must surely be unaware of) set yourself up as an Arbiter of Taste. When do you ever ask, 'What do you think? Do you like . . . ? What do you feel about . . . ?' or say, 'It seems to me that . . .'? These forms of address are alien to you because you have so long set yourself up as The Authority, stating your opinions as unquestionable dogmas, de haut en bas" (675). Here, Levertov

demands rhetorical responsibility from Duncan. It is interesting also that Duncan, at least to Levertov, takes a rhetorical position against "taste," and yet enacts a kind of belletristic attitude toward her in his letters, presenting himself as an authority rather than a participant in conversations.

65. Duncan and Levertov, *Letters,* 677.

66. Ibid., 678.

67. See Donald Allen's *New American Poetry: 1945–1960* (Berkeley: University of California Press, 1999).

68. Allen Ginsberg's "Howl" shows one use of poetry in the 1950s that attempted to describe the political and social situation of a community of artists, writers, and others who rejected the Cold War cultural values of postwar America. By confronting a public space dominated by state and corporate interests with a communal notion of social rebellion, Ginsberg and others brought an agonistic and politically conscious poetry to popular audiences.

69. Duncan and Levertov, *Letters,* 679.

70. Ibid., 680.

71. Ibid., 666.

72. Ibid., 697.

73. Robert Duncan, *Bending the Bow* (New York: New Directions, 1968), iii.

74. Duncan, *Bending,* v.

75. Duncan's arguments are similar in ways to Kenneth Burke, particularly his understanding of literature as rhetorical discourse that provides "*strategies* for dealing with *situations*" through "perspective by incongruity." See "Literature as Equipment for Living," in *The Philosophy of Literary Form* (Berkeley: University of California Press, 1973).

76. Duncan, *Bending,* 71–72.

77. Ibid., 81.

78. Ibid., 81–82.

79. Robert Duncan, *Groundwork: Before the War ★ In the Dark,* ed. Robert J. Bertholf and James Maynard (New York: New Directions, 2006), 79.

80. Levertov suggests as much in "TO R. D., MARCH 4th, 1988," a poem written only a few weeks after his death:

You were my mentor. Without knowing it,
I outgrew the need for a mentor.
Without knowing it, you resented that,
and attacked me. I bitterly resented
the attack, and without knowing it
freed myself to move forward
without a mentor. Love and long friendship
corroded, shrank, and vanished from sight
into some underlayer of being.

As the poem continues, they meet in Levertov's dream inside a church, where they reunite in a "reality our foolish pride extinguished." There, Levertov writes, "I had no need / for a mentor, nor you to be one; / but I was once more / your chosen sister, and you / my chosen brother" (754–55).

81. See Anne Waldman's title poem in *Manatee/Humanity* (New York: Penguin, 2009); Amiri Baraka's "Somebody Blew Up America," available at http://www .amiribaraka.com/blew.html, accessed February 28, 2011; and Clayton Eshleman, "The Assault," Poetry Foundation, available at http://www.poetryfoundation.org/ harriet/2008/09/clayton-eshleman-on-911/, accessed February 28, 2011.

Chapter 3

1. Habermas describes the significance of printed media in the formation of public opinion in eighteenth- and early nineteenth-century salons and coffee houses, noting how, finally, only in 1803 were journalists legally allowed into the House of Commons to report on the debates and proceedings of government. (See *Structural Transformation of the Public Sphere,* 57–73.) Today it is difficult to understand contemporary media as a public vehicle in the sense Habermas describes. The concentration of media ownership has created a situation now where six companies, including General Electric, Time/Warner, and Walt Disney, control nearly all of the traditional broadcast resources. Efforts are underway in Congress, moreover, to restrict the comparatively more open features of Internet bandwidth. See Freepress's "Ownership Chart," at http://www.freepress.net/ownership/chart/main, accessed October 23, 2010; and for recent efforts by the FCC to exert authority to set broadband policy, see Amy Schatz, "FCC Split as It Launches Internet Regulation Effort," *Wall Street Journal,* June 18, 2010, available at http://online.wsj.com/ article/SB10001424052748704289504575312742566475122.html?mod=WSJ_hpp _MIDDLETopStories, accessed October 23, 2010.

2. For more on the sensory experience of television and electronic media on viewers, see Marshall McLuhan, *The Medium Is the Massage* (Berkeley: Ginko Press, 2005); Walter Ong, "The Shifting Sensorium," in *The Varieties of Sensory Experience: A Sourcebook in the Anthropology of the Senses,* ed. David Howes (Toronto: University of Toronto Press, 1991), 47–60; and more recently, Nicholas Carr, *The Shallows: What the Internet Is Doing to Our Brains* (New York: W. W. Norton, 2010).

3. J. B. Jackson provides a fascinating discussion of American homes and lifestyles based on a study of three different houses from the seventeenth, nineteenth, and mid-twentieth centuries. The home, he argues, modulates a family's needs and mediates social space between privacy and the community. For Jackson, the home results from ongoing changes in definitions of human relationships to particular environments. See "The Westward-Moving House: Three American Houses and the People Who Lived in Them," in *Landscapes: Selected Writings of J. B. Jackson,* ed. Ervin H. Zube (Amherst: University of Massachusetts Press, 1970), 10–42.

4. For more on the legal, moral, and symbolic interactions that impose legibility on society, see Taylor, *Modern Social Imaginaries.*

5. See Michael Warner on the categorical significance of "circulation" in the formation of public space in *Publics and Counterpublics,* 90–114.

6. Filmmaker Werner Herzog argued in a 1970 interview with film critic Roger Ebert that contemporary culture needs to renew its images and its capacities for understanding them. "At the present time," he said, "I think that we do not know very much about the process of vision itself. We know so very little about it, and, with this kind of experimental work that I have been describing, we might soon be able to learn a little bit more. This kind of knowledge is precisely what we need. We need it very urgently because we live in a society that has no adequate images anymore, and, if we do not find adequate images and an adequate language for our civilization with which to express them, we will die out like the dinosaurs. It's as simple as that! We have already recognized that problems like the energy shortage or the overpopulation of the world or the environmental crisis are great dangers for our society and for our kind of civilization, but I think it has not yet been understood widely enough that we also absolutely *need* new images." See Gene Walsh, *Images at the Horizon: A Workshop with Werner Herzog Conducted by Roger Ebert* (Chicago: Facets Multimedia Center, 1979).

7. For more biographical information, see Tom Dent, *Dictionary of Literary Biography, Volume 41: Afro-American Poets since 1955,* ed. Trudier Harris and Thadius M. Davis (Detroit: The Gale Group, 1985), at http://www.writing.upenn.edu/epc/authors/thomas/thomas_gale_essay_2.html, accessed August 10, 2009; see also Aldon Lynn Nielsen, "A New York State of Mind," in *Black Chant: Languages of African-American Postmodernism* (Cambridge: Cambridge University Press, 1997), 146–48.

8. The Black Arts movement was a broad cultural formation that linked art with social change. Initiated by Amiri Baraka, the Black Arts movement associated art with activism as a way to implement social change in areas of New York and Newark in the 1960s and '70s. "One of the goals of the Black Arts movement was the creation of a mass art." See Lorenzo Thomas, "Neon Griot," in *Extraordinary Measures* (Tuscaloosa: The University of Alabama Press, 2000), 197; and Nielsen, *Black Chant,* 78–169.

9. Maria Damon, "Lorenzo Thomas's Literary Historiography." Paper delivered for the Lorenzo Thomas Panel at the American Studies Association Conference, Houston, November 15, 2002, 1–2.

10. See Thomas, *Extraordinary Measures,* 187–218; and *Don't Deny My Name: Words and Music and the Black Intellectual Tradition* (Ann Arbor: University of Michigan Press, 2008).

11. Thomas, *Extraordinary Measures,* 196.

12. Ibid., 197.

13. Ibid.

14. Ibid., 197–98.

15. Ibid., 199–200.

16. Ibid., 200.

17. Ibid., 201.

18. As Thomas argues, "whether or not one is religious, the influence of the black church within the African American community is basic and unavoidable. One can hear the rich, emphatic voice that distinguishes much Black Arts poetry in the speeches of Martin Luther King, Jr. Listening to a recorded sermon such as *I'm into Something I Can't Shake Loose* by W. C. Thomas, Jr., of the Canaan Baptist church in Dayton, Ohio—Paul Laurence Dunbar's hometown—we can experience the full power of the African American sermonic tradition." See Thomas, *Extraordinary Measures,* 203; and see Henry Louis Gates Jr., "The Church," in *Come Sunday: Photographs by Thomas Roma* (New York: Museum of Modern Art, 1996).

19. Thomas, *Extraordinary Measures,* 203.

20. Ibid., 218.

21. Damon, "Historiography," 1–2.

22. Lorenzo Thomas, *The Bathers* (New York: I. Reed Books, 1981).

23. Thomas observes "the psychological dysfunction that [W. E. B.] Du Bois diagnosed as 'double consciousness'" in his introduction to *Extraordinary Measures.* Maria Damon discusses the significance of "double consciousness" further, arguing: "First, the term 'double consciousness,' which W. E. B. Du Bois, borrowing from the language of clinical psychology, intended as a descriptor of pathology, and which intent Thomas echoes in the opening pages of *Extraordinary Measures* by calling it a 'psychological dysfunction,' must be described and documented. It has been given a redemptive twist by recent theorists who point out that double vision, or even multiple perspective, can be an asset when one is trying to understand the whole of a phenomenon, to hear the whole voice, see the whole picture. As much as slavery is the ur-trope of modernity and the plantation the ur-trope of the new world, double consciousness is the mode of seeing and processing the experience of modernity—one that manages a self-as-other consciousness that enables documentation, analysis, and, we hope, reconciliation." See Thomas, *Extraordinary Measures,* 5; and Damon, "Historiography," 4. By contrast, Paul Gilroy considers the philosophical and cultural situation of double consciousness through his reading of Frederick Douglass via Hegel, arguing that "[it] is the slave rather than the master who emerges from Douglass's account possessed of 'consciousness that exists for itself,' while the master becomes representative of a 'consciousness that is repressed within itself.'" See Paul Gilroy, *The Black Atlantic: Modernity and Double-Consciousness* (Cambridge, MA: Harvard University Press, 1993), 60.

24. For a historical account of the Birmingham campaign, see David J. Garrow, *Bearing the Cross: Martin Luther King, Jr., and the Southern Christian Leadership Conference* (New York: Vintage Books, 1988), 236–60.

25. Adam Fairclough, *To Redeem the Soul of America: The Southern Christian Leadership Conference and Martin Luther King, Jr.* (Athens: University of Georgia Press, 1987), 138.

26. Damon, "Historiography," 1–2.

27. Nielsen, *Black Chant*, 155.

28. Thomas, *The Bathers*, 59.

29. Ibid.

30. Nielsen reports that Thomas was influenced by Gerald Massey's *The Book of the Beginnings* and *Egypt the Light of the World,* developing from those a "scribal concept, which parallels both later sub-Saharan African scribal practices and African-American spirit writing, [and] was a writing of the mysteries, a writing of signs that, when pronounced, would bring God into evidence. That scribal concept acknowledges writing as both marker of absence and means of bringing the ineffable into our thoughts. In the title poem of *The Bathers,* Thomas transcribed Egyptian glyphs within the context of present political struggle, writing the present as predicated upon the past of writing. In the act of bringing an ancient African text to bear upon the contemporary and local texts of American racial politics, Thomas reenacted Martin Delany's audacious acts of signifying in his book *The Origin of Races and Color,* when that nineteenth-century writer copies the texts of ancient Africa into his text as a means of contesting the textual power of racist Americans. Delany's text might almost be taken as a sort of Rosetta Stone permitting us to read the unpronounceable hieroglyphs of Thomas's poem within a polyglot context of black writings." See Nielsen, *Black Chant*, 154.

31. Thomas, *The Bathers*, 59–60.

32. See Ishmael Reed, *Mumbo Jumbo* (New York: Scribner, 1996) for more on African American readings of North American history and culture.

33. Thomas, *The Bathers*, 60.

34. Ibid., 61–62.

35. For more on the exhibit and on Warhol's paintings, see Anne M. Wagner, "Warhol Paints History, or, Race in America," *Representations* 55 (Summer 1996): 98–119.

36. For a study of Martin Luther King Jr.'s Birmingham campaign as "image event," with a discussion of responses to Charles Moore's photographs, see Davi Johnson, "Martin Luther King, Jr.'s 1963 Birmingham Campaign as Image Event," *Rhetoric & Public Affairs* 10, no. 1 (2007): 1–26.

37. Wagner, in "Warhol Paints History, or, Race in America," rehearses some of the critical challenges to Warhol's images, asking: "Does Warhol's art expose or reflect the culture it images?" (101). Her compelling response is formulated around an inquiry into the opposing material forms of photography and painting, examining the circulation and representation of images rendered in both. "While I think that Warhol's canvases likewise imagine white viewers, I am less confident that he grasped the complexity of his imagery and its central metaphor," she writes. "He did know that photography was central and why this was the case. Photography not only communicated the image of racism, it gave racism historic form" (113). Although he was politically and socially liberal, "Warhol was caught in the circuitry—the circularity—of racism, more or less despite himself" (114).

38. It is crucial to note that Thomas would have read his work—and circulated it—to large public audiences. He observes how in the 1960s "the poetry of the Black Arts movement was *popular.* It reached a visible and enthusiastic audience even if the movement's leaders tended to exaggerate the proletarian profile of their mostly collegiate following." See *Extraordinary Measures,* 218.

39. Thomas, *The Bathers,* 126.

40. Ibid., 127.

41. Ibid., 129.

42. Ibid., 130.

43. For more on how postwar consumer culture diminishes public and private spheres through tensions between representation and reality, "the sign [and] thing[s] signified," see Guy Debord, *The Society of the Spectacle* (1967; New York: Zone Books, 1995).

44. Despite public outrage at the student deaths, Thomas insists that the accumulation of images like those taken at Kent State shape public feelings with a sense of futile outcome. Images of events reinforce attitudes and beliefs without providing the resolutions and potential satisfactions that can come through deliberation. The passive reception of "news" accumulates without relief for domestic consumption.

45. Lorenzo Thomas, *Dancing on Main Street* (Minneapolis: Coffee House Press, 2004), 113.

46. Thomas, *Dancing on Main Street,* 114.

47. Ibid., 112.

48. Ibid., 96–97.

49. Ibid., 97–98.

50. Ibid., 98.

51. Ibid., 99.

52. Dent, *Dictionary.*

53. Peter Bürger argues that the historical avant-garde attempts to bring about social change, whereas the aesthetic avant-garde isolates artistic experimentation from the social and popular production of language. Jochen Schulte-Sasse, in his introduction to Bürger, argues that the aesthetic avant-garde is invested in epistemology, and therefore issues of truth, whereas the historical avant-garde pursues contingent cultural and historical issues regarding what is right and wrong. Dorn's work, like Lorenzo Thomas's, would associate with this latter sense. See Peter Bürger, *Theory of the Avant-Garde,* trans. Michael Shaw (Minneapolis: University of Minnesota Press, 1984).

54. For a general overview of Dorn's career, see Dale Smith, "Edward Dorn: An Introduction," in *Way More West: New and Selected Poems,* ed. Michael Rothenberg (New York: Penguin Books, 2007), xiii–xvii.

55. Olson, *Collected Prose,* 298.

56. Dorn, *Way More West,* 39.

57. Robert Creeley recalls that "Charles [Olson] spoke of [Dorn] as having an 'Elizabethan ear' years ago and marveled at his grace." See "On Charles Olson,"

Jacket magazine 12 (July 2000), available at http://jacketmagazine.com/12/olson -p-cree.html, accessed November 8, 2010).

58. Dorn, *Way More West,* 91.

59. Edward Dorn, *Interviews,* ed. Donald Allen (Bolinas, CA: Four Seasons, 1980), 106.

60. Edward Dorn, *Abhorrences* (Santa Rosa: Black Sparrow Press, 1990), 62.

61. Edward Dorn, *Ed Dorn Live: Lectures, Interviews, and Outtakes,* ed. Joseph Richey (Ann Arbor: University of Michigan Press, 2007), 70.

62. Struever, *Rhetoric, Modality, Modernity,* 110.

63. See Burke, "Literature as Equipment for Living."

64. For a discussion of Dorn's literary construction of his satiric epigrams from classical and eighteenth-century sources, see Alan Golding, "Dorn's 'Pontificatory Use of the Art,'" in *Internal Resistances: The Poetry of Edward Dorn* (Berkeley: University of California Press, 1985), 212–15.

65. Dorn's work can be seen addressing in many ways what Habermas calls a "culture-consuming public," which came to replace a "culture-debating public." Habermas describes the distinction thus: "Religious academies, political forums, and literary organizations owe their existence to the critical review of a culture worthy of discussion and in need of commentary; radio stations, publishers, and associations have turned the staging of panel discussions into a flourishing secondary business. Thus, discussions seem to be carefully cultivated and there seems to be no barrier to its proliferation. But surreptitiously it has changed in a specific way: it assumes the form of a consumer item." Such a public distinction associates with Dorn's public understanding, and in many ways his work attempts to resolve this by interrupting the habits of a "culture-consuming" public. See Habermas, *Structural Transformation of the Public Sphere,* 159–75.

66. See Dorn, "Correction," in *Ed Dorn Live,* 69–77.

67. Dorn, *Abhorrences,* 15.

68. For a recent estimation and critical response to Dorn's cultural attitudes, see Silliman's Blog, Tuesday, March 20, 2007, at http://ronsilliman.blogspot.com/ 2007/03/for-reader-of-my-generation-collection.html, accessed August 11, 2009, wherein Ron Silliman reviews *Way More West.*

69. Dorn, *Abhorrences,* 174.

70. Dorn, *Ed Dorn Live,* 70–71.

71. For a decade, beginning in June 1981, *Rolling Stock* was a newspaper-style publication that "chronicled the eighties" in terms of social, political, and artistic scenes. Published from Boulder, Colorado, where Dorn taught at the University of Colorado, the journal had many contributing editors and writers, including Duncan McNaughton, Tom Clark, Sidney Goldfarb, Lucia Berlin, Robert Creeley, and others. According to Jennifer Dunbar Dorn, "*Rolling Stock* was a collaborative effort involving our correspondents, artists, writers, art director, student interns, volunteers—too many to mention by name—but it remained a cottage industry endeavor with me at its shaky helm. By now we had about 1,000 subscribers, sev-

eral distributors, and another list of independent bookstores." See Jennifer Dunbar Dorn, "*Rolling Stock:* A Chronicle of the Eighties," *Chicago Review* 49, no. 3/4 and 50, no. 1 (2004): 152–59.

72. Nielsen, *Black Chant,* 146.

Chapter 4

1. For instance, see Jules Boykoff and Kaia Sand, *Landscapes of Dissent: Guerrilla Poetry and Public Space* (Long Beach, CA: Palm Press, 2008).

2. See John Robb, *Brave New War: The Next Stage of Terrorism and the End of Globalization* (Hoboken, NJ: John Wiley and Sons, 2007) for an account of nation-state decline and how nonstate actors are increasingly effective at disrupting global communication and state agendas; Nassim Nicholas Taleb considers the vulnerability of contemporary global culture and markets in *The Black Swan: The Impact of the Highly Improbable* (New York: Random House, 2007); Howard J. Bunker, ed., *Networks, Terrorism, and Global Insurgency* (New York: Routledge, 2005), presents analysis by military strategists on the shifting technological and organizational networks of global warfare where the influence of nation-states is increasingly threatened by terrorists and other nonstate actors; a detailed analysis of the failure of nation-states can be found in Martin van Creveld's *The Rise and Decline of the State* (Cambridge: Cambridge University Press, 1999).

3. Barack Obama's 2008 election suggests that ideological conditions shifted slightly after eight years of Bush administration policy. While causal relations between oppositional views to Bush-era policies and the shift in direction toward Obama's election to the presidency are impossible to locate in this study, I argue that a minority of culture workers in New York and other large cities contributed to the formation of attitudes and beliefs during both Bush administrations. See Malcolm Gladwell's *The Tipping Point* for arguments about the effectiveness of word-of-mouth communication and how the efforts of a few can reach the attention of a majority over time.

4. Certain poems are highlighted in a "Poems for the Month." One poem by Leslie McClintock, featured in January 2009, describes how "fourteen children," in Kabul, "eight to ten / years old, / walking to / school the last / day of term are / blown up / by a suicide bomber." The short lines bring emphasis to each word as the poem relates the horrific incident captured by a "grainy AP photo." By appropriating the image from a photograph, the poet depicts with staccato urgency the scene's horror, identifying for readers "one textbook fanned / open on the road." While the poem persuades readers of the atrocities of war and brings into print the blunt frame of photographic witness, it relies on rhetorical techniques that make present the aftermath of the event, telling readers what most should understand: war's violence brings terrifying consequences. See Leslie McClintock, "Fourteen School Children Murdered in Kabul," Poems of the Month, Poets Against War at

http://poetsagainstthewar.org/displaypoem.asp?AuthorID=67973#453124012, accessed August 17, 2009.

5. Sam Hamill, Poets Against War, at http://www.poetsagainstthewar.org/, accessed August 17, 2009.

6. Hamill, "A Short History of Poets Against War," Poets Against War, at http://www.poetsagainstthewar.org/paw_background.asp, accessed August 17, 2009.

7. Sam Hamill, ed., *Poets Against the War* (New York: Nation Books, 2003).

8. Hamill, PAW, at http://www.poetsagainstthewar.org/whoweare.asp, accessed March 22, 2009.

9. Interestingly, Charles Weatherford's prowar poetry website, Poets For the War, launched in March 2003, is no longer available online, while Hamill's site remains active and, until recently, was growing. See "Pro-War Poetry Website Launched," BBC News, Wednesday, March 5, 2003, available at http://news.bbc.co.uk/2/hi/entertainment/2821455.stm, accessed October 30, 2010.

10. See Warner, *Publics and Counterpublics*, 90–114, for a discussion of circulation as a category of the public sphere. By contrast, Alexander R. Galloway argues for insights to networked computing through the concept of *protocol*. For Galloway, "a computer protocol is a set of recommendations and rules that outline specific technical standards. The protocols that govern much of the Internet are contained in what are called RFC (Request For Comments) documents. . . . [T]hese technical memoranda detail the vast majority of standards and protocols in use on the Internet today" (6). See Alexander R. Galloway, *Protocol: How Control Exists after Decentralization* (Cambridge, MA: MIT Press, 2004).

11. Galloway, *Protocol*, 9.

12. Dale Smith, "Essay on War," Poets Against War, at http://poetsagainstthewar.org/displaypoem.asp?AuthorID=346#453056541, accessed March 21, 2009.

13. It should be noted here, too, that Hamill and Levertov were friends and correspondents for many years. In one essay, "In Her Company: Denise Levertov," *Jacket* magazine 36 (2008), at http://jacketmagazine.com/36/lev-hamill.shtml, accessed March 21, 2009, he writes: "As 'engaged poets,' we shared a common struggle to resist bending one's art to the purpose of mere propagandizing while acknowledging one's politics within the living arts of poetry."

14. For recent discussions of public engagement online, see Barbara Warnick, *Rhetoric Online: Persuasion and Politics on the World Wide Web* (New York: Peter Lang, 2007); and Raley, *Tactical Media*. Malcolm McCullough considers the interaction of machine interfaces with user interactivity and considers the ways pervasive computing are transforming interactions in many types of social environments in *Digital Ground: Architecture, Pervasive Computing, and Environmental Knowing* (Cambridge, MA: MIT Press, 2004).

15. Several important Supreme Court decisions contribute to public forum doctrine, notably culminating in Perry Education Association v. Perry Local Educators' Association, 460 U.S. 37 (1983), where the court established a three-part

categorization of public forums placing restrictions on speech in public spaces. According to Boykoff and Sand, the "three categories of public space" include: "(1) the traditional public forum, (2) the designated public forum, and (3) the non-public forum." Examples of these types of spaces include (1) "streets, sidewalks, and parks," and (2) "college and university meeting facilities, plazas in front of federal buildings, municipal theaters and school meeting rooms." The final category "includes all spaces that don't fall into the prior two categories but are still public property." Examples include "airports," "military bases, prisons and streetlight posts." In these places, "speech acts can be unreservedly regulated by the state, which can apply time, place, and manner restrictions, as long as the regulation on speech is reasonable and not an attempt to squelch expression only because state officials oppose the point of view of the speaker." See Boykoff and Sand, *Landscapes,* 19–22.

16. Boykoff and Sand, *Landscapes,* 21.

17. Ibid., 25–26.

18. Ibid., 31.

19. Ibid., 32.

20. Kristin Prevallet, *Shadow Evidence Intelligence* (New York: Factory School, 2006), 47.

21. See the "disclaimer" appearing in the form of a footnote following this text. It reads: "PIPA officially (but not because there are any officials) denies any allegiance to hierarchy or status within the collective but unidentified mind-which-is-PIPA. There are no members as such of PIPA, and no official spokesperson. This documentation is not to be confused with any official statement. Regardless, YOU are PIPA if you choose to participate in the endeavor to create site-specific poetry interventions into public spaces. Often such interventions are against the law. Check with the particular legal apparatus of your state (if you care) before embracing PIPA. (Which is not an ideology, and therefore cannot be embraced. Only manifested.)" See Prevallet, *Shadow Evidence Intelligence,* 48.

22. Ibid., 47–48.

23. For theoretical perspectives, see discussions of biopolitics and swarm behavior by Michael Hardt and Antonio Negri in *Multitude: War and Democracy in the Age of Empire* (New York: Penguin, 2004). For military theory on the confrontation of states by nonstate actors, see Robb, *Brave.*

24. Prevallet, *Shadow Evidence Intelligence,* 47.

25. "There are plenty of advertising executives," Gladwell notes, "who think that precisely because of the sheer ubiquity of marketing efforts these days, word-of-mouth appeals have become the only kind of persuasion that most of us respond to anymore." See *Tipping Point,* 11, 32.

26. Prevallet, *Shadow Evidence Intelligence,* 49.

27. Ibid., 54.

28. Ibid., 56.

29. Ibid.

30. Ibid.

31. Ibid., 57.

32. Ibid.

33. Ibid., 61.

34. Ibid.

35. Ibid.

36. Ibid., 60.

37. See Perloff, *Poetry On and Off the Page.*

38. The term "resilient communities" is advanced most persuasively by John Robb, whose blog provides informative and practical commentary on community building during the decline of the influence of nation-states. See http:// globalguerrillas.typepad.com/.

39. In "Cultural Criticism and Society," in *Prisms* (Cambridge, MA: MIT Press, 1994), first published in 1951, Adorno makes the claim that *all* poetry is implicated in a kind of cultural "barbarism": "Even the most extreme consciousness of doom threatens to degenerate into idle chatter. Cultural criticism finds itself faced with the final stage of the dialectic of culture and barbarism. To write poetry after Auschwitz is barbaric. And this corrodes even the knowledge of why it has become impossible to write poetry today." In "On Lyric Poetry and Society," in *Notes to Literature,* vol. 1 (1954; New York: Columbia University Press, 1991), Adorno narrows his claim to focus on lyric poetry in particular, arguing that since the Holocaust, such writing is no longer possible in the West.

40. It is worth noting that Levertov's pathos-driven appeals might inspire Adorno's distrust of lyrical poetry in the final half of the twentieth century. Without experiencing the specific suffering of the Vietnamese, she wrote as a witness to their experience in work such as *To Stay Alive.* The discordance between experience and pathetic representation introduces problems of ethos. How do we, as readers, trust the words of a westerner attempting to manipulate the understanding of events for which, say, no witnesses are able to speak out on behalf of their experience? The My Lai massacre, for instance, resists reconciliation by the constructed pathos of a Western lyric strategist. Similarly, images, such as Nick Út's 1972 Pulitzer Prize–winning photograph, taken as Phan Thị Kim Phúc and her siblings fled Trang Bang after a South Vietnamese airstrike dropped napalm on their village, mediate the horrific details of war through the urgency and terror of circumstance. Such photos bear testament and witness to a reality burdened by the imaginary of war. For Adorno, Western lyricism is bound to the subjectivity of the poet and therefore too often exists at a representational distance from the event. The stubborn testament of the camera's lens, however, offers a drama and a tension of motive and suffering that disturbs with visceral urgency: where the lyric might persuade through representation, the war photo resists identification, working instead at the level of drive and desire. For more on affective identification, see Diane Davis in "Identification: Burke and Freud on Who You Are," in *Rhetoric Society Quarterly* 38, no. 2 (2008): 123–47.

41. See Theodor Adorno, *Minima Moralia: Reflections from Damaged Life* (New York: Verso, 1974) for investigations of the moral and psychological problems associated with Western social and economic systems.

42. The readers of contemporary poetry, of course, are numerous and various. Many, including Johnson, use Ron Silliman's problematic phrase "post-avant" to describe contemporary poetry associated with "experimental" strategies of composition rooted in avant-garde aesthetic traditions. Johnson's writing in many ways aims at this audience of "post-avant" readers. See Silliman's Blog, at http://ronsilliman.blogspot.com, for current discussions of "post-avant" poetics.

43. For a discussion of these tendencies in avant-garde art, see Renato Poggioli, *The Theory of the Avant-Garde*, trans. Gerald Fitzgerald (Cambridge, MA: Harvard University Press, 1968), 61–77.

44. Johnson was for many years a railroad mechanic and active member of the Socialist Workers Party; in the 1980s, he worked on two occasions as a literacy teacher in war zones in Sandinista Nicaragua.

45. Johnson also translates modernist poetry from Latin America, and he often points out the differences in avant-garde traditions of Anglophone poetry and the South American adaptations of European modernism, which is usually more socially and politically motivated. His translations with Forrest Gander of the Bolivian poet Jaime Saenz have been recognized by PEN American center, including *The Night* (Princeton, NJ: Princeton University Press, 2007) and *Immanent Visitor* (Berkeley: University of California Press, 2002).

46. Although he publishes work in traditional book formats, he maintains a complicated public presence in the comments sections of many of the most frequented poetry blogs. Such public action online has been read as willful self-promotion, and yet Johnson also remains consistent with his critique of both expressivist and experimental poetry that neglects to engage social conditions.

47. Kent Johnson, *Homage to the Last Avant-Garde* (Exeter: Shearsman Books, 2008).

48. Johnson, *Homage*, 12.

49. Ibid., 15.

50. I do not mean to imply that such complicity is overtly conscious or self-aware on the part of poets and artists in post–World War II US culture. For Adorno, however, the conditions have been such that artists under global capitalism have been able to explore an extraordinary range of meanings and formal possibilities with a great deal of structural support. Kenneth Burke, perhaps says it better, in a brief review of Thomas Mann's trilogy, *Joseph and His Brothers:* "To live by contingencies alone is unquestionably the most comforting way to live—and contented ages have probably been those in which the concepts of duty were wholly of this specific sort, harvesting when the crops were ripe, shearing when the sheep were heavy, and coupling when the body felt the need of its counterbody. But the world of contingencies is now wholly in disarray. In our despicable economic structure, to do the things thus immediately required of us is too often to do despicable things.

It is at such times, I imagine, that the question of duty naturally becomes more generalized, and attempts at defining the 'ultimate vocation' seem most apropos." See Burke, "Permanence and Change," in *The Philosophy of Literary Form: Studies in Symbolic Action* (Berkeley: University of California Press, 1973), 429.

51. Georges Ribémont-Dessaignes quoted in Poggioli, "Agonism and Futurism," *The Theory of the Avant-Garde*, 63.

52. Today, reality shocks with much greater speed and suddenness than art. Since 9/11 we have witnessed wars, occupations, and US-sanctioned torture in the Middle East (with photographs that border on the pornographic), more recently along with shocks to the global financial system. Contemporary avant-garde poetry, Johnson suggests in his work, must move against the spectacles created by contemporary culture. It does this not by shocking bourgeois audiences, but by persuasively revealing other ethical perspectives to them.

53. Johnson, *Homage*, 122.

54. "Enough," statement for a public reading of *Enough: An Anthology of Poetry and Writing against the War*, ed. Rick London and Leslie Scalapino (Berkeley: O Books, 2003), on the website Circulars: Poets and Critics Respond to U.S. Global Policy, at http://www.arras.net/circulars/archives/000253.html#000253, accessed March 21, 2009.

55. As an interesting side note, PAW, which regularly promoted all manner of "anti-war" poetry publications in the wake of the initial promotion of the site, refused to support Johnson's work, even though his poem "Baghdad" had appeared in the selected PAW anthology and had been included as one of the fifteen or so poems featured (from approximately 15,000 at the site) in a special *Monthly Review* journal portfolio. The editors of PAW presumably were taken aback by the "self-critical" reference to PAW in the title poem, which validates much of the poem's critique.

Afterword

1. Struever, *Rhetoric, Modality, Modernity*, 107.

2. "Modernist inquiry," I realize, is not an ideal term. Alan Gilbert reminds us in *Another Future: Poetry and Art in a Postmodern Twilight* (Middletown, CT: Wesleyan University Press, 2006) how even "postmodernity" accounts for literary and artistic practices with little satisfaction. Struever's sense of the dynamic possibilities latent in modernist inquiry, however, invites critical inspection of modernism as dynamic potential. The tensions of modernity necessarily sharpen the back-and-forth between formalist practice and institutional formations on one hand, against heterogeneous proliferation of forms deployed with tactical (and rhetorical) skill on the other. My point here is not to try and resolve these recurring tensions but to acknowledge the controversial terms that orient critical and creative practices in dynamic cultural contexts.

3. Struever, *Rhetoric, Modality, Modernity*, 110.

4. Ibid.

5. Ibid., 112.

6. Ibid., 117.

7. Ibid., 120.

8. Ibid., 124.

9. Because of this "reflexivity," "modal interest perhaps replicates defamiliarization as a critical gesture," and such defamiliarization has, of course, been a standard objective of modernism. See Struever, *Rhetoric, Modality, Modernity,* 127.

10. Des Pres, *Praises and Dispraises,* 225.

Bibliography

Adorno, Theodor W. *Aesthetic Theory.* Translated by C. Lenhardt. 1970. London: Routledge and Kegan Paul, 1984.

———. "Cultural Criticism and Society." In *Prisms.* Translated by Shierry Weber Nicholsen and Samuel Weber. 1951. Cambridge, MA: MIT Press, 1983.

———. *Minima Moralia: Reflections from Damaged Life.* Translated by E. F. N. Jephcott. New York: Verso, 1974.

———. "On Lyric Poetry and Society." In *Notes to Literature.* Vol. 1. Edited by Rolf Teidemann. Translated by Shierry Weber Nicholsen. 1954. New York: Columbia University Press, 1991.

Allen, Donald, ed. *New American Poetry: 1945–1960.* Berkeley: University of California Press, 1999.

Arendt, Hannah. *The Human Condition.* Chicago: University of Chicago Press, 1998.

Aristotle. *On Rhetoric: A Theory of Civic Discourse.* Translated by George A. Kennedy. Oxford: Oxford University Press, 2006.

Armentrout, Rae. *Versed.* Middletown, CT: Wesleyan University Press, 2009.

Arnold, Matthew. "Culture and Anarchy: An Essay in Political and Social Criticism (1867–69)." In *Culture and Anarchy and Other Writings,* edited by Stefan Collini. Cambridge: Cambridge University Press, 1993.

Bakhtin, Mikhail. *Rabelais and His World.* Translated by Helene Iswolsky. Bloomington: Indiana University Press, 1984.

Baraka, Amiri. *Ed Dorn & the Western World.* Austin: Skanky Possum and Effing Press, 2009.

Bernstein, Charles. "Enough." At the website Circulars: Poets and Critics Respond to U.S. Global Policy. Available at http://www.arras.net/circulars/archives/000253.html#000253.

———. "State of the Art." In *A Poetics.* Cambridge, MA: Harvard University Press, 1992.

Bertholf, Robert J. "Decision at the Apogee." In *Robert Duncan and Denise Levertov: The Poetry of Politics, the Politics of Poetry,* edited by Albert Gelpi and Robert J. Bertholf. Stanford, CA: Stanford University Press, 2006.

Boykoff, Jules. "Surveillance, Spatial Compression, and Scale: The FBI and Martin

Luther King Jr." *Antipode: A Radical Journal of Geography* 39 (September 2007). Available at http://www.blackwellsynergy.com.ezproxy.lib.utexas.edu/action/showFullText?submitFullText=Full+Text+HTML&doi=10.1111%2Fj.1467-8330.2007.00549.x.

Boykoff, Jules, and Kaia Sand. *Landscapes of Dissent: Guerrilla Poetry and Public Space.* Long Beach, CA: Palm Press, 2008.

Brenner, Neil. *New State Spaces: Urban Governance and the Rescaling of Statehood.* Oxford: Oxford University Press, 2004.

Brouwer, Daniel C., and Robert Asen. "Introduction: Public Modalities, or the Metaphors We Theorize By." In *Public Modalities: Rhetoric, Culture, Media, and the Shape of Public Life,* edited by Daniel C. Brouwer and Robert Asen. Tuscaloosa: The University of Alabama Press, 2010.

Bunker, Howard J., ed. *Networks, Terrorism, and Global Insurgency.* New York: Routledge, 2005.

Bürger, Peter. *Theory of the Avant-Garde.* Translated by Michael Shaw. Minneapolis: University of Minnesota Press, 1984.

Burke, Kenneth. "Definition of Man." In *Language as Symbolic Action: Essays on Life, Literature, and Method.* Berkeley: University of California Press, 1966.

———. "Literature as Equipment for Living." In *The Philosophy of Literary Form: Studies in Symbolic Action.* Berkeley: University of California Press, 1973.

———. "Permanence and Change." In *The Philosophy of Literary Form: Studies in Symbolic Action.* Berkeley: University of California Press, 1973.

———. *A Rhetoric of Motives.* Berkeley: University of California Press, 1969.

Burnham, Christopher. "Expressive Pedagogy: Practice/Theory, Theory/Practice." In *A Guide to Composition Pedagogies,* edited by Gary Tate, Amy Rupiper, and Kurt Schick. Oxford: Oxford University Press, 2001.

Butler, Judith. *Gender Trouble: Feminism and the Subversion of Identity.* New York: Routledge, 1999.

Calhoun, Craig, ed. *Habermas and the Public Sphere.* Cambridge, MA: MIT Press, 1993.

Capinha, Graça. "Robert Duncan and the Question of Law." In *Robert Duncan and Denise Levertov: The Poetry of Politics, the Politics of Poetry,* edited by Albert Gelpi and Robert J. Bertholf. Stanford, CA: Stanford University Press, 2006.

Carr, Nicholas. *The Shallows: What the Internet Is Doing to Our Brains.* New York: W. W. Norton, 2010.

Casillo, Robert. *The Genealogy of Demons: Anti-Semitism, Fascism, and the Myths of Ezra Pound.* Evanston, IL: Northwestern University Press, 1988.

Codrescu, Andrei. *The Posthuman Dada Guide: Tzara and Lenin Play Chess.* Princeton, NJ: Princeton University Press, 2009.

Creeley, Robert. "On Charles Olson." *Jacket* magazine 12 (July 2000). Available at http://jacketmagazine.com/12/olson-p-cree.html/.

Crowley, Sharon. *Toward a Civil Discourse: Rhetoric and Fundamentalism.* Pittsburgh: University of Pittsburgh Press, 2006.

Damon, Maria. *Dark End of the Street: Margins in American Vanguard Poetry.* Minneapolis: University of Minnesota Press, 1993.

———. "Lorenzo Thomas's Literary Historiography." Paper delivered at the Lorenzo Thomas Panel at the American Studies Association Conference, Houston, November 15, 2002.

D'Arcus, Bruce. *Boundaries of Dissent: Protest and State Power in the Media Age.* New York: Routledge, 1996.

Davidson, Michael. *Guys Like Us: Citing Masculinity in Cold War Poetics.* Chicago: University of Chicago Press, 2004.

———. *The San Francisco Renaissance: Poetics and Community at Mid-Century.* Cambridge: Cambridge University Press, 1989.

Davis, Diane, "Identification: Burke and Freud on Who You Are." *Rhetoric Society Quarterly* 38, no. 2 (2008): 123–47.

Dean, Jodi. "Cyber Salons and Civil Society: Rethinking the Public Sphere in Transnational Technoculture." *Public Culture* 13, no. 2 (2002): 243–65.

———. *Publicity's Secret: How Technoculture Capitalizes on Democracy.* Ithaca, NY: Cornell University Press, 2002.

Debord, Guy. *The Society of the Spectacle.* 1967. New York: Zone Books, 1995.

Deleuze, Gilles. "Postscript on Control Societies." In *Negotiations, 1972–1990.* New York: Columbia University Press, 1995.

Dent, Tom. *Dictionary of Literary Biography, Volume 41: Afro-American Poets since 1955.* Edited by Trudier Harris and Thadius M. Davis. Detroit: The Gale Group, 1985.

Des Pres, Terrence. *Praises and Dispraises: Poetry and Politics, the Twentieth Century.* New York: Viking Penguin, 1988.

Dewey, Anne. *Beyond Maximus: The Construction of Public Voice in Black Mountain Poetry.* Stanford, CA: Stanford University Press, 2007.

———. "Poetic Authority and the Public Sphere of Politics in the Activist 1960s: The Duncan-Levertov Debate." In *Robert Duncan and Denise Levertov: The Poetry of Politics, the Politics of Poetry,* edited by Albert Gelpi and Robert J. Bertholf. Stanford, CA: Stanford University Press, 2006.

Dorn, Edward. *Abhorrences.* Santa Rosa: Black Sparrow Press, 1990.

———. *Ed Dorn Live: Lectures, Interviews, and Outtakes.* Edited by Joseph Richey. Ann Arbor: University of Michigan Press, 2007.

———. *Interviews.* Edited by Donald Allen. Bolinas, CA: Four Seasons, 1980.

———. *Way More West: New and Selected Poems.* Edited by Michael Rothenberg. New York: Penguin Books, 2007.

Dorn, Jennifer Dunbar. "*Rolling Stock:* A Chronicle of the Eighties." *Chicago Review* 49, no. 3/4 and 50, no. 1 (2004).

"The Draft: Doctor's Dilemma." *Time* magazine, January 12, 1968. Available at http://www.time.com/time/magazine/article/0,9171,837647,00.html.

Duncan, Robert. *Bending the Bow.* New York: New Directions, 1968.

———. *Groundwork: Before the War * In the Dark.* Edited by Robert J. Bertholf and James Maynard. New York: New Directions, 2006.

Duncan, Robert, and Denise Levertov. *The Letters of Robert Duncan and Denise Levertov.* Edited by Robert J. Bertholf and Albert Gelpi. Stanford, CA: Stanford University Press, 2004.

Eberly, Rosa A. *Citizen Critics: Literary Public Spheres.* Champaign, IL: University of Illinois Press, 2000.

Echols, Alice. "Review of *The Feminist Promise: 1792 to the Present.*" *Women's Review of Books* 27 (September/October 2010).

Faigley, Lester. "Rhetorics Fast and Slow." In *Rhetorical Agendas: Political, Ethical, Spiritual,* edited by Patricia Bizzell. Mahwah, NJ: Erlbaum, 2005.

Fairclough, Adam. *To Redeem the Soul of America: The Southern Christian Leadership Conference and Martin Luther King, Jr.* Athens: University of Georgia Press, 1987.

Foley, Michael S. *Confronting the War Machine: Draft Resistance during the Vietnam War.* Chapel Hill: University of North Carolina Press, 2003.

Foucault, Michel. *The Birth of Biopolitics: Lectures at the Collège de France, 1978–1979.* Edited by Michel Senellart. New York: Picador, 2008.

Freepress. "Ownership Chart." Available at http://www.freepress.net/ownership/chart/main/.

Galloway, Alexander R. *Protocol: How Control Exists after Decentralization.* Cambridge, MA: MIT Press, 2004.

Garland, Joseph E. *Down to the Sea: The Fishing Schooners of Gloucester.* Boston: David R. Godine, 2000.

———. *Gloucester on the Wind: America's Greatest Fishing Port in the Days of Sail.* Mount Pleasant, SC: Arcadia Publishing, 1995.

———. *Lone Voyager: The Extraordinary Adventures of Howard Blackburn Hero Fisherman of Gloucester.* New York: Touchstone, 1998.

Garrow, David J. *Bearing the Cross: Martin Luther King, Jr., and the Southern Christian Leadership Conference.* New York: Vintage Books, 1988.

Gates, Henry Louis, Jr. "The Church." In *Come Sunday: Photographs by Thomas Roma.* New York: Museum of Modern Art, 1996.

Gilbert, Alan. *Another Future: Poetry and Art in a Postmodern Twilight.* Middletown, CT: Wesleyan University Press, 2006.

Gilroy, Paul. *The Black Atlantic: Modernity and Double-Consciousness.* Cambridge, MA: Harvard University Press, 1993.

Ginsberg, Allen. "Howl." In *Howl and Other Poems.* 1956. San Francisco: City Lights Publishers, 2001.

Gladwell, Malcolm. *The Tipping Point: How Little Things Can Make a Big Difference.* New York: Back Bay Books, 2002.

Golding, Alan. "Dorn's 'Pontificatory Use of the Art.'" In *Internal Resistances: The Poetry of Edward Dorn.* Berkeley: University of California Press, 1985.

Gorgias. "Gorgias' Encomium of Helen." In *The Older Sophists,* edited by Rosamond Kent Sprague. Indianapolis: Hackett Publishing, 2001.

Greenwald, Glenn. "On the Claimed 'War Exception' to the Constitution." *Salon,* February 4, 2010. Available at http://www.salon.com/opinion/greenwald/2010/02/04/assassinations/.

Habermas, Jürgen. *The Structural Transformation of the Public Sphere: An Inquiry into a Category of Bourgeois Society.* Translated by Thomas Burger. Studies in Contemporary German Social Thought. Cambridge, MA: MIT Press, 1991.

Hallberg, Robert von. "Olson's Relation to Pound and Williams." *Contemporary Literature* 15 (Winter 1974). Available at http://www.jstor.org/stable/1207708/.

Hamill, Sam. "In Her Company: Denise Levertov." *Jacket* magazine. Available at http://jacketmagazine.com/36/lev-hamill.shtml.

———. "A Short History of Poets Against War." *Poets Against War.* Edited by Sam Hamill. Available at http://www.poetsagainstthewar.org/paw_background.asp.

Hamill, Sam, ed. *Poets Against the War.* New York: Nation Books, 2003.

Hanisch, Carol. "The Personal Is Political." 1969. In *Notes from the Second Year: Women's Liberation: Major Writings of the Radical Feminists,* edited by Shulamith Firestone and Anne Koedt. New York: Pamphlet, 1970. Available at http://www.carolhanisch.org/CHwritings/PIP.html/.

Hardt, Michael, and Antonio Negri. *Multitude: War and Democracy in the Age of Empire.* New York: Penguin, 2004.

Harrington, Joseph. *Poetry and the Public: The Social Form of Modern U.S. Poetics.* Middletown, CT: Wesleyan University Press, 2002.

Hauser, Gerard A. *Vernacular Voices: The Rhetoric of Publics and Public Spheres.* Columbia: University of South Carolina Press, 2008.

Hennessey, Kathleen. "'Tea Party' Activists March on Capitol Hill." *Los Angeles Times,* September 13, 2010. Available at http://articles.latimes.com/2010/sep/13/nation/la-na-tea-party-rally-20100913/.

Jackson, J. B. "The Westward-Moving House: Three American Houses and the People Who Lived in Them." In *Landscapes: Selected Writings of J. B. Jackson,* edited by Ervin H. Zube. Amherst: University of Massachusetts Press, 1970.

Johnson, Davi. "Martin Luther King, Jr.'s 1963 Birmingham Campaign as Image Event." *Rhetoric & Public Affairs* 10, no. 1 (2007): 1–25.

Johnson, Kent. *Homage to the Last Avant-Garde.* Exeter: Shearsman Books, 2008.

Kane, Daniel. *All Poets Welcome: The Lower East Side Poetry Scene in the 1960s.* Berkeley: University of California Press, 2004.

Levertov, Denise. *O Taste and See.* New York: New Directions, 1964.

———. "Politics and the Poet: An Interview with Denise Levertov." Conducted by E. G. Burrows (1968). In *Conversations with Denise Levertov,* edited by Jewel Spears Brooker. Oxford: University Press of Mississippi, 1998.

———. *To Stay Alive.* New York: New Directions, 1971.

Longinus. "'Longinus' on the Sublime." Translated by W. Hamilton Fyfe. 1927. The Loeb Classical Library. Cambridge, MA: Harvard University Press, 1982.

McCarthy, Gail. "Charles Olson Today: 20th-Century Gloucester Poet Remains Relevant into the 21st Century." *Gloucester Daily Times,* December 31, 2008. Available at http://www.gloucestertimes.com/pulife/local_story_366210543.html.

McClintock, Leslie. "Fourteen School Children Murdered in Kabul." *Poets Against War.* Edited by Sam Hamill. January 2009. Available at http://poetsagainstthewar.org/displaypoem.asp?AuthorID=67973#453124012.

McCullough, Malcolm. *Digital Ground: Architecture, Pervasive Computing, and Environmental Knowing.* Cambridge, MA: MIT Press, 2004.

McLuhan, Marshall. *The Medium Is the Massage.* Berkeley: Ginko Press, 2005.

Michaels, Walter Benn. "Empires of the Senseless: (The Response to) Terror and (the End of) History." *Radical History Review* 85 (Winter 2003).

Murphy, Richard. *Theorizing the Avant-Garde: Modernism, Expressionism, and the Problem of Postmodernity.* Cambridge: Cambridge University Press, 1998.

Nelson, Cary. *Repression and Recovery: Modern American Poetry and the Politics of Cultural Memory, 1910–1945.* Madison: University of Wisconsin Press, 1989.

Nielsen, Aldon Lynn. *Black Chant: Languages of African-American Postmodernism.* Cambridge: Cambridge University Press, 1997.

Olson, Charles. *Collected Prose.* Edited by Donald Allen and Benjamin Friedlander. Berkeley: University of California Press, 1997.

———. *The Maximus Poems.* Edited by George F. Butterick. Berkeley: University of California Press, 1983.

———. *Maximus to Gloucester: The Letters and Poems of Charles Olson to the Editor of the Gloucester Daily Times, 1962–1969.* Edited by Peter Anastas. Gloucester, MA: Ten Pound Island Book Company, 1992.

Ong, Walter. "The Shifting Sensorium." In *The Varieties of Sensory Experience: A Sourcebook in the Anthropology of the Senses,* edited by David Howes. Toronto: University of Toronto Press, 1991.

Perloff, Marjorie. "A Conversation with Charles Bernstein." Electronic Poetry Center, SUNY-Buffalo. Available at http://epc.buffalo.edu/authors/perloff/articles/mp_cb.html/.

———. *Poetry On and Off the Page: Essays for Emergent Occasions.* Evanston, IL: Northwestern University Press, 1998.

Plato. "Gorgias." Translated by D. J. Zeyl. In *Complete Works,* edited by John M. Cooper and D. S. Hutchinson. Indianapolis: Hackett Publishing, 1997.

Poets Against War. Edited by Sam Hamill. Available at http://www.poetsagainstthewar.org/.

Poggioli, Renato. *The Theory of the Avant-Garde.* Translated by Gerald Fitzgerald. Cambridge, MA: Harvard University Press, 1968.

Pohl, R. D. "Slow Poetry: Recipe for a New Avant-Garde." BuffaloNews.com. Available at http://blogs.buffalonews.com/artsbeat/2009/07/slow-poetry-recipe-for-a-new-avantgarde-1.html/.

Polis Is This: Charles Olson and the Persistence of Place. DVD. Directed by Henry Ferrini. Information on the film is available at http://www.polisisthis.com/.

Prevallet, Kristin. *Shadow Evidence Intelligence.* New York: Factory School, 2006.

"Pro-War Poetry Website Launched." BBC News. Wednesday, March 5, 2003. Available at http://news.bbc.co.uk/2/hi/entertainment/2821455.stm/.

Raley, Rita. *Tactical Media.* Minneapolis: University of Minnesota Press, 2009.

Rebhorn, Wayne A. *The Emperor of Men's Minds: Literature and the Renaissance Discourse of Rhetoric.* Ithaca, NY: Cornell University Press, 1995.

Reed, Ishmael. *Mumbo Jumbo.* New York: Scribner, 1996.

Rich, David, ed. *Charles Olson: Letters Home, 1949–1969.* Gloucester, MA: Cape Ann Museum, 2010.

Rifkin, Libbie. *Career Moves: Olson, Creeley, Zukofsky, Berrigan and the American Avant-Garde.* Madison: University of Wisconsin Press, 2000.

Robb, John. *Brave New War: The Next Stage of Terrorism and the End of Globalization.* Hoboken, NJ: John Wiley and Sons, 2007.

Roberts, Adam. "Good Poetry Is Like Good Food: How to Find It . . . and Savor It." *The Atlantic,* November 10, 2010. Available at http://www.theatlantic.com/culture/archive/2010/11/good-poetry-is-like-good-food-how-to-find-it-and-savor-it/66308/.

Roberts-Miller, Patricia. *Deliberate Conflict: Argument, Political Theory, and Composition Classes.* Carbondale: Southern Illinois University Press, 2004.

Saenz, Jaime. *Immanent Visitor.* Berkeley: University of California Press, 2002.

———. *The Night.* Princeton, NJ: Princeton University Press, 2007.

Sandqvist, Tom. *Dada East: The Romanians of Cabaret Voltaire.* Cambridge, MA: MIT Press, 2005.

Schatz, Amy. "FCC Split as It Launches Internet Regulation Effort." *Wall Street Journal.* June 18, 2010. Available at http://online.wsj.com/article/SB10001424052748704289504575312742566475122.html?mod=WSJ_hpp_MIDDLETopStories/.

Seelye, Catherine, ed. *Charles Olson and Ezra Pound: An Encounter at St. Elizabeths.* New York: Paragon House, 1991.

Shurin, Aaron. "The People's P★★★k." In *Robert Duncan and Denise Levertov: The Poetry of Politics, the Politics of Poetry,* edited by Albert Gelpi and Robert J. Bertholf. Stanford, CA: Stanford University Press, 2006.

Side, Jeffrey. "Interview with Marjorie Perloff." *Poetry Salzburg Review* 10 (Autumn 2006). Available at *The Argoist Online,* at *http://www.argotistonline.co.uk/Perloff%20interview%202.htm/.*

Silliman, Ron. *The New Sentence.* New York: Roof Books, 1987.

Smith, Dale. "Edward Dorn: An Introduction." In *Way More West: New and Selected Poems.* By Edward Dorn. Edited by Michael Rothenberg. New York: Penguin Books, 2007.

———. "Essay on War." *Poets Against War.* Edited by Sam Hamill. Available at http://poetsagainstthewar.org/displaypoem.asp?AuthorID=346#453056541.

Smith, Neil. "Contours of a Spatialized Politics: Homeless Vehicles and the Production of Geographical Scale." *Social Text* 33 (1992): 54–81. *JSTOR.* Edited by Bruce Robbins and Andrew Ross. Duke University Press. Available at http://www.jstor.org/stable/view/466434.

Somers-Willett, Susan B. A. *The Cultural Politics of Slam Poetry: Race, Identity, and the Performance of Popular Verse in America.* Ann Arbor: University of Michigan Press, 2009.

Spicer, Jack. "For Joe." In *The Collected Books of Jack Spicer,* edited by Robin Blaser. Los Angeles: Black Sparrow Press, 1975.

Struever, Nancy S. *Rhetoric, Modality, Modernity.* Chicago: University of Chicago Press, 2009.

Taleb, Nassim Nicholas. *The Black Swan: The Impact of the Highly Improbable.* New York: Random House, 2007.

Taylor, Charles. *Modern Social Imaginaries.* Durham, NC: Duke University Press, 2004.

Thomas, Lorenzo. *The Bathers.* New York: I. Reed Books, 1981.

———. *Dancing on Main Street.* Minneapolis: Coffee House Press, 2004.

———. *Don't Deny My Name: Words and Music and the Black Intellectual Tradition.* Ann Arbor: University of Michigan Press, 2008.

———. *Extraordinary Measures: Afrocentric Modernism and Twentieth-Century American Poetry.* Tuscaloosa: The University of Alabama Press, 2000.

Van Creveld, Martin. *The Rise and Decline of the State.* Cambridge: Cambridge University Press, 1999.

Vickers, Brian. *Classical Rhetoric in English Poetry.* Carbondale: Southern Illinois University Press, 1970.

Wagner, Anne M. "Warhol Paints History, or, Race in America." *Representations* 55 (Summer 1996).

Waldman, Anne. *Manatee/Humanity.* New York: Penguin, 2009.

Walker, Jeffrey. *Bardic Ethos and the American Epic Poem: Whitman, Pound, Crane, Williams, Olson.* Baton Rouge: Louisiana State University Press, 1989.

———. *Rhetoric and Poetics in Antiquity.* Oxford: Oxford University Press, 2000.

Walsh, Gene. *Images at the Horizon: A Workshop with Werner Herzog Conducted by Roger Ebert.* Chicago: Facets Multimedia Center, 1979.

Warner, Michael. *Publics and Counterpublics.* New York: Zone Books, 2002.

Warnick, Barbara. *Rhetoric Online: Persuasion and Politics on the World Wide Web.* New York: Peter Lang, 2007.

———. *The Sixth Canon: Belletristic Rhetorical Theory and Its French Antecedents.* Columbia: University of South Carolina Press, 1993.

"Who We Are." *Poets Against War.* Edited by Sam Hamill. Available at http://www.poetsagainstthewar.org/whoweare.asp.

Williams, Raymond. *The Long Revolution.* 1961. Calgary: Broadview Press, 2001.

Williams, William Carlos. "The Poem as a Field of Action" (1948). In *Selected Essays.* New York: New Directions, 1969.

Žižek, Slavoj. *Living in the End Times.* New York: Verso, 2010.

Index